Woman – The Full Story

'An astute, humorous and moving insight into the lives of women from Eve to the 21st century woman ... An enormous amount of valuable research has gone into the writing of this book, including anecdotes of the lives of pioneering women, such as Gladys Aylwood and Mary Slessor, whose courage is earth-shattering and a profound lesson for us all. They prove that we can all have a voice and that a few can make a difference for many ... I underlined pearls of wisdom on nearly every page!'

FIONA CASTLE

'Michele Guinness discusses important issues for Christians today, both women and men. Her writing is perceptive, informed and challenging – a blend of personal experience and biblical and sociological insights – full of the wisdom, spiced with wit, we have come to expect from her.'

BISHOP MICHAEL NAZIR-ALI

'A terrific tour de force. It will get under your skin, challenge your assumptions, make you laugh at your silly prejudices and dare you to live equally alongside the wonder that is woman.'

RUSS PARKER

'A delightfully humorous biography. Graphic revelations and great insights. Challenging, very readable and refreshingly original. Sell your bed and buy this book! You will love it!'

BISHOP DAVID PYTCHES

⊗

'If there is one book that will really serve to liberate women from centuries of male dominated Bible interpretation, it's this one! This book provides a truly emancipating reading experience – both for women who have been bound by masculine misreadings, and for men who have misinterpreted the true picture of women provided in the Bible. I cannot recommend this book more enthusiastically. It is beautifully written and immensely perceptive. It's greatest strength lies in the fact that its author comes at the Bible texts from a Jewish perspective, thereby exposing the true context and meaning of Biblical passages about women. Every woman and man should read this!'

MARK STIBBE

For Joel and Abby
who urged me to write a book
I didn't know was there

Contents

Acknowledgements   9

Sometimes It's Hard to Be a Woman   13

PART 1: *The Kosher Woman – A Jewish,*
Matriarchal Heritage

   1 The Life-Giving Woman   27

   2 The Manipulative Woman   55

   3 The Assertive Woman   81

PART 2: *The Christian Woman – A Liberating,*
Life-Changing Inheritance

   4 A Woman of Little Status?   107

   5 The Silent Woman?   133

   6 The Submissive Woman?   167

PART 3: *The Contemporary Woman – Living*
our Bequest in Today's World

   7 The Sexual Woman   199

   8 The Mothering Woman   233

   9 The Working Woman   263

  10 A Woman of Experience and Maturity   293

Acknowledgements

*Writing an autobiography and making a spiritual
will are practically the same.*

SHALOM ALEICHEM

I never intended to write another book. Writing is such a terribly presumptuous occupation. Who am I to add my few drops to the ocean of words already in existence? How can I justify sharing my paltry experience with the world? My only defence is that I was spurred on by a passion that has pursued me day and night for years, for today's women of faith to set aside our diffidence and take up the challenge of our calling. Only then will we see the rise of an army of evangelists, campaigners, reformers and missionaries, like Catherine Booth, Mary Slessor, Florence Nightingale and Josephine Butler, who risked their reputations, and even their very lives, to change the face of their nineteenth-century world.

So thank you to everyone who made a contribution, however unwitting – to those who goaded me into speaking on the subject (especially *Woman Alive* magazine and *Crusade for World Revival* for organizing the *Alive to God* events that made me do the initial homework), and to those unknown individuals who heard me and challenged me afterwards on my woolly thinking and made me go back and study again; to the congregation of St Thomas's, Lancaster, who allowed me to try out a seminar on women and authority, then moaned that I hadn't prepared any notes for them to take away; and to my children especially, who came home from university in immense frustration and said, 'We know it must be right for women to be able to play a leading role in the Church, as they do in the rest of society, but we don't know how to argue it. You believe it. So now write it down for us.'

Abby didn't know then that I would commandeer her help. I didn't know she would go way beyond her remit. I thought she thought I was the perfect woman and mother; I thought she valued my common sense, not to mention my fashion sense. As you'll see, it all goes to show what illusions we weave. But then, she is her mother's daughter. I should have guessed I'd get more than I bargained for. I do appreciate her ruthless honesty. On good days.

When I first told friends in publishing about my idea for a book on woman, they all said, 'Amy Boucher Pye at Zondervan's your woman.' And they were absolutely right. The literary liposuction wasn't always painless – but the svelte, slimmer product at the end is a tribute to her skill and I am immensely grateful for it.

Thank you to those who read chapters and scribbled painstaking and helpful comments on them, or inadvertently released tiny treasures I snatched from the ether – Sue Kiernan, Judy Crowther, Ruth Hassall, Serena Lailey and many more. I apologize if I didn't warn you that I was going to regurgitate your words. I'm a journalist. Everything I see and hear is grist to the mill. Please don't stop speaking to me. Everything we say will be shouted from the rooftops one day anyway. Thank you, too, to Mary Audrey Raycroft of Toronto, who encouraged me to believe I wasn't completely off the wall in my interpretation of God's plans for women, wound me up with even more ideas, and set me spinning in dozens of new directions.

Dr Stephen Travis, Vice Principal of St John's Theological College in Nottingham, England, gave some of his invaluable leisure time one Christmas in our home to checking my New

Testament theology, correcting my faux pas in his usual gracious, sensitive and encouraging manner. I am deeply indebted to his gentle wisdom and advice. If I have omitted to act on all of it, it is because of my inability to comprehend some of the more subtle nuances of his arguments, rather than a post-Christmas lapse of concentration on his part.

And a special big thank you to my husband, who has been a 'head' in the true sense of the word – a source of life, release, encouragement, confidence, love and IT know-how, who has been as much a partner in the production of books as he has of babies, and for whom I have never merely been a 'back-up'. But then, show me the Jewish mama who is!

> Risk being unliked. Tell the truth as you understand it. If you're a writer you have a moral obligation to do this. And it is a revolutionary act – truth is always subversive.
>
> ANNE LAMOTT

Sometimes It's Hard to Be a Woman

My lifetime has witnessed one of the greatest revolutions in the history of the West – the change in the status of women. Was it just over a quarter of a century ago that I sat in a café in Manchester and, starry eyed, told my newly acquired, long-adored man that I could think of no more blissful future than staying at home to darn his socks and iron his shirts? How old fashioned and quaint it sounds now – positively antique. To be fair, the self-sacrificial romantic idealism didn't last long. For women of my generation the world was already spinning on its axis. It was full of new opportunities I didn't want to miss. And each has caused me a great deal of heart-searching about what it means to be woman as God intended, bringing our unique gifts to the home, community, workplace and church.

I was a first child and my father, like most Jewish men, had desperately wanted a boy to carry on the family name. In fact he had a bet on it – £5 each way – with his father-in-law. So when the formidable, starched-white sister crinkled her way into the hospital waiting room to tell the expectant father he could stop pacing the floor because he had a lovely daughter, this skilled and competent medical practitioner asked her, 'Are you saying it is a girl, or you only think it's a girl?'

'Doctor,' she said disparagingly, for those were the days when a senior nurse could reduce even a competent medical man to blancmange with one twitch of her winged hat, 'we do have ways of knowing these things.'

By the time this anecdote passed into my conscious history, my father not only had his son, but had also discovered the joys of having an adoring daughter, and though he dismissed women doctors as 'horses', he had convinced himself that when I grew up I would break the mould. Unlike my mother, whose choices were hidebound by the double whammy of both British and Jewish middle-class cultural expectations – to hook not just a fish, but a prize fish of a provider, I must have the best education and the opportunity of university and a career.

Despite being Jewish, therefore, I was sent to a good Church of England private school for girls. Dad would have been horrified had I told him that the careers advice reluctantly dispensed by the tweedy Miss Calderbank in bun and brogues consisted of, 'You have three choices, my dear: teaching, nursing or the army.' That was how it was in the 1950s. The sighing Miss Calderbank suspected that few of the young women sent to see her would heed a word of her advice anyway, since they would not be reduced, as she had been by a world war and male shortage, to the necessity of a career. Even the teaching staff still resigned themselves to throwing their gems before unappreciative little wretches who at the first opportunity would exchange their brains for something in trousers, and flush away a shining future to become wives and mothers. As their mothers had no doubt done before them.

My mother, in blue nylon overalls, dusting and polishing, cooking and cleaning, straightening pictures, armchair castors and curtain folds, was hardly the stuff of my female teenage fantasies. 'What's life all about?' I asked her one day, in desperation.

She was in the process of moving the left-hand candle of a pair on the dining room sideboard one centimetre towards its opposite number, half a centimetre from the wall, and didn't even look up.

'You'll meet a nice Jewish boy, marry, have a nice home, children, a car. . .'

'And then what?'

'What more do you want?'

Was this then my destiny, this drudgery my mother evidently resented? Every day, as she banged his lunch down on the table in front of him, she would say to my father, 'Next time I'm coming back as a man'. As a good Jewish mama she didn't actually believe in reincarnation, but she did believe in making sure her man appreciated her long-suffering and self-sacrifice. I always wondered why she bothered making him lunch if she hated doing it so much. Couldn't he get his own? But had one of his Jewish male friends ever learned to cook, it would have meant the overturning of civilization as my father knew it. My father took his role as breadwinner very seriously, was convinced he worked far harder than my mother ever did in the home, and let her know without saying so that she was lucky to be 'a kept woman'. That she didn't need to go out to work was a sign of the status which he, the son of poor Jewish immigrants, had won for them both.

A new world for women

I was born several years after the end of the Second World War, when the men had been away at the front and the women had been expected to take on their jobs. But when the men came home, in order to ensure there was enough work for them to do, the government made it socially unacceptable for middle-class women to abandon the safety of hearth and home and the love of a good man. Those who did were usually single, and were treated with a mixture of pity and fear – the stern, forbidding teachers who terrified pupils and parents alike; the big-breasted nursing sisters and matrons who ran their hospitals with military precision, tyrannizing the poor patients; the dedicated personal assistant who organized her male boss, buying flowers for his wife, birthday cards for his mother and Christmas presents for his children, letting him know that behind an obsequious façade was a woman who, given half a chance, could do a better job than him. These women, whose rightful husbands were lying in the graves of unknown soldiers in France, Italy and North Africa, were often seen as formidable, unfeminine, unnatural – battle-axes. No woman could possibly combine a career with a fulfilling emotional and domestic life.

As women were given greater access to education, however, social attitudes began to be shaken. In the 1960s the contraceptive pill gave women new freedom and choices. My mother opened a pram shop in a mining town in County Durham and turned out to be a shrewd, successful businesswoman until the pits were closed. She couldn't do much about that, but after all, my father said sympathetically, as his lunch was once again bounced onto the table in front of him, she had only been earning herself some pocket money.

In 1971 women were awarded equal rights and equal pay in the workplace. Although they have never yet achieved that in reality, change was accelerating at such a pace that the writer Gloria Steinem could say with satisfaction, 'Some of us are becoming the men we wanted to marry'. For many women, not being forced to depend on a man for status or fulfilment has had a liberating impact on their marriage. In the past, denied any outlet for her education, gifts and skills, the wife was forced to invest all her ambitions and dreams in her man. In some cases he was kind, thoughtful and sensitive, but didn't have enough oomph for his partner, who chivvied and bullied her poor Harry or Norman to achieve all she felt she could have done, given half the chance. She ended up nursing a lasting sense of disappointment, while he was left feeling a failure.

Today women no longer have to become a nurse in order to grow up and marry a doctor. They can become a doctor. They don't have to marry into the army for the excitement of an army life. They can become a colonel. They don't even have to go to theological college to snap up a minister, to become a minister's wife. They can be the minister in all but the Roman Catholic, Orthodox, free evangelical and some of the newer churches – despite the fact that women often run them, even if they don't lead them.

Nonetheless, there have also been pitfalls in thinking that a career alone will give women a sense of identity and meaning. The Swiss psychologist of the 1950s and '60s, Paul Tournier, one of the first Christian voices to challenge the Church's attitude to gender, believed that from the time of the Renaissance, Western civilization had been dominated by the cold, objective 'male' values of reason and rationalism, while the 'feminine' qualities of emotion, feelings and relationship, dismissed as inferior, had all but disappeared. That, he maintained, had led to the death of small communities, the emphasis on centralization, the growth of multinationals and the increase in bureaucracy. Tournier was a prophet before his time. He believed that once women were allowed to be leaders in the workplace, the balance would be restored. What he couldn't foresee was that to get to the top, some women would deny their distinctly female God-given gifts and characteristics and become more like a man than a man.

Like Tournier, I believed that if we eschewed the shoulder-padded, power-dressing, cut-and-thrust image bequeathed to us by our longest-serving prime minister, Margaret Thatcher, that if we remained resolutely feminine, we would make the world a gentler place – even for the men. But then, while our differences from men are our greatest strength, they can be seen as weaknesses and used to keep us in our place beneath the glass ceiling, and it isn't hard to understand why some women reject them. Some feel they have so much to prove that they have no choice but to be tougher than the men to beat them at their own game. Others don't feel they fit the accepted stereotype. In surveys no man wishes he had been born a woman, while about 25 per cent of women, given a chance, would rather have been a man. In today's world being a woman isn't always easy.

It's all about image

But being a woman has its compensations.

Once a month we have an excuse for being cranky and difficult. If a spot suddenly breaks out in the middle of our chin, we have ways and means of concealing it. Girlfriends are often grateful when we tell them, gently, that they have broccoli stuck between their front teeth. When we feel fragile and in need of male sympathy, a mysterious gynaecological ailment can usually do the trick. And there's nothing like a new lipstick to give us a whole new lease of life.

While Orthodox Jewish men thank God daily they're not a woman, I thank God I'm not a man. Imagine being condemned to an entire working life in virtually identical dark suits, stiff collars and uncomfortable ties. No access to instant brotherhood for him, no sharing recipes and make-up tips, no whingeing about the way the wife's snoring keeps him awake at night, or moaning about the ladders in his tights. No giggling about the predictability of the opposite sex or sharing his anxieties about his prostate – in the gents.

Men simply do not have access to the bond of understanding amongst women that can unite virtually complete strangers. It's almost impossible to compliment a man – embarrassing enough if a woman does it, let alone another male. The recipient will usually back up against the wall with a look of wild panic in his eyes, clear his throat, and start wittering about football.

It is important to celebrate our femininity, especially in a world where youth and body shape are what matters, and a woman riper than 30 and bigger than 36 inches in the key places can feel she has been weighed and found wanting. Small wonder we're not as comfortable with our sexuality as we were meant to be. But few women are satisfied with their shape. Even diminutive size tens seem to think they should be a minimalist size six. On a recent television programme about body image, one woman thought life would really begin when she became a size fourteen, but when she had achieved her goal, she was still waiting. Nothing had changed. Another young woman who was anorexic said, 'I wish I'd been taught to accept myself the way I was taught to cook.'

A friend of mine saw a text over a beauty salon in Uganda: 'With God all things are possible.' With God they may be, but sadly not with the beauty therapist. The contemporary stereotype of beauty is sun-kissed, blonde and leggy. I am therefore, by definition, a nonstarter. My legs end at my husband's knees. In fact, he is so much taller than I am that his head was cut off on our wedding photos. There's not much I can do about that, but bleaching my hair was a possibility – had it not been for the painful necessity of touching up the roots every week. I would like to have been a perfect English rose – demure and delicate, rather than a swarthy-looking continental with a big nose and a wonky ear. I never summoned up enough courage or cash to flatten the ear and de-Jewish the nose. These days a face-lift is ever more tempting – except that my daughter Abby insists she couldn't conceive of my 'natural laughter lines' (read 'wrinkles') being replaced with a taut and permanent look of surprise.

The cult of youth and beauty isn't new. One of the most popular ditties of the 1940s urged women to 'Stay young and beautiful, it's your duty to be beautiful if you want to be loved'. It seems that we've been crooning a lot of rubbish for a very long time. Perhaps it isn't surprising that we've begun to believe it at last.

So blonde and leggy I shall never be, but my bone structure and inexhaustible nervous energy do mean I look fairly slim – in clothes at least. But why do shops always reserve the most flamboyant, exciting clothes for big women, while 'petites', as we're patronizingly called, end up with one or two rows of neat, dull little suits? When I worked in local radio I used to interview a woman who had her own retail chain for big women. She walked into the studio in bright red suits and bold jewellery, turning every head. 'I've never been short of a cuddle from the men,' she said, 'whereas you, if we were in Africa, the Oxfam lorry would be calling at your door.'

At certain stages of her life a woman becomes invisible altogether – when she pushes a screaming or disruptive toddler in a buggy round the shops, when her hair goes grey, her figure sags, varicose veins create a road map on her legs, and she's too frail to stand up for herself. If women are 'past it' at thirty, past what, I want to know? What can a teenager do that I can't, and a whole lot better because I have experience and wisdom and maturity on my side? Gypsy Rose Lee, the stripper, said, 'I still have everything I ever had twenty years ago. It just happens to be two inches lower.'

Looking through the newspaper obituaries and noticing that one in four were of men, the journalist Irma Kurtz came to the conclusion that only men die; women go through the change. It is at that moment when we can no longer procreate that we become worthless in the eyes of the world. The truth is that, with the freedom of the children leaving home, we may be entering our most useful and effective years.

But it's not so different in the Church

Until recently I thought that all there was to say on the subject of women had been said and that the issue of how equal women were was now well and truly passé – in Western society at least. No more books on the subject were needed.

Then I saw a poster sent out by the Equal Opportunities Commission which said, 'Prepare your daughter for working life. Give her less pocket money than your son.' Apparently, in this equal world of ours, women still earn approximately 20 per cent less than their male colleagues for the same secular job.

In the Church of England, when husband and wife are both ordained, the women have often found it hard to get paid work at all, and find themselves acting as voluntary assistant curates.

In fact, when I asked Abby why she never considered becoming a minister, she suggested wryly that the Church should have its own version of the equal opportunities poster: 'Prepare your daughter for Christian ministry. Don't give her any pocket money at all.'

Both my son and daughter, now young adults, have been staggered to come across flagrant sexism outside their home circle at their respective universities. It seems that, despite the fact that women are now headteachers, senior managers, chief constables and even prime ministers, some churches and Christian organizations still persist in not giving women any chance to engage in preaching or leadership. In an article in *Renewal* magazine written in September 2000, Andy and Jane Fitz-Gibbon described how their fifteen-year-old daughter came home from school one day looking rather subdued. When they quizzed her about what was wrong, she described how she had responded to a request to lead the school Christian club the following week, but had been turned down because 'you're a girl, and only boys can lead'.

At the consecration of a bishop in Southwark Cathedral recently, I have to admit it was a very strange sensation to climb over two rather dour-looking clergymen in black suits who resolutely remained in the pew during Communion. They wouldn't take the bread and wine from the hands of the Archbishop of Canterbury – he was tainted because he had ordained women to the priesthood. The irony was that the Church happened to be celebrating a feast day dedicated to Saints Felicity and Perpetua, horribly and publicly tortured and killed for their Christian faith as Roman sport in the third century.

Why is it that a Church called to follow its leader's radical example and stand at the cutting edge of society, demanding the equality of all human beings, regardless of colour, race or gender, is so often a reactionary, outdated voice, out of kilter with the contemporary world and of little relevance? For many years, while it has been led by men, it has been run by an army of dedicated women, happy to roll up their sleeves and do the menial tasks like dusting the pews and polishing the brasses, making the tea and attending to the flowers. Today our wonderful church cleaner, the best ever, is a man. He mends the vacuum cleaner when it breaks down, replaces duff light bulbs, and is a wizard at general maintenance.

Yet despite the breakdown of traditional roles in society, we persist in the unspoken notion that certain areas of church life are more feminine than others – the prayer ministry team rather than the pulpit, the Sunday school rather than home group leadership. When we arrived at our present church they had never had a female churchwarden. 'Not a suitable job for a woman,' said the then churchwarden. 'She couldn't scramble up on the roof to check the gutters.' Within a year Peter and I visited Bath Abbey and in the bookshop met their feisty female churchwarden. 'The first thing I did on my appointment,' she confided, totally unprompted, 'was to buy a boiler suit so that I could get up on the roof to check the gutters.' The very thought gave me vertigo.

Abby says most of the young women she meets at university who have any religious faith are confident about their potential in the job market, but struggle with their role in the Church. They think Paul was a misogynist. They presume whole chunks of the Bible must be out of date and out of touch. If that's the case, what might it say about what they really think of God himself and his feelings for the female he has created?

On another level, if Western women are fed the myth that we're past our best at thirty, if women in the workplace feel forced to behave more like the men than a man, if the Church compounds the problem by giving us little encouragement to explore our gifting at any age, what is God's perspective on this particular half of the species he created? Why were the achievements of twentieth-century women of faith so slim compared to so many of their daring, outspoken nineteenth-century sisters? And must the twenty-first-century Church be condemned to lack the fearless female leadership it so desperately needs?

These questions are not passé. They demand answers, and I have spent many years trying to find those answers, weighing up a mass of differing biblical interpretations, historical attitudes and cultural expectations in an effort to piece together the full story.

It's time to set the record straight. In doing so, we'll be going back to the original sources – the Hebrew Scriptures and the New Testament, as well as looking at women's stories from history and today. We'll delve deep, turning the texts inside out, playing with every nuance, for this is a very Jewish way of handling biblical material. Sadly, the Church has inherited a Hellenistic or Graeco-Roman approach to all study, including theology. Learning is cerebral. The brain must be fed, reason satisfied. The Jewish tradition, in contrast, is to learn with the heart, not the head. Doing is more important than knowing. That is why story is the very fabric of the Hebrew Scriptures, and Jesus, immersed in that tradition, continually resorted to parables. He knew they could be milked repeatedly and never run dry. Each time they are told, new revelation dawns. Aspects of the tale, hidden before, suddenly emerge. 'With stories, you don't ask questions,' goes an old Jewish saying.

I apologize in advance if, as I share my own journey and write from my limited perspective, I may appear to overlook those with very different experiences from my own – the ever-increasing number of women who are single because of separation or divorce, or who have never married, or who do not have children, whether by choice, circumstances or in great sorrow. I hope nonetheless that much of what I say will be relevant to all my sisters under the skin – and to all the men who share the world and our journey with us.

Ultimately, I have come to the conclusion that from the beginning of time, woman has had an equal part to play in the story God has been writing about his people – demonstrated by the extraordinary place they have carved out for themselves in history. I am constantly amazed by how timeless the Bible is, more, not less, relevant to our culture, as we dig for the essence of what it really says, and discover precious nuggets of great price.

This is an opportunity to celebrate all that women have been, are and will be, so let's embark on a new adventure through the texts and history books, in search of the challenges, achievements, failures and joys of women as they have wrestled through the ages to take their place in the universe. The journey will take us from the beginning of time as we know it, across the centuries, to the place we have reached today. We'll revisit the tough Jewish matriarchs and risk-taking leaders of the Old Testament, and their loving, liberated counterparts in the New, and we'll meet a host of women who, through the years, have inherited that same passionate determination to rise to the challenge of God's radical call – before we look at what it means to be a woman now.

Today's woman of faith may not be able to have it all – at least, not all at once, but, like her sisters past, present and future, she has the power to fulfil her God-given potential and change the world in ways he always knew we would. This is our story – the full story.

PART 1

The Kosher Woman

A Jewish, Matriarchal Heritage

CHAPTER 1

The Life-Giving Woman

Her story, and not just history, begins at creation. There is Adam all alone in his breathtaking, pristine, resplendent new inheritance. There is no one to share his pleasure in the landscape – the pure white puffballs of clouds that scud like clumps of cotton wool across the magnificent, encircling vault of a Wedgwood sky, or the dew that drips in diamond earrings from the heads of a riot of multicoloured flowers, nodding happily between the blades of endless acres of sweet-smelling grasses and stout, shady trees, or the foam-tipped, pie-crust edges of the vast expanse of dappled royal blue and aquamarine ocean that laps gently and rhythmically at the borders of his property. He tries to decide whether it's possible to have a meaningful relationship with any of the creatures roaming freely on his land, but, strangely enough, none of the animals meets his particular requirements.

Since 'the fall' hasn't yet occurred, the job spec is fairly straightforward at this stage – someone who will share his heart, body, soul and mind. Only later, once the human rot has set in, does he add cook, dishwasher, cleaner, childminder and general drudge to the list, someone to run the home and kids to free him to be the successful leader, to iron his shirts so that he looks the part, to fill his belly so that he doesn't suffer malnutrition on the way up, and to meet his bodily needs by becoming a sex strumpet in the bedroom as the clock turns midnight.

For most of the twentieth century, particularly after two world wars when women showed how tough and competent they could be, given the opportunity, a wife in the parlour contributed to a man's success. Singleness was not an advantage in the career stakes. Marriage meant upward mobility and a pay rise. He, in turn, kept a policy in the bottom drawer, providing for the little woman in the event of her being careless enough to lose her man. I remember as a child in the 1950s that when women did indeed face the trauma and ignominy of being without their breadwinner – for far less noble reasons than an unpredictable death – they often discovered that, despite their years of selfless service, when the bounder left them for a younger model they were in fact destitute, and since he hadn't done them the favour of dying, they were unable to claim the benefits of insurance.

The early part of the twentieth century could be cruel to women. Yet this rigid middle-class division of roles – the superior male doing the work, the inferior woman seeing to his domestic needs – was regarded as a Christian principle, supported by the Church and often based on an extremely convenient misinterpretation of the creation story in the book of Genesis.

Woman is the image of her Father

> In the image of God he created them; male and female he created them.
>
> GENESIS 1:27 NIVI

The first account of creation in Genesis 1 reveals an amazing truth. Individually and corporately, men and women are repro versions of their Father in heaven. We have his capacity to love, laugh and form intimate relationships. We are his ambassadors or representatives. Small wonder God is so hard on graven images. Who needs them? 'You want to know what I'm like?' he asks all created beings. 'Then all you have to do is take a look in the mirror to see the pinnacle of my creative powers.'

Male and female are entirely separate beings, yet incomplete without each other. Both are given dominion over the created order and are told to reproduce. They are different biologically for reproductive purposes, but in no other obvious way. In fact, they are more alike than different – made from the same design, of the same stuff, two sides of the same coin, the image of the Father and Creator.

So how was it possible for the great Early Church Father Augustine to write in the fourth century AD, 'The woman herself alone is not the image of God, whereas the man alone is the image of God as fully and completely as when the woman is joined with him'?[1] As early as the second century AD, Origen, the founder of systematic theology, said, 'What is seen with the eyes of the creator is masculine, and not feminine, for God does not stoop to look at what is feminine and of the flesh.'[2]

How could they wilfully ignore what was written in the first chapter of the Bible? The key is in the writings of yet another second-century Christian sage. Clement of Alexandria said, 'Nothing for men is shameful, for man is endowed with reason; but for woman it brings shame even to reflect on what her nature is.'[3] The Early Church Fathers, steeped in classical Greek culture, admired reason above all other human qualities. It followed, then, that for them, being made in the image of God meant that, unlike the animals, man had an intellect – he was an eminently reasonable being. Man, here, is the operative, not generic word. It was abundantly clear to every man that woman wasn't reasonable. She was irrational and incomprehensible, given to sudden mood swings and strange intuitions. You couldn't talk to a woman man to man. There was no way, then, that she could have been made in the image of God. Whatever the book of Genesis said, it was manifestly obvious that she was intellectually inferior, and a lesser being spiritually.

It never seems to have occurred to the Early Fathers that it takes a very practical, rational person to run a home, a husband, children, a dog, a rabbit and a budgie, let alone fulfil the other jobs most women do. It never seems to have crossed their minds that men simply don't understand women's logic. Instead, they reasoned, women's so-called moods, their contrariness, their sheer illogicality, must have something to do with that monthly mystery they found so distasteful. Nowhere in the Bible is there any suggestion that female hormones, whether they're kind or contrary, have any major effect on our ability to make decisions. Yet until recently in the West, and still in many Muslim countries, that imagined monthly emotional nosedive has meant that women have been deemed unsuited to certain jobs – usually ones that involve thinking.

The tragedy is that the clear and special message at the beginning of creation, the innate equality of men and women, was entrusted to all those with eyes to see it, no longer blinkered by history and culture and the fall from grace that was to come – in other words, the Church. It certainly isn't preached by orthodox Judaism, or Islam, or Hinduism, which all put a far greater value on boys than girls. For instance, from a Muslim point of view:

> A woman should conceal her husband's secrets. If she is experiencing a difficult time she should not reveal this to anyone. She should always express joy so that the husband is not grieved. In this manner she will win him over and her respect will increase in his sight.
>
> A successful wife is one that recognises the husband's nature. You should try and understand his temperament. If he is angry do not utter something that will increase his anger. Always watch his mood before speaking. If he responds to jokes by expressing happiness then continue doing so, otherwise not. If he is displeased with you, do not sit with a sullen face. Instead, plead with him for forgiveness and try to win

him over whether it is your fault or not. This will result in his love increasing for you.[4]

Sadly, instead of proclaiming a radically different message from Islam, the Christian Church banged the same drum.

The abuse of creation and the environment is deplorable, but the wholesale tyranny of men over women throughout the world is even worse. In many developing countries women die in childbirth, often because the man still has to give his permission for his wife to have a Caesarian section and is missing at the crucial moment. Anne Garden, consultant gynaecologist at the Liverpool Women's Hospital, who has also worked in India, told me she discovered that, 'When men own women's bodies they abuse them'. She claims to be the world's most reluctant feminist, but seeing how dispensable women can be changed her mind – at least about campaigning for the rights of women overseas.

In the Afghanistan of the 1960s women had the vote. In the 1980s seven women were members of parliament. Before the *mujahedin* took power in 1992, 50 per cent of university students in Kabul were female. They were interested in fashion, wore make-up and miniskirts and took education and a career for granted, much as women in the West do. In 1996, when the Taliban filled the power vacuum created by the Russians, women were threatened with a lashing if they dared leave the home without being robed from head to toe in the heavy, scratchy *burqa* with its small, crocheted grille that barely allows the wearer to breathe, let alone see out. Professional women were denied any right to their careers and ended up destitute, begging on the streets for food for their children. One in four women died giving birth in filthy, infested maternity hospitals. Education for girls was forbidden. Half of the population were dehumanized and made invisible. And while their world closed down around them, we in the Western world forgot them, too hidebound by personal political considerations to care – until our worlds collided.

In fact, contrary to what we would like to believe, the culture has changed very little since the Taliban lost control. Women are still the property of their husbands and are often subject to domestic violence. In some places little girls have had acid thrown in their faces as they walk to school, young women are beaten if they appear in public without the *burqa*, twelve- and thirteen-year-olds are sold into marriage to much older men and, as wife number three or four, end up as servants.[5]

In this day and age a woman can still face death by stoning for having a child after she has been raped. Female circumcision is becoming more, not less, prevalent. In Saudi Arabia fifteen teenage girls were burned to death in a school fire, as the religious police would not allow them to flee the building unveiled. But the oppression of women hardly receives any political consideration, though we would be naive to think it couldn't happen to millions more women, even in the West.

So when the Early Church Fathers turned their backs on the message of equality in Genesis, they failed to lead the Church in fulfilling part of its special commission, and therefore failed the world. What a radical message it was. It challenges the reduction of the female to a commodity and the wholesale abuse of girls and women everywhere – by inferior status and lack of human rights, genital mutilation, child prostitution, sexual exploitation and domestic violence.

Throughout history, Christian women, mostly acting alone or in small, radical, often despised groups, have attacked basic injustices to achieve suffrage, improve the lot of prostitutes and proclaim new freedoms such as unbound feet. Largely, however, the Church dropped the ball. The feminist movement caught it before it touched the ground and ran with it. They rose to the challenge laid down by early Christian feminists, changed basic attitudes in Western countries to divorce, domestic violence, child abuse and rape, then went way beyond the God-given remit, claiming that women were morally superior and men dispensable. In today's post-feminist era, men in the West are struggling to redefine what it means to be a male in this strange new world, while the Church, at least twenty-five years behind the times, still can't decide whether and what a woman should be allowed to do, and blames feminists for creating the problem in the first place. Before Christians lay many of society's ills at that particular door, we need to take account of what they did achieve, and grieve for the trophy that should have been ours.

Man's little helper?

> It is not good for the man to be alone. I will make a helper suitable for him.
>
> GENESIS 2:18

It is the second, more detailed account of creation in Genesis 2 – 'I will make [Adam] a helper suitable for him' – that is used to justify the notion that woman was an afterthought, a PS at the end of God's correspondence. That one little English word, 'helper', appears to be the root of the problem – a justification for relegating woman to a supporting role. Of course, it could be argued that God's first attempt at creating humankind was a trial run, that he took one look at Adam, stood back, scratched his head and said, 'I must be able to do better than that!' – but that wouldn't be very generous.

The Hebrew for helper is *ezer,* used fifteen times in the Hebrew Scriptures, fourteen of them to refer to God himself. *Ezer* is used in Psalm 30:10, where the writer cries out, 'O LORD, be my help', and in Psalm 54:4, where he proclaims that God is indeed his helper. If God is our helper, is he therefore inferior to the humans he has made, a general factotum and servant? No doubt like any father he may have to change our nappies and clear up our messes from time to time, but that doesn't make him subordinate to us, an enabler of all our little schemes and projects, ambitions and goals, much as we're tempted to behave as if he was.

When my husband Peter's old headmaster at Monkton Combe, a public school with a Christian foundation, retired, he remained available for consultation and support, should it be needed. 'Derek Wigram,' announced an old boys' magazine, 'is now serving the Lord in an advisory capacity.' Don't we all? And a fat lot of good it is – fortunately.

There is no hierarchical implication in the word 'helper'. It isn't man the male, but man as male and female, who is made in the image of God. Together we reflect differing male and female aspects of one who has no gender. God doesn't establish a primary and secondary authority over creation. There is no chief executive and vice chief, no sheriff and deputy. Woman isn't even back-up, let alone a helpless dependent. *Ezer* is verb as well as noun, and means 'to protect, surround, defend, cherish'. These words are much more in keeping with the overall context of the creation story than 'back-up' or 'support' – paralleled in *Roget's Thesaurus* as 'prop', 'crutch' and 'backbone'. Are men really flattered by the notion of being as spineless as a jellyfish without a woman to lean on? On the other hand, if I help you cross the road, which of us is the stronger?

In 1971 President Richard Nixon of the USA, a close family friend of evangelist Billy Graham, addressed a public event in Crutchfield and said in Graham's presence, 'We all think of Billy Graham as a strong man. But as I look at the Graham family, if I am asked who are the stronger, Billy Graham or the women in his family, I'd say the women every time . . . God made man out of the soft earth, but he made woman out of a hard rib – the woman is the stronger of the two.'[6] The truth is, women are often resourceful and resilient, and when we really love, cherish and protect a man, it has the power to transform him into the giant he was meant to be. We also know how to reduce him to mincemeat. It is a fearful responsibility.

This 'helper' God creates is 'fit' or 'suitable' for Adam. These are fairly weak translations of what is a unique propositional expression, *knegedu*, not used anywhere else in the

Bible. *Knegedu* comes from *neged,* which means 'opposite'. *Knegedu* is even stronger. It actually means 'opposite against', or 'standing boldly opposite'. In other words, Eve is right in Adam's face, nose to nose, eyeball to eyeball. They can gaze at each other with love and longing, or confront if necessary, and it often is.

Archbishop Desmond Tutu unwittingly described *knegedu* when he spoke of his relationship with his wife, Leah. 'I have a very strong weakness for being liked . . . I am guilty of the sin of pride. Sometimes I find it very difficult to be humble – that is why it is so good to have Leah. She pulls me down a peg or two. To her I am not an archbishop with a Nobel prize. I'm just a not-very-good husband who loves gardens but won't do any gardening.'[7]

My friend Sharon waited a long time for a prince to arrive on his charger and sweep her off her feet. When he eventually cantered in, he turned out to be a free church minister in his forties who had managed to ride out the relentless advances of the many single women in his congregations who quite liked the idea of being the pastor's wife. But Sharon didn't simply swoon into his arms and let him carry her away. She had learned to stand up for herself and resisted all attempts to tame her. 'All these years,' he said to her, not a little exasperated, 'I could have had any one of countless women, who hung on my every word and agreed with all I said – and God has to give me you.'

'Ah,' Sharon said to him, 'that's because he knew it was me you needed.'

Knegedu isn't just about marriage. Although it also means 'corresponding to' or 'answering to', although woman appears to supplement and complement the male, Jesus never married and he was certainly not incomplete. He did, however, have many significant, equal relationships with women that answered some of the emotional needs of a young man.

So away with the notion that God looks down on poor li tle man and says, 'There you are, all on your owny-oh.'

make you a teddy bear to keep you company, and drive the nasty loneliness away.' Nor did God create woman because he knew Adam would never go out and buy himself a new fig leaf when the old one wore out.

When God declares, 'It's not good for man to be alone,' he isn't simply plagiarizing the sixteenth-century poet John Donne, who said no man was an island. For one thing, John Donne hadn't been born – though God no doubt had access to a preview of his poems.

But what I want to know is this: if, before the creation of Eve, Adam was told he could eat from any tree in the garden except the Tree of the Knowledge of Good and Evil, why didn't he head straight for the Tree of Life? For at this stage, although he hasn't yet disobeyed his Maker, he has human life but not God's life. It was imperative that he swallowed a chunk of fruit from the Tree of Life, to move, as Watchman Nee puts it, 'from simply being created by God, to being born of him as well'.[8] But he doesn't. Is it possible that the male tendency to isolationism and independence is manifesting itself from the very beginning? Could it be that this tendency is profoundly understood by a Maker who creates a being to meet Adam's deepest need – someone who will look him in the eye and draw him gently out of his self-sufficiency, so that they can serve God more fully together than apart?

Here in Genesis is the answer to the very contemporary question posed by *Bridget Jones's Diary* as to whether men and women really need each other at all in this enlightened age of ours. Vexed female columnists denounced Bridget as a bad female role model for daring to suggest that life might be better with a man. After all, countless women now choose to live and raise children without any male presence. But Bridget gets her man and life is richer for both of them because of it. Men and women are made for each other, yet we can only truly enjoy the full benefits of that extraordinary relationship when we stand boldly, but lovingly, opposite each other.

So this is what I've been missing

So God says, 'Adam, I have the perfect answer. I will create someone who will fulfil all your deepest longings. She will be wife, friend, confidante, colleague and lover, but it will cost you an arm and a leg.'

'Tell you what,' Adam says to God, 'what will you give me for just a rib?'

Much has been made of the fact that woman was formed from an entirely dispensable part of the male anatomy, but forty-two other references in the Bible to the Hebrew word *sela*, used here for 'rib', are translated 'side'. More than 250 years ago, in his great commentary on the Bible, Matthew Henry wrote:

> The woman was made out of rib out of the side of Adam; not made out of his head to rule over him; nor out of his feet to be trampled upon by him; but out of his side to be equal with him, under his arm to be protected, and near to his heart to be beloved.[9]

When he sees woman, Adam recognizes her at once. This is what he has been waiting for, 'bone of my bones and flesh of my flesh' (Genesis 2:23). In other words, 'Nice as they are, God, I really didn't fancy any of the animals, but this time you've excelled yourself. This one's just like me – sister, wife, colleague, friend and partner.' There is no mention here of any physical, anatomical or biological differences, no order of tasks. Man and woman are biologically, psychologically, sociologically and spiritually the same. It is the sameness Adam welcomes. The differences are only skin deep.

Our son Joel was three when his sister Abby was born. 'It was like having a human doll,' he said, 'especially when she began to communicate in words I could recognize. She was a person just like me who could respond and it was so exciting.' All was well while she remained dependent, adoring and malleable. But imperceptibly the little girl with seraphic face and

golden curls grew into an adolescent who rejected his protectiveness and pedantic ideas. She realized her big brother wasn't
a giant after all, and had developed a vocabulary finely honed
enough to highlight his foibles and failures and demolish him
in front of his friends.

It's the story of all men and women in a microcosm. For
two teenagers loving was no longer automatic. It had to be
learned. Once he was no longer threatened by her independent mind, nor she by his need to dominate her, a deeper relationship was formed on the foundation of mutual respect. It
amuses me how fiercely they refuse to enter into any inferred
criticism of the other by a parent. And of course, in their loyalty to each other they're absolutely right. He still takes a great
deal of pride in her feminine attractions, and she in his bois-
terous male energy, but now they recognize an innate, God-
given sameness and equality. Having discovered the personal
benefits of having a strong and gifted sister for a friend, Joel
cannot bear to see restrictions on any woman simply on the
basis of her gender.

Leaving, cleaving and coming unstuck

Adam calls his wife Eve. In Hebrew, Eve is called *Chava,* which
means a great deal more than just plain 'life', or *chai.* As a child,
like many Jewish people, I was given a representation of *chai* in
gold to wear around my neck. It's a bit of superstition, but I
simply found it ostentatious and got tired of having to explain
what it was. *Chai* is at the root of *l'chaim,* 'to life', the Jewish
version of 'cheers', said before downing a pint or a glass of wine.
Jews place a high value on human life. For the moment it is all
we know. But 'Mother of all Living' is not an adequate translation of Eve's name (Genesis 3:20). She may well be the means
whereby man manages to procreate, but she is a great deal more
than a walking reproductive system. In the Hebrew Scriptures
the verb *chavah* is consistently translated 'to declare'. In other

words, the name given to woman has a verbal implication. It actually means 'spoken word of life'. Woman not only gives, she also speaks life to the man, and therefore to all humanity. She is created a communicator, instinctively relational.

It is interesting that throughout their lives, men will find it harder than women to express their feelings. Men who resort to domestic violence tend to do so because they are often unable to find the right words to give vent to their anger.

It may be a very elastic point, but some contemporary medical research suggests that woman's gift with language, and her ability to verbalize her emotions, could come from the way the brain is constructed. Speech is located in the left side of the brain, emotional responses in the right. In the early weeks of development a foetus is not obviously male or female. It is the sudden surge of androgens, the male hormones, at sixteen weeks that precipitates the development of the distinctive male characteristics. The hormones also appear to cause a slight thickening of the central column in the brain, so that messages cannot be so easily transferred from one side to the other, possibly making it harder for men to express their feelings.

Italian men, it must be said, appear to defy the 'Berlin Wall in the brain' concept. Not that I have ever been close enough to one to know whether they are really as emotionally articulate as they appear. On the other hand, I have worked as a communications manager in the National Health Service for many years and I do know that boys develop motor skills much later than girls, and that from childhood, men outnumber women by as many as ten to one in needing the specialist attention of a speech and language therapist.

If God created woman to speak words of life, that can only be of benefit to the whole of society, including the men. It is hardly surprising, therefore, that throughout history Satan has had a vested interest in keeping her silent and subjugated. His attempt to achieve that goal begins here.

At first all is well in the land of romance. Adam and Eve 'cleave' to one another. The Hebrew word is *dabaq*, meaning to 'cling', 'stick' or 'adhere'. It is as if they have been attached with superglue. Any parent knows that separating flesh that has been unintentionally joined by this pervasive substance can only be achieved with pain and trauma. The principle of leaving the parental home behind and cleaving to the new partner is reiterated by Jesus himself. It is therefore foundational. The past may not impinge on this present. Adam and Eve had no parents or family to leave, but Adam seems to have been quite happy to exchange his nights out with the animals for nights at home with the wife. In other words, Eve now has a prime call on his commitment, while he must be the priority in her life, even when the children come.

It is amazing how many couples come unstuck on this particular principle. My mother used to ring her mother every day for advice, support and commiseration, even though they lived a mere ten miles apart and saw each other at least once a week. My grandmother's word was law in our home. 'I've always been a better mother than a wife,' my grandmother used to say with some pride. 'A woman will always be better at one role than the other,' she assured me. I disagree. It was a justification for being a very possessive, demanding parent, and that was never an ideal arrangement for my father or my grandfather.

So Adam and Eve are stuck to or with each other – naked and without shame. I remember being shocked by a response to an article I wrote for *Woman Alive* magazine about enjoying our sexuality. A young woman wrote to criticize my suggestion that there should be any pleasure in sex. She and her husband had been so horrified at the sight of each others' naked bodies on their wedding night that they never managed to consummate the relationship. I could hardly believe that in this so-called 'open' society of ours such repression could exist. It does, and I hope they got the help they so obviously needed.

The first couple's nakedness in the garden is mental and emotional, as well as physical. In fact, in most marriages, the three are interdependent – reflecting the indivisibility of mind, body and spirit in Jewish thinking. The man and woman have nothing to hide from each other. No negative childhood experience, no youthful foolishness, no rejection complex or hurtful past memory can rise up like bile to sour the spontaneous, joyous moments of mutual discovery and companionship. Until that one moment of disobedience.

Where was Adam when Eve was deceived by the serpent and took the fruit she knew wasn't hers to take? Was he at the bottom of the garden on a deckchair reading the newspaper or having a nap? Had he gone to watch a football match? No. 'She also gave some to her husband, who was with her' (Genesis 3:6). He was right beside her, at her elbow. In fact, Adam doesn't appear to have tried very hard to fulfil his duty to protect this being who was his to cherish, or to exercise the authority he had been given over every living thing, including the serpent. He is fully implicated in Eve's decision to ignore the words of her Maker, and from that moment the relationship between men and women is doomed to difficulty. One cock-a-snook at the Creator, and suddenly, 'It's all his fault,' or, 'She made me do it.' Farewell to trust, harmony and intimacy. Enter vulnerability, insecurity and isolation.

I'm rather fond of this description of a noncommunicative husband by a frustrated wife, recounted by Paul Tournier. He suggested she tell her husband how she felt. 'Oh,' she blurted out, 'my husband is a mysterious island. I am forever circling round it but never finding a beach where I may land.' Tournier writes:

> I understood her, for it is true. There are men who are like mysterious islands. They protect themselves against any approach. They no longer express themselves, nor do they take a stand on anything. When their wife consults them on something important, they hide themselves behind their paper. They look deeply absorbed. They answer without even looking up, in a tone impersonal, anonymous, and vague, which excludes all argument. Or else they make a joke of it.[10]

History goes pear-shaped

I will greatly increase your pains in childbearing;
with pain you will give birth to children.
Your desire will be for your husband,
and he will rule over you.

GENESIS 3:16

The foundation for the often dysfunctional nature of many male–female relationships is laid in the Genesis story in this one little verse. Commentators are very divided about what it means, but one thing is certain: despite how it may appear superficially, there is no sexual connotation in the word 'desire'. Common sense should tell us that. Which of the two genders has the bigger problem with the basic instinct? The one with the testosterone, actually. Surely God knew that would be the case, so had no reason to suggest that the woman would be permanently on heat.

Yet throughout the glorious and sorry history of the Church, woman has continually been cast in the role of temptress – and all because of this verse. This particular interpretation began during the period between the end of the Old Testament and the beginning of the New, when some Jewish scholars were trying to reconcile their Scriptures with the pagan Greek and Roman tales of gods and goddesses that were an inherent part of the culture in which they lived. They began to confuse the biblical story of Eve with the mythical Pandora, a beautiful but deceitful woman sent to earth by the gods with a box full of misery for the human race.

The Babylonian Talmud, a compilation of traditional Jewish sayings passed down orally from one generation to the next but not committed to writing until the seventh or eighth century, claimed that Eve – or was it Pandora? – brought ten curses on herself when she opened the forbidden box. Number 5 is 'Your desire shall be for your husband', followed by a rather coarse and explicit description of what that entailed –

enough to make a twenty-first-century husband reckon half the chance would be a fine thing.

The apocryphal book Ecclesiasticus, written between 200 and 100 BC, claims, 'From woman a beginning of sin; and because of her all die.' This does not tie in with the theology of the apostle Paul, who would say in his letter to the Romans that death and sin came through Adam, but it certainly does reflect the Greek and Roman attitude of the time. So the Apocrypha simply gave a theological justification for an erroneous cultural and secular attitude prevalent at the time.

Even the King James and Revised Standard Versions of the Bible add an English 'yet' before 'your desire will be for your husband', establishing a tenuous connection between childbirth and a woman's supposed indefatigable sexual desire. A loose interpretation would be, 'Sorry girls, having babies is going to be horrible, but since you'll keep on having the hots for a man, you'll keep on putting yourselves through that particular misery.' That link isn't there in the original Hebrew. Nowhere in the text is there any suggestion that a woman has masochistic tendencies. So what does the verse mean?

'I will greatly increase your pains [*tsavon*] in childbearing; with pain [*etzev*] you will give birth to children.' *Tsavon* normally means 'sorrow', and *etzev* 'toil'. They are not the most common words used in the Bible to describe the pain of childbirth. In fact, they are a direct parallel to the 'sorrow' and 'toil' that are Adam's lot as he struggles to make the ground productive.[11] There is no reference here to any basic biological differences between a woman and a man that predispose women to running the home and men to running the world. Work will involve the same degree of sorrow and toil for both. Man's greater physical strength is of little relevance. In fact, childbearing probably takes more physical stamina and a higher pain threshold than any other human activity.

Hard work, pain and discomfort are not a curse. Satan is cursed. The ground is now cursed. But God will not and cannot curse the creatures he has created with such love and hope.

He simply describes the inevitable consequences of their determination to follow their own propensities. In fact, Eve is given a special blessing. Woman will give birth to the Messiah, the one who will ultimately grind the serpent into oblivion and restore human beings to their original fellowship with God. With such a promise for humankind, the process of having babies was never going to be easy. Since Messiah will be born of a woman, Satan will have a vested interest in making sure every birth will be threatened.

I suspect that this is the moment when the hitherto serene and seamless female reproductive system suddenly suffers meltdown and becomes completely scrambled. Periods never arrive at the right time, desire between spouses is guaranteed never to coincide, fertility is a hit-and-miss affair, pregnancy means nausea, stretch marks, high blood pressure, gastric reflux and the slow disintegration of the teeth, and the menopause is a minefield of irrational behaviour and hot flushes. Confronted with the vagaries of my menstrual cycle, my husband said he understood the feeling behind the traditional Jewish morning prayer said by a man, in which he thanks God he's not a Gentile or a woman. I think he has grossly exaggerated these minor inconveniences. On the other hand, would men have coped with periods? The poet Carol Ann Duffy tries to imagine it and thinks not.

> Then he started his period.
> One week in bed.
> Two doctors in.
> Three painkillers four times a day.
>
> And later
> a letter
> to the powers that be
> demanding full-paid menstrual leave twelve weeks per year.
> I see him still,
> his selfish pale face peering at the moon
> through the bathroom window.
> *The curse*, he said, *the curse*.[12]

If, as some suggest, the text means 'I will greatly increase your sorrows and conceptions', we could assume God never originally intended that pregnancy would be the potential outcome of every experience of intercourse, ruining the fun and enjoyment factor for millions of women through the centuries, condemning them to serial childbearing and an early grave. I believe God gave sex for mutual pleasure and intimacy, and not just to turn women into baby-making machines. But presumably he foresaw, and may actually have been rooting for us to invent, such things as contraception, tampons, epidurals and HRT, creating hitherto unknown freedoms for twentieth-century women.

It isn't only women who are blessed with problems in the reproductive department, of course. When her patients complain about the lot of women, obstetrician and gynaecologist Anne Garden suggests they bide their time until that moment when they are tucked up comfortably in bed and, tyrannized by his prostate, their partner is trotting backwards and forwards to the loo.

So what is the woman's desire?

Despite the benefits of our culture, those of us blessed with having children will find it does have a way of bringing its own inevitable pain. My mother used to say, 'When your children are little, your fears are little. As they get bigger, so do the fears.' I didn't believe her. I was too busy juggling the child-minding, worrying about feeding, teething and minor developmental and behavioural difficulties. But there is no anxiety to equal a mother's. Every new adventure of theirs spells danger and terror for me. I feel their every hurt, sorrow, pain, disappointment and rejection much more vividly than any of my own. They are my daily breath, hope and prayer, an integral part of me, yet completely separate. I can't imagine the pain of losing one of them permanently, or of having them reject me.

It was difficult enough letting them walk out of the door and down the path into their own lives. I realized then that I raised them only to give them up, and never knew how hard that would be.

The bonus is that Peter and I are alone together again, and we still love each other. My desire, or *teshuqah,* for my husband is still very much alive, but I'm not sure that has anything to do with this verse, since possible impregnation at our stage of life really would be a miracle. *Teshuqah* was translated 'lust' by Jerome in his Latin version of the Bible known as the Vulgate, published in AD 382. The first English translation in 1380 by Wycliffe, based on the Vulgate, also spoke of woman's 'lust'. In his fairly recent commentary on Genesis, Gordon Wenham still seems to think that the word he translates as 'urge' has sexual overtones. 'Women often allow themselves to be exploited ... because of their urge towards their husband: their sexual appetite may sometimes make them submit to quite unreasonable male demands.'[13] This simply doesn't ring true for me. Women submit to abusive male demands out of fear and poor self-esteem, for money, or, in developing countries, because they have no alternative. Some may do so out of a misguided sense of love – but generally, sex is not the driving force for women that it is for men.

Susan Foh agrees that *teshuqah,* or 'desire', cannot be sexual in this context, then argues that woman's real urge is not for sex, but independence.[14] Her desire is to dominate the male. Apart from the fact that this simply isn't in the text, there is no universal or historical evidence to back it up. Until the last forty years, independence wasn't on a woman's agenda – especially if she was poor. Women simply learned ways of manipulating, or even emasculating, a man to get what they wanted. In the north of England it was an art every young woman learned from a master – her mother – but at the end of the day, independence was outside the realms of possibility. Divorce could leave even a well-to-do woman disenfranchised and destitute. Or imagine a young Indian woman, condemned to slavery in her in-laws' home for not having a big enough dowry, even dreaming of being in control of her life. Today, in most countries outside the West, the very idea of independence is so far removed from a woman's experience that even the fantasy is too cruel.

The wonder of the Scriptures for me is their ability both by text and story to transcend cultural, international and historical boundaries. If it doesn't make connections with my experience as a woman, wherever I live, whoever I am, it cannot truly be the inspired word of God. But time and time again, as I dig deeper into the text, it challenges aspects not just of my life but of every life, with a wisdom which belies its age.

Teshuqah is only used to translate 'desire' in two other places in the Hebrew Scriptures, and neither have a sexual connotation. In Genesis 4:7 God warns Cain, 'Sin is crouching at the door; its desire [or pull] is for you, but you must master it' (RSV). And in Song of Songs 7:10 the writer says, 'I am my beloved's, and his desire [longing] is for me' (RSV).

Missionary doctor Katherine Bushnell (1865–1946), who campaigned against the white slave trade and abuse of women throughout the world, shattered preconceived stereotypes of the role of women in 1923, in her book *God's Word to Women*. During her time in China she was horrified at the way culturally biased translations of the Bible brought women into greater, not lesser, bondage. She was convinced that this was totally at odds with the liberating, healing power of the Gospel, and spent forty years learning biblical languages and studying the original texts so that women everywhere would have a solid, biblical foundation for their freedom. Dr Bushnell points out that most of the ancient translations of the texts, including the Septuagint of 285 BC, kept the literal translation of *teshuqah,* which is 'turning'. In other words, Eve is told that from now on her turning, or natural gravitation, will be towards man rather than towards God.

That translation makes a great deal of sense to me. As a single woman I relied on an hour of meditation and prayer each morning. Once married, especially when the babies arrived, there wasn't time. But in all honesty the erosion of that hour pre-dated motherhood. In fact, it began on the first morning of our marriage. I simply didn't need to depend on God in the same way – not when there was a flesh-and-blood source of wisdom, comfort and company sitting in the bed next to me. For some things a girl must be alone – and one of them is private prayer. But it was abundantly clear, as Peter picked up his Bible and tucked himself happily into the sheets, that he had no intention of vacating his warm little space to move elsewhere.

That was the beginning of many years of negotiation for the quiet I needed to re-establish the primary relationship I had lost. It's all too easy to become a little dependent when you are married to a rock like my man. But it isn't only in marriage that women have a tendency to revolve around men like the moon around the sun. It was once the accepted culture of the workplace. Nurses scurried around male doctors, air hostesses around the pilots, office clerks around the male managers. We may think that socio-economic independence for women in the West has changed all that, but there are still secretaries who would lie down in a puddle rather than let the boss dirty his shoes; and in some churches, the minister still has a bevy of good ladies at his beck and call. Whenever she comes home, Abby is still asked repeatedly if there is a man in her life, as if being without one is the worst thing that could happen to her. It is too easy to invest our all – our attractiveness as women, our value as people, our justification for living – in male acceptance, pleasure and approval. It is oh-so-instinctive to bask in reflected glory.

A friend described recently how the teenage girls for whom she was responsible at Soul Survivor (an under-canvas conference for thousands of young people) got up at 5.30 a.m. to get the hot showers, shampoo and blow-dry their hair and put on full make-up before the boys got up, while the boys didn't wash for a week and certainly didn't notice the efforts made for their benefit.

In its extreme form, the unspoken expectation that only a man can meet our deepest needs leads to an obsession with body image, the diet and fitness craze, and ultimately anorexia and bulimia. In developing countries, many of the inhumane practices imposed on women, such as circumcision, are condoned and even encouraged by women themselves, terrified that their daughters won't attract a man.

And what does the man do with the woman's desire?

'And he will rule over you,' says God – with a long sigh, I suspect. Woman's very need of man will make her vulnerable to man's domination. The relationship becomes co-dependent. The secretary needs to be trodden on to feel a sense of worth, and the boss is happy to oblige, for it gives him a sense of power. The mistress stays with a man who has no intention of leaving his wife for her, because she thinks she cannot face life without him and any crumb of affection is better than none at all. Women will marry, not for love, but because they cannot face the possibility of being single. Co-dependency does not lead to healthy compatibility. When two people feed on rather than feed each other, it reduces rather than releases.

For God, this is a sad and sorry irony. Men were never intended to live with the intolerable burden of having to fulfil a woman's every emotional need. As Paul Tournier's client had seen only too well, the man can be perfectly happy on his own little desert island – behind a newspaper, in front of a television or computer, at the football match or lost in a piece of work brought home from the office. Then he looks up and sees her boat. She's rowing for all she's worth, making dozens of different approaches in her determination to find a landing space. He throws up his hands in horror and heads for the trees. But the harder she tries to find him, the more determined he is to hide, for he knows that whatever he does, whatever he says, it will never be enough to fill what Jane Hanson calls 'the great canyon' in a woman.[15] For the sake of self-preservation, he must find one way or another to keep her in her place, either by becoming the absent, workaholic male of the West, or the subjugating, desensitized male of many developing countries. How can the behaviour of Afghan, Saudi Arabian and Iraqi be understood, except by a deep-seated, almost instinctive fear? They cannot live *knegedu* with their women, for they know that if the women are allowed to express their views, the men will be forced to live with confrontation, criticism and disapproval. Repression means freedom for the men to do as they please, a way of stamping on the tender, loving part of themselves.

At face value it seems as if there is little distinction between the man's and the woman's sin and its consequences. Both make a bid for divinity, and both, for their pains, are condemned to hard work and grief. But a closer look at the story reveals that both the initial failure and its implications are different. Woman is given dominion, authority and supremacy over the entire created order – with one restriction. She may not eat from one particular tree. Nonetheless, she reaches out and takes the one thing that is not hers to have. She fails in the area of authority or dominion, and it is her dominion and authority she forfeits, for man will now dominate and subjugate her.

Adam, on the other hand, is given a relationship that is the very key to his wellbeing. But he sins in the area of relationship. He colludes with Eve when he should have protected her, and he forfeits the benefits of that relationship. In dominating woman he loses an equal, a partner and a friend. Every society where woman is a second-class citizen is only half alive. Unwittingly, man cuts himself off from the intimacy and closeness for which his entire being will always yearn. Here is the foundation for the evidence described by contemporary sociolinguist Deborah Tannen, who claims that in the West women use language to connect while men use it to compete.

The eternal tragedy of male and female relationships is encapsulated in this story for all time. Behind Adam and Eve the garden gate slams shut. No more frolics. Both are now condemned to the daily grind of creating a viable economy and raising a family.

I was intrigued by a recent television series on Channel 4 called *Sex BC*, because I saw for the first time how new historic research could bear the book of Genesis out, and give some justification for my instincts about female sexuality. Professors of ancient history claimed that in the earliest recorded time, men and women had indeed been equal, hunting, gathering and cooking side by side. The women breastfed their babies to early childhood and that tended to act as a natural contraceptive. But then civilization changed. Society became agricultural. A large workforce was needed to till the land. Babies were fed cows' milk. Women succumbed to one pregnancy after another, and their exhausted bodies often gave out in childbirth. Those who survived were domesticated, tied to the hearth. Women's sexuality began to feel more like a curse than a blessing.

Mary Stewart van Leeuwen puts it like this: 'The fall ripped apart the organic unity of homes and communities and turned us into a society of commuting wage earners (mostly men) and domestically isolated homemakers (mostly women).' In other words, from then on human beings simply accepted that man's dominion had become domination and woman's sociability had become 'social enmeshment'.[16] We are both trapped in the stereotypes, the separate cages, that society, and often the Church, has created for us. Men are locked into expectations of achievement, success and invulnerability, and women into nurturing, caring and self-sacrifice. If we don't fit the stereotypes, we can feel more like Frankenstein's monster than God's created handiwork.

Adam and Eve before the fall are male and female as God intended, enjoying mutuality, compatibility and equality. Sometimes we catch a glimpse of what that can mean – in a marriage where we take the risk of exposing ourselves emotionally in a new way to our partner and it leads to an intimacy we only imagined in our dreams, or in a working relationship where, as colleagues, we use our gender differences dynamically to contribute to the success of a project and discover a heady satisfaction in complementary companionship.

That is because redemption, that undeserved, life-transforming gift of Christ from his cross, has opened up the possibility of a restoration of the relationship that was lost through Adam's and Eve's disobedience. When a man hands over his autonomy to Christ, he need no longer feel threatened when a gifted woman takes her place at his side, looking him straight in the eye. When God is the centre of a woman's life, the repository of all her expectations, aspirations and desires, she will no longer need to drain a man, nor depend on him for her sense of self-worth. Then, with dignity and independence re-established, we will be able to lay down the anger and resentment that has pursued us through the centuries. Women can grasp hold of the key, then release our men, husbands, colleagues, fathers, brothers, sons, from their self-imposed isolation in the fortress of the mind, the cages they build to protect themselves from hurt, pain and failure. We will take up the calling for which we were created, to speak life into our homes, workplaces, communities and society. The world has been waiting for that for a very long time.

Notes

1. Augustine, *On the Trinity*, 7.7.10.
2. Origen, *Selecta in Exodus*, 17.7.
3. Quoted by Elaine Storkey, *Contributions to Christian Feminism* (Christian Impact, 1995), p. 48.
4. Moulana Majaz Azami, *Guidance for a Muslim Wife* (Madrasah Arabia Islamia, 1990). There is a good deal of wise advice for women on relationships and raising children in this little booklet, but also the undoubted message that she serves God by serving her man.
5. 'Beyond the Veil', *Dispatches*, ITV, 10 November 2002.
6. Patricia Daniels Cornwell, *A Time for Remembering: The Ruth Bell Graham Story* (Harper and Row, 1983), p. 202.
7. Archbishop Desmond Tutu quoted from an interview with Gyles Brandreth, 'My Idea of Heaven', *The Sunday Telegraph*, 5 April 2001. © Telegraph Group Limited 2001.
8. Watchman Nee, *The Messenger of the Cross* (Christian Fellowship Publishers, 1980), pp. 136–37.
9. Leslie F. Church, ed., *Matthew Henry's Commentary on the Whole Bible* (Zondervan, 1961), p. 7.
10. Paul Tournier, *Marriage Difficulties* (SCM, 1967).
11. Derek Kidner, *Genesis: An Introduction and Commentary*, Tyndale Old Testament Commentaries, ed. D.J. Wiseman (IVP, 1967).
12. Carol Ann Duffy, from 'Mrs Tiresias', *The World's Wife* (Picador, 1999), reprinted with the permission of Macmillan, London, UK.
13. Gordon J. Wenham, *Word Biblical Commentary, Genesis 1–15* (Word Books, 1987), p. 81.
14. Susan Foh, 'What is the Woman's Desire?' *Westminster Theological Journal*, 37, 1974–75, pp. 376–83.
15. Jane Hanson with Marie Powers, *Fashioned for Intimacy* (Regal, 1997).
16. Mary Stewart van Leeuwen, *Gender and Grace: Women and Men in a Changing World* (IVP, 1990), p. 117.

CHAPTER 2

The Manipulative Woman

After Eve, women had no voice, no power, few rights. For many centuries they didn't appear to miss what they hadn't known, largely because they found subtle ways of exerting their influence. In the well-established tradition of the four founding matriarchs of the Judaeo-Christian culture, they resorted to the only means at their disposal – manipulation. Many of the matriarchs in my own family were masters of the art. Take, for example, my Grandmother Rose.

Rose and her husband Michael, my father's father, were both asylum seekers from aggressive anti-Semitism in Latvia. Why Grandfather Michael chose to seek his fortune in the United Kingdom, rather than France like most of his cousins, no one knew for certain, but he kept in close touch with them and old, dog-eared, sepia photographs testify that for many years they exchanged regular visits in the summer. He was an only child and eventually they were the only relatives he had.

Rose, whom he met and married in Britain, was not an easy woman. Crippled by a badly treated hip injury after a childhood fall, she was aged before her time by arthritis and disappointment. I remember a small, bent old woman with a pudding-basin cut of thinning white hair, whose eyes were like raisins in a sponge cake and whose tongue was as sharp as her nose.

My mother thought her the original mother-in-law from hell, critical and complaining whatever was done for her. She was incredibly possessive of my father. No one was good enough for her only son, born unexpectedly eight years after his sister and the only glimmer of light in her old age. He could do no wrong. When my mother told her she was expecting my younger sister, a third child, she snapped, 'How could you do that to my son?' My mother assured her, 'Your son had a part to play'. And my father would make excuses for her, citing the hard and lonely life she had endured after Michael's premature death. But even he had no idea of the lengths to which her unforgiving nature had driven her.

Long before my parents' marriage, probably some time shortly before the Second World War, a disagreement arose between her and Michael's family in France, probably a minor tiff which grew into epic proportions in Rose's eyes. From that moment on she intercepted and destroyed every letter they wrote to her husband. My grandfather was deeply saddened by their silence, but gradually, as the years went by, when his letters were never acknowledged, he resigned himself to the fact that they must have perished at the hands of the Nazis. He used to tell my father repeatedly how aggrieved he was that the only family he possessed had died in the Holocaust. It was the sad tale my father always told us, lamenting his lack of relatives on his father's side.

So when, some time after my father's death, my sister suddenly received a letter from cousins in France, we were all rather shocked. Peter and I went to visit them in Nancy one year on our way home from a holiday. The tale they told was very different from the myth that had been handed down to us. They had indeed been in grave danger during the Nazi occupation, but had managed to flee to the Alps, where they had been hidden for several years by a small community of Italians unsympathetic – as so many had been – to Mussolini. They had tried to reinstate the correspondence with their cousin Michael once the war was over, and couldn't understand why he had never replied to their letters. In the end, bitterly disappointed, they had simply given up.

I was appalled. What a bequest to leave to any family. Here we were, years after my grandmother's death, struggling to understand what on earth could have driven her so doggedly to engineer the termination of the relationship with her husband's family. What vindictiveness could have induced her to destroy those letters, year in, year out, when she could see the pain it caused her husband? How could she have allowed such a sad misapprehension to continue, with its consequences for successive generations?

I was twelve when she died, and all I remember of her are weekly visits to the bed-sitting-room that was her self-inflicted prison in my aunt's house. She hated living with her daughter and son-in-law, and felt she should really be living with her beloved son instead. So she took her revenge on both her children.

'Michael has appeared to me in a dream and told me I must join him,' I overheard her say to my father one icy Christmas Eve. 'Nonsense, Mother,' he reassured her, but she died the next day. I thought it must be wonderful to have a premonition like that, until I learned – years later – that she had committed suicide. Never again would my father spend a single Christmas Day without the memory of seeing her body, calling the undertaker, making the harrowing arrangements. No Christmas Day would ever be without the sorrow, regrets and guilt. This was the ultimate in family manipulation – and we all paid the price for it.

Four kinds of women

As a Jewish child at a private Church of England girls' school in Newcastle with predominantly non-Jewish friends, I was very conscious of how different the lives of our women were from the lives of the women in their families. One or two of their mothers went out to work, mainly as teachers, while others were stalwarts of fundraising or other voluntary organizations, but most appeared to have a great deal of time on their hands. They attended coffee mornings, went into Newcastle to buy bits and bobs for the family cottage in Bamburgh, or a new evening dress for the Northumberland Hunt Ball. They took tea in town at Tilleys, eating little fancy cakes with a fork, to the accompaniment of a wizened female string trio. They never appeared to make decisions about anything that really mattered. That was the father's domain.

Not in my family. My mother socialized very little during the day. She was far too busy cleaning, tidying, organizing, and preparing for the next festival. In our home she reigned supreme. Her kingdom ran like clockwork. Well might my father be the omnipotent, omnicompetent local doctor, but once over the threshold of our home, he abdicated almost all responsibility.

The differences between our grandmothers were even more marked. My friends' grandmothers were sweet, silent, self-effacing seventy-year-olds in black or grey, whose only mission in life was not to be a burden to the younger generations. My maternal grandmother was fifty and a fashion guru. She smoked Woodbines, drank a great deal of whisky, expected a minimum weekly visit and a daily phone call, and her word was law in our home.

The local women in the pit village where my father had his medical practice were more like her, tough and feisty. They controlled the purse strings. The men handed over their weekly pay packet and were given an allowance or drinking money. As the pits began to close there was less to give and life was hard. Those women shouted a lot, but unlike my father and grandfather, who wouldn't have dared answer back, their men told them to shut up and went out anyway.

Most women, it seemed to me, if they did have influence, exercised it from behind, rather than beside, the men in their lives. Most were too afraid of being found unattractive or unlovable to express their needs, wants or real feelings. Those who did, like some of the women in my family, did it in such a way that it provoked a Pavlov's dog reaction. The Sabbath bunch of flowers is hardly a gift of love and affection when the giver knows that the alternative is to be subjected to several hours of haranguing or sulking.

I have a very vivid memory of a schoolfriend's birthday party. She was the daughter of a consultant surgeon, revered by my father, as all consultants were in those days. I was about seven or eight years old and went feeling a little overawed, but with high expectations. It was a horrid party. Mrs Consultant Surgeon, endowed, apparently, with every benefit of her husband's status, income and prestige, showed little evidence of enjoying any of it. Every time a record was played she had a fit of hysterics, whined about having a headache, swore she couldn't cope and demanded that the music be turned off. Since virtually every game, from Musical Chairs to Pass the Parcel, required musical accompaniment, it left her plenty of opportunity to be the centre of attention in a room full of uncomfortable, unhappy little girls.

Later, when my father willed me to tell him what a wonderful time I'd had, I simply nodded. It was my first conscious experience that all was not always well in the world of adults and I couldn't begin to put that into words – especially words he didn't want to hear. Yet in a strange way I was disturbed by the woman's obvious misery, and both embarrassed and sorry for my friend. What would induce a mother to spoil her daughter's birthday party?

As I reflect on it now, I can still feel the strange electricity that passed between the parents – he, impassive behind his half-spectacles; she, demanding and difficult. What was she trying to tell him? Even then I knew the performance was for him. The relationship was the key to the woman's profound unhappiness.

Many years passed before I woke up to the fact that the strange behaviour of several of my schoolfriends' mothers was due to depression or alcohol. Now I understand that behind the façade of the perfect wife and mother, women of their generation had few means of keeping at bay an all-pervading sense of boredom and worthlessness, and were often deeply angry and frustrated. They had no choice but to resort to underhand ways of establishing their presence or achieving their own ends. It hardly led to open, honest, loving relationships. In fact, like my Grandmother Rose's extraordinary piece of deceit, it diminished all the people concerned in one way or another.

As society underwent a major upheaval in the 1970s and '80s, women's expectations of both their personal and working lives soared. Nonetheless, it took some time for them to realize that equal rights and equal pay were all very well, but legislation would never enable them to fulfil their bright, new destiny. Change must come from within as well as from without. To maximize the new opportunities they needed to regain their sense of self-worth, and acquire a more appropriate, confident way of communicating. They would have to learn to kick the need for approval, express their wishes in a more honest manner and take responsibility for their own actions. Seminal books like *A Woman in Your Own Right – Assertiveness and You*[1] by psychologist and counsellor Anne Dickson began to prepare women for the new world of the 1980s.

I found that book incredibly releasing and empowering, and it helped me to regain my sense of being a person, rather than simply an extension of my children, when I went back into the workplace after they had gone to school. But some in the Church, suspicious of any new-fangled, secular ideas, dismissed assertiveness training for women as a licence for self-indulgence, domination and control. This was a complete misunderstanding of the meaning of assertiveness, defined in the dictionary as 'to state positively and confidently'. Anne Dickson explained that her goal was to enable women to rediscover 'the art of clear, honest, direct communication'. This sounds very much like a call to reappropriate God's gift to woman at creation, lost in the annals of male dominance and female co-dependency, or the old *teshuqah*. It is also consistent with instructions in the Bible to be honest and truthful in our relationships.

I was convinced about the need to become lovingly assertive when I confronted the three familiar, predominantly female, unattractive alternatives: aggression, passive acquiescence or manipulation.

Imagine this fairly commonplace scenario. Mum crawls through the back door after a manic day at work, laden with the shopping, to find the sink stacked with dirty dishes, the ironing piled high on a food-bespattered counter, no sign of preparations for the evening meal, and two senseless teenagers stretched out in front of the TV.

She can react in one of four ways. An aggressive woman will scream and shout, bang the doors, throw a few plates, or try to bully or even kick their lifeless forms into action. The passive martyr will sigh sadly, set to, tidy up, put the shopping away and the tea in the oven, then retire early to bed with a headache, feeling depressingly used. A manipulative woman will probably nag, whine and mutter, just loud enough for the children to hear, then look for some way of spoiling the meal for the whole family as a subtle form of punishment and revenge. The problem is that none of these three reactions will bring any benefits for her or for her teenagers. She is left dissatisfied and they learn nothing about decent behaviour and meaningful relationships.

If, however, she were to say, firmly but pleasantly, 'Would you mind putting the video on and recording that programme you're watching, as I'm dog tired and would really appreciate some help,' she might get a more reasonable response, not to mention a modicum of respect. On the other hand, she could make herself a cup of tea, join them in front of the TV, and wait until hunger forces them into the kitchen. But she might be waiting until bedtime.

The aggressive woman can appear competitive, domineering, sarcastic, cold or superior. She tends not to listen, states opinions as facts and is an expert at creating hurt and havoc. She is often caricatured as the bullying boss who reduces her juniors to tears, the domineering wife and mother who always manages to get her own way, the strident feminist for whom every innocent comment is a deliberate slight, dominating men from boardroom to bedroom. But that loud and forceful manner may well be a cover for a lack of self-esteem.

The passive woman feels permanently put-upon, yet won't say so because she can't cope with conflict. She is the minister's wife who has allowed herself to become the parish doormat, wearer of cast-offs from the endless jumble sales she resents having to organize. She is the mother who always picks up the dirty clothes left in a trail from bedroom to bathroom door, silently berating her selfish family. She is the office junior or PA who can't get on with her work because the boss keeps sending her out for aspirin for his toothache or a birthday card for the wife. She is the teacher who always covers for sick leave because she can't say no, but bitterly resents the way she is put upon. Ms Passive is a pushover. She only wants to be nice, but she has 'victim' written all over her. Ironically, in the end, she loses the respect of those she set out to please, and may well suffer from depression as a result of all that repressed anger.

Like my Grandmother Rose, the manipulative woman is cunning enough to gain her own ends without resorting to open confrontation. She uses guilt-inducing tactics instead, like a minister's wife I know who spends her life engineering members of the congregation into doing what she wants them to do without their consciously knowing it. Rather than admit she doesn't want to teach in Sunday school any more, she says, 'If I tell them I'm not well, they'll feel they have to take over my class'. At her worst, like my schoolfriend's mother, the manipulative woman may ruin her child's birthday party or even her child's life, for she simply cannot see how frighteningly destructive her behaviour can be.

I meet all three of those women every day. I see them everywhere, in everyone else – but not in me. Yet most of us oscillate between those personality types all the time, and it's like trying to stand up in the middle of a see-saw. Frustrated with being passive, we swing in the other direction in an attempt to regain our power. But then we fear we're being domineering, so we stagger back towards a more central position and try a more subtle approach to getting our own way. In the end, the see-saw swings to and fro at such a pace that it leaves us feeling exhausted and giddy.

Assertiveness helps us keep our balance. Because the assertive woman accepts herself as she is, she finds it easier to accept other people as they are, with all their faults and foibles. She doesn't need to put others down to increase her own sense of self-worth. She doesn't think they're to blame for what happens to her. She doesn't make them feel guilty for not recognizing her needs. She listens to what others have to say, then expresses her own views openly and honestly, quite prepared to risk the rejection they may incur.

Yet I don't think Anne Dickson had the whole truth. She claims that the assertive woman doesn't suffer from feelings of rejection because her self-esteem is anchored in herself. I know myself too well to have any confidence in that department. I will settle instead for the biblical definition of an assertive woman, preceding Anne Dickson's by several centuries. The assertive woman of faith is never completely crushed because her self-esteem is anchored in God. Her *teshuqah,* her cravings for love and fulfilment, are satisfied by him alone. She knows that he loves and accepts her and has only her good at heart. Therefore she can be as merciful to herself and to others as he is to her. No longer driven by her own insecurities, she is not afraid to speak out with dignity and clarity, or to stand her ground calmly when necessary. If she is hurt, she forgives. And if she is wrong, she apologizes with grace.

The Bible is full of assertive women of calibre – steady and wise, loving and good, open and honest, like Ruth, Esther and Hannah. These are women who know the will of God, adhere to it and speak up for it, whatever the risk, whatever the cost.

They do not achieve that measure of godly assertiveness overnight. Obedience must be learned and embraced. Sadly, Eve did not obey and for a while, as far as woman's story goes, the plot was lost. The evidence is all in the book of Genesis.

Four great matriarchs

Jewish historians often ascribe the survival of the Jewish people, through thousands of years of persecution in the Diaspora, to the Jewish mama. I suspect this may be a rather romanticized notion. Personal experience tells me that it was held together by a curious mixture of chopped liver and emotional blackmail rather than worship, love and peace. Comedian Jackie Mason, a rabbi in a previous life, tells Jewish men to beware. Once they marry their lives will be seriously proscribed. The Jewish woman is so houseproud that he will only be able to sit in the one armchair she sets aside for him. The rest, kept in a pristine, plumped-up, grease-free condition, are strictly for guests. He recommends to Jewish men that they court a woman for as long as they like, but whatever they do, never marry her. 'That way you get to stay a guest and sit in whatever chair you like.'

Eve's tragedy has brought us to this – to a grandfather who thought he had lost his only relatives in the Holocaust, and to a father restricted to one armchair in the multi-armchaired home of my childhood. The *ezer* or helper who has lost her equality is bent on regaining control. She makes her man think he is the centre of the universe, but it is the universe she has constructed and where she reigns supreme. The gentle art of *knegedu*, of loving negotiation and healthy confrontation, has been lost. Be she mother, wife or colleague, when she manipulates, he may wittingly or unwittingly submit – and the outcome, as with my Grandmother Rose's meddling, leaves a bad taste.

According to tradition, Jewish mamas have four role models – the four great, founding mothers of the faith: Sarah,

Rebecca, Leah and Rachel. There is no doubt they were all exceptional, a force to be reckoned with. But women of faith? Their very problem was that they started well, with great faith, but then more immediate pressures crowded in and clouded their vision. In fact, like the many mamas who followed them, they couldn't see beyond the end of their own noses. All that mattered was the success of their myopic, family-centred projects in the here and now, and that led them into a scant disregard for their part in the mighty epic God was writing. I often wonder whether that other, later, quintessentially British matriarchal figure, Prime Minister Margaret Thatcher, would have acted any differently had she been given a preview of how the history books and twenty-first-century documentaries would judge her. Perhaps we are all too blinkered, too tied to the mundane and immediate, to appreciate that whether we are a walk-on extra or have a tiny speaking part, our lives are essential to the bigger picture.

The Christian tradition has tended to pass over the four biblical matriarchs altogether. They simply don't fit our preferred conceptions of saintliness, our stereotypes of true spirituality – especially in a woman. They are tough, dynamic, fearless, outspoken, sensual, passionate, jealous, impatient, frustrated, rational, argumentative, entertaining – and highly manipulative. They are just too flesh-and-blood, too uncomfortably like us.

The level of equality and respect they enjoy is remarkable for the time in which they lived, their husbands (apart from Jacob and that was a costly, if unintentional, mistake) committed to a reasonable measure of monogamy. At the start of their married lives each is definitely an *ezer* or helper, journeying side by side with her man, sharing in his pioneering adventures, enduring the dangers and discomfort without question or protest, protecting and confronting him when necessity demands it. And, apart from Leah, they are loved and valued, and deeply mourned when they die.

Nonetheless, the consequences of Adam's and Eve's fall from grace are already taking effect. Sarah, Rebecca and Rachel have problems with their reproductive systems and there are no fertility clinics to help – although surrogacy seems to have been in vogue, with consequences no less traumatic than they can be today. All four need to be the centre of their man's universe, and deeply resent any intrusion from an outside source, whether it be a slave girl and her offspring, a firstborn son or a sister. No matter how affectionate their husbands are, their world is already proscribed by men – foreign kings and leaders, brothers and fathers. They have already become a tool, a bargaining point, property up for barter. Small wonder they become masters in the manipulative arts. Survival tactics are imperative.

The first great Jewish mama

Sarah is my favourite – the quintessential Jewish mama, rational and reasonable, wanting only the best for her man, and going out to get it with the self-restraint of a steamroller on a hill without brakes – but sadly on the wrong hill. She must have been quite a woman. When Abraham sets out on his virtually incomprehensible mission from Ur to the land of promise, she accompanies him, despite the fact that she hasn't yet managed to give him children. Why does Abraham keep a barren wife? What future was there in that? He must have loved her a great deal.

In fact she is such a stunning-looking woman that Abraham persuades her to tell the local people she is his sister. It is only a half-lie, after all, since she is his half-sister. That he exposes her to rape doesn't appear to bother him unduly. Twice foreign kings take a fancy to her and make off with her. On the second occasion she's well past middle age – an encouraging thought in our twenty-first, youth-worshipping century. It's a sad fact that where wolf whistles from workmen once made me bristle with self-righteous female indignation, they now make me purr with pride, for I know that if the lads were closer to the wrinkles and droops, they would be horrified by their mistake. Oh the vanity of setting any store by fading female attractiveness! It is almost Sarah's undoing – especially as Abraham's duty to protect and cherish his mate is subsumed by his fear of confrontation. Fortunately, God defends his wife's honour, even if Abraham won't.

That same character flaw in Abraham makes its reappearance when he agrees to sleep with Sarah's Egyptian maid, Hagar. This may well have been Sarah's suggestion, but ten years earlier he, not Sarah, had been told that Sarah's son would be his heir. Had he ever passed this piece of information on to his wife? I suspect not, for she is simply looking for a practical way to fulfil his need to father. It is a relatively unselfish gesture and he doesn't appear to have had any objections – perhaps because ten years seemed too long to wait for God to keep his word, and he simply couldn't resist the attractions of a younger model.

When Hagar becomes pregnant and starts to laugh at Sarah behind her back, the scene is set for high drama and Abraham's peace is over. Living in close proximity with Hagar's humiliating behaviour must have been almost unbearable for Sarah. After all, the girl was her protégé. She had been generous to her, opened the door of opportunity, and this was her thanks. I can't say I really blame Sarah for throwing Hagar out, though it wasn't perhaps the best way to deal with the situation, and might not have been necessary if Abraham had sorted out the little upstart himself.

Over the years Sarah has discovered, probably with some disappointment and disillusionment, that her man is weak. He doesn't always make the best decisions. He opts for the peaceful life – compromise by any other name. And, like so many women since, she believes that for his good she will have to take matters into her own hands.

A couple of years ago, American writer Laura Doyle wrote a contentious book called *The Surrendered Wife* that attracted a fair amount of publicity for its reactionary views. I wasn't at all convinced by many of her arguments. 'For greatest intimacy, agree with your husband's ideas even when it scares you', for example, sounds like a recipe for manipulation, and not nearly as constructive as employing a little gentle confrontation. On the other hand, when, at the start of a televised group session, she told the participants that if they gave up their desire for control they would lose their disrespect for their men and forget they had ever thought them incompetent, I had to admit she had a point. Sarah is concocting a recipe for disaster.

Hagar is allowed to return and, for another fourteen years, remains part of the uneasy *ménage à trois* that Abe's and Sarah's foolishness has created. But then, one day, listening behind the tent door – presumably the Old Testament equivalent of a keyhole – Sarah hears a strange visitor remind her husband that she herself will have a son. Judging by her reaction, this is the first she knows of it. She has to stuff her pinny in her mouth to stop herself laughing – and not just because she can't remember the menopause, let alone periods. Every preacher I have ever heard on this subject claims she says, 'But I am too old'. That may be delicate, but it isn't accurate. What she actually says is, 'After I am worn out and my husband is old, will I now have this pleasure?' (Genesis 18:12). The spiritual destiny of humankind is hanging in the balance, and Sarah is wondering whether Abraham can rise to the occasion. Meanwhile, it is her faith that fails to rise to the challenge. But even her shallow cynicism has to give way to awe and wonder when God reminds her that nothing – not even an anachronistic dose of spiritual Viagra – is too hard for him.

To her credit, Sarah's sense of humour never deserts her. She has the chutzpah, the barefaced cheek, to call her son Isaac, which means 'laughter', for she knows that however entertaining her story, whatever hilarity it will induce, she will always have the last laugh.

There has already been too much human meddling, however, for the fulfilment of God's promise to bring this tense little family an automatic happy ending. The medieval nun and mystic Teresa of Avila said that our answered, not our unanswered, prayers would cause us the greatest heartaches. With the arrival of a new baby the discord in the home spirals out of control. On the face of it, a trivial incident lights the blue touchpaper that will provoke the final explosion. In the Revised Standard Version of the Bible Sarah sees and resents Hagar's child playing with Isaac (Genesis 21:9). The obvious implication is that Sarah is insanely jealous. Here is a familiar typecasting of woman in the role of green-eyed monster. The New International Version, however, translates the Hebrew word *tachaq* more accurately, not as 'playing', but as 'mocking', or 'behaving with malice'. Hagar's son Ishmael is not a toddler. This jealous sibling is in his mid-teens and presents a serious risk to the baby. This is certainly the apostle Paul's interpretation of events in his letter to the Galatians, where he says, 'The son born in the ordinary way persecuted [or bullied] the son born by the power of the Spirit' (Galatians 4:29). Ishmael's treatment of Isaac is only a little more aggressive than Hagar's treatment of Sarah. He has probably picked up his mother's derisive attitude. Children have a tendency to mimic their parents.

Sarah's eyes are finally opened to the enormity of the problem she and Abraham have unwittingly unleashed, and from which they will never now be free. The time for manipulation has finally run out. There will never be an easy way to resolve the situation, but for the sake of succeeding generations they have to try.

This time Hagar and Ishmael are banished once and for all. Abraham is reluctant, not because he cares for Hagar, but because he loves Ishmael, and because he would like to wriggle out of the consequences of his actions. 'Do what you usually do,' God tells him, with more than just a hint of sarcasm, 'whatever Sarah tells you.' Within this apparently male-dominated story is a woman who repeatedly gets her own way. On this occasion her decision may not appear the most generous, but it is inspired. In his letter to the Galatians, Paul turns Sarah's relationship with Hagar into a picture of the ultimate triumph of true faith over oppressive, man-made religion. '"Get rid of the slave woman and her son, for the slave woman's son will never share in the inheritance with the free woman's son." Therefore, brothers, we are not children of the slave woman, but of the free woman' (Galatians 4:30–31).

Hagar and Ishmael are not left to die in the desert because they don't fit into the original plan. God is not at all impressed with Hagar's crocodile tears. After all these years in Abraham's and Sarah's home, witnessing some of the most extraordinary events in history, does she know nothing of God's mercy? What does she take him for? God responds to Ishmael's prayers, not Hagar's self-pity, and takes care of both of them. But meanwhile Sarah, for all her faults, her impetuosity, tetchiness, faithlessness, lack of vision and manipulative ways, becomes, with a wonderful touch of divine irony, a truly matriarchal figure – the mother of all who truly believe.

The second mama's sedition

Rebecca is very different from the mother-in-law she never meets – self-assured and gracious. She isn't too on her dignity to draw drinking water for a mere servant and his camels (Genesis 24:46). She has learned that humility pays greater dividends than high-handedness. When she discovers he is looking for a wife for his master and that she fulfils the job spec, she pursues her destiny with single-minded determination. When the will of God is clear, why procrastinate?

Isaac recognizes the outstanding inner qualities reflected in her external beauty and adores her from the moment he sets eyes on her. It is a love which grows and deepens over the years. He still can't keep his hands off her well past their silver wedding anniversary, and is cavorting with her in a field when the king of the Philistines passes by and is appalled to see him virtually *in flagrante delicto* with the woman he has passed off as his sister. Evidently, Isaac has learned little from his father's mistakes. I imagine that when the king suddenly appeared on the scene with a look of undisguised horror on his face, Rebecca rearranged her robe and stomped off with as much dignity as she could muster, leaving Isaac to wangle his way out of this one.

In fact, Rebecca eventually saves Isaac from far greater folly. Sadly, however, she doesn't do it *knegedu,* or eyeball to eyeball. In most relationships there are times for straight talking, for gentle assertiveness in the name of common sense, but Rebecca opts for deception rather than reasoned confrontation. But then, she is a Jewish mama. Why change the habit of a lifetime? To be fair, like so many women after her, she probably finds confrontation difficult. Perhaps she tried it when Isaac suggested calling her his sister – and failed.

Men don't find confrontation easy either. We had a senior manager in my previous workplace who always resorted to manoeuvring behind his colleagues' backs. He connived, wheeled and dealed, and usually got what he wanted, but ultimately set us against each other, destroying trust and team spirit in the process. As Rebecca discovers, deceit and manipulation may seem the easier, even safer option, but the long-term cost can be immense.

In her case, making a favourite of one particular child is a fatal mistake. When it comes to children, women are at their most vulnerable. Mothering can turn an intelligent, rational human being into a fond and doting idiot. In my days as a youth worker it never ceased to amaze me that mothers would turn up for a court appearance with an absolute reprobate of a son and still believe, just because he said so, that he had been wronged, yet again, by the criminal justice system. It was simply that her son had got into bad company. It never crossed her mind that he could be the bad company that everyone else's son was getting into. We may love our children, but we're not always good for them.

Isaac and Rebecca wait a long time for their twins, Esau and Jacob, but the foetuses fight even before they leave the uterus. The boxing match in the space between Rebecca's diaphragm and bladder is so intense she actually cries out in pain and is told there are two nations inside her – no wonder it hurts – and that the elder will serve the younger. As they emerge Jacob, the second-born, whose name means 'deceiver', is hanging on to Esau's heel.

Was Isaac around at the time? Surely he can have no doubt about the future of his two boys – yet he seems determined to thwart God's plans because of his own irrational preference for Esau. Rebecca, because of her love for Jacob, is not prepared to leave God to sort the situation out. It's too much of a risk. Her faith deserts her and she decides to give God a hand, and though her intervention to secure the future of the dynasty is crucial in the light of history, neither she nor Jacob act with love and generosity. Ironically, had she challenged rather than tricked Isaac into giving Jacob the blessing of the firstborn, such was his dependence on her wisdom and judgement that her husband may have given her what she wanted, and she would never have lost her sons. Instead, she forges ahead and takes destiny into her own hands.

Every Jewish mama knows the way to a man's heart – through his stomach. Now Esau is the Bible's answer to a celebrity chef and knows how to make his father's gastric juices flow. But Rebecca has no doubt that, while her son is out hunting for game, she can reproduce the gastronomic masterpiece Isaac loves so much in a fraction of the time. Had Isaac's preference for Esau's gourmet cuisine stung her in the past? No Jewish woman can bear to hear an unfavourable comparison of her roast chicken or gefüllte fish. She'll show this foolish husband of hers how stupid he is to let his belly govern his heart and make his appetite an arbiter between nations! Was this the first man to be ruled and then defeated by his stomach? He probably wasn't the last.

Rebecca ensures that Jacob gets the coveted blessing, but he dare not stay to enjoy it. Esau is determined to kill him. Rebecca now sees that she is caught in a web of her own making. Her dysfunctional family is falling apart. She realizes with the most dreadful, searing pain that through her own actions she must lose what she loves most in the world, and that her son's safety will depend not only on her manipulative skills, but on every ounce of inner resourcefulness she can muster. With a calm which belies her true feelings, she must untie her home-loving boy from her apron strings and send him away as far as she can. Nonetheless, he must go to her family not as a fugitive but with his father's backing, and Isaac, the old fool, must be made to believe it was his idea in the first place.

Using the excuse of Jacob's need to find a wife, she plays masterfully on the instrument of Isaac's self-interest. It is a stroke of genius. Esau has married foreign women and it hasn't gone down well with his father. The prospect of welcoming a third foreign daughter-in-law into the house – more noise, more squabbling, more ungodly behaviour – is altogether more than Isaac can face, as Rebecca knows only too well. Her diplomatic triumph is complete. But the price is almost more than she can bear. She will never see Jacob again.

If Rebecca had not taken matters into her own hands, might history have been so very different? Surely God would have found some way of fulfilling his intentions for the two boys, foretold at their birth. But Rebecca cannot rely on it, cannot allow herself to trust, cannot resist the urge to be guided by her own cleverness and intelligence. For her two sons, the result is a mess. She sows seeds of suspicion and hatred that will have repercussions for years to come. And throughout the centuries there have been many women, guided by the best and worst of motives, who have done exactly the same. Manipulation is a fearful and dangerous weapon in the hands of an unwitting expert.

My friend Janet, a minister's wife in the Midlands, claims it is an art passed through the generations from one woman to another. They learn it at their mother's knee. She was no exception. By the time she grew up, the habit was so ingrained that she couldn't admit its existence, let alone break its hold.

Year upon year I watched my mother browbeat my father. Whatever she wanted, whether it was a new outfit, new curtains, her children's education or a holiday abroad, she would get. My father was a gentle, generous man, but if he expressed caution she would nag. If he endeavoured to open up a sensible discussion of the subject, she would throw a tantrum. Only once, after nearly forty years of marriage, did he ever admit the truth – that she simply wore him down.

When I married Phil, I automatically followed her example. I knew no other way. As soon as he walked into the house from work I would hit him with my agenda. But I had a husband who recognized my behaviour for what it was and said, 'I will not be manipulated'. I was devastated. It left me completely powerless. I ground my teeth to such an extent that my dentist asked me what I was doing to them. Gradually I began to see that when I divested Phil of the right to any argument or debate I made him feel like a lion in a cage. Through counselling I learned the dangers of trying to use people to fulfil your own goals.

But not until in sheer desperation I begged several friends to pray for me was my need for control well and truly broken. And that was after a particular event in the church in which we ministered brought me to my senses. I'm still horrified when I think about what I did even now.

We needed a steering committee – I can't even remember what for – and a very shy, quiet woman in the congregation agreed to stand as secretary. She was a dear, faithful woman, but her shyness made her quite draining.

There was another candidate, new to the church, vibrant, dynamic, impressive, and I thought, 'This is the kind of person we need on the committee,' so – and I can't believe I did this – I went around the congregation quietly canvassing on his behalf.

He won the vote – with or without my help I will never know – but he was a disaster. He has left the church now, but in the meantime caused us the greatest heartache we had ever known in the whole of our ministry. The woman was gracious enough to take his place on the committee, and has been absolutely wonderful.

I learned the hard way that we really don't need to do God's work for him. But we will get it into our heads that we know what is needed, and it's a terrible lack of trust. I certainly paid for my foolishness – but so did others.

A church with a manipulative minister's wife is in peril. I once attended a conference in York where a nun persisted in challenging me about my role. 'Yes, but what is your place in the church?' she demanded. I blinked. It was obviously a leading question, and I hunted around for the proper answer. 'I suppose I'm a member of the congregation like any other,' I said. 'Right,' she said triumphantly. It was evidently what she wanted to hear and I was relieved, but it left me feeling uneasy.

Only later did the truth dawn. As the minister's wife, it was naive of me to suggest I had no more power than anyone else in the congregation. It is not appropriate for me to sit on the church council or any other committee where I might be tempted to challenge my husband in public. I do not have access to the accepted channels for expressing a viewpoint. My democratic powers are severely curtailed. I am therefore not a member of the congregation like any other. But I also know from my experiences in the workplace that the person with the most power is she who shares the boss's bed. That gives me power in a league of its own. I can influence my husband's attitudes, sway his opinions, simply by dropping in the odd word here and there, over a meal or at bedtime. That kind of power, if unrecognized, can easily be abused.

In the 1950s, Kathleen Bliss, a lecturer in religious studies at Sussex University, claimed that because women had no real voice in the Church, they were all restricted to what she calls this kind of underhand or 'irresponsible power'.

It is nonsense to say that women have never had any power in the churches: they have had immense power, but power in the form of influence, which is irresponsible power. Nobody can call to account the wife or mother who gets her way with husband or son and is known to be the real director of his opinion and vote. This is the form of power to which women, particularly very able women, have been confined by their exclusion from responsible power. Wherever democratic ideals prevail in society, influence of all kinds is discredited. Open attempts are made to prevent pressure on political leaders and on those who make appointments, issue honours and privileges and make executive decisions in every walk of life. That influence is influence with very great skill over the centuries and many still prefer it to any form of responsibility which brings them out into the open. But the choice between influence and responsibility is one that women have to make, and churches have to make in relation to women.[2]

For generations, from Sarah and Rebecca to Grandmother Rose, women resorted to using indirect rather than open methods of persuasion. Achievement and success could only be attained through a husband, brother or son. Necessity became a habit and, as Janet saw only too well, habits are hard to break.

Sleeping with the sister

Manipulation is self-perpetuating, even if it isn't genetic. It permeates and poisons whole families. Jacob, the master deceiver, son of an inspirational teacher, is subjected to the ultimate deception. Welcomed into the home of his mother's brother, he falls hopelessly in love with Rachel, his Uncle Laban's luscious younger daughter. For seven years, he subjects himself to abusive working practices to get the girl of his dreams, but they simply flash by in a haze of romantic passion. The wedding finally takes place – and 'in the morning, behold, it was Leah' (Genesis 29:25 RSV). How on earth did he not know he had spent his wedding night with the elder sister? I have often wondered what it says about the Judaeo-Christian tradition of sexual foreplay and have come to the conclusion, very little. Jacob was probably drunk after the traditional party. Laban had a vested interest in ensuring that he was. There was no electricity at the time and, unless there is a moon, a tent in the desert can be very dark. But in the light of day Jacob's ignominy is complete. Our great romantic hero didn't even notice he had slept with the wrong girl. From that day on, the bride's veil has always been lifted during the Jewish wedding ceremony, for no Jewish man is fool enough to make the same mistake twice.

As for Leah, we can only guess at her feelings. Did she really have no choice? Or did she comply with her father's wishes because she had always found Jacob attractive and thought that this was her only way of winning him and she could make him love her in the end? Or, perhaps, knowing she wasn't as good looking as her sister, she feared her chances were passing her by? Too many women find themselves in dismal, loveless relationships because they have married for similar reasons. Leah's hopes are doomed from the start. She is her father's pawn. Jacob also acquires his true love and his penalty is life with two warring women. In fact, the consequences of sibling rivalry are so catastrophic that marrying sisters in their lifetime is subsequently forbidden in the book of Leviticus.

I have often mused on what can be learned from Leah's plight, and have wondered whether her story, though desperately sad, isn't also tragically familiar. She is any woman locked in an unreciprocated, sterile relationship, denied the love and affection she needs. She is the woman whose partner walks out and abandons her for another. She is every woman who feels frustrated in love, rejected, let down and passed over. I had a favourite aunt, trapped by her lack of financial independence in a barren, desolate marriage to a rude, unloving man. He turned a vivacious, carefree young woman into a wistful, lonely hypochondriac. Nonetheless, she was a surrogate mother to me, and there were moments when her irrepressible generosity and sense of humour would break through – especially when we went on a shopping spree – and I loved her for it.

However it may seem, Leah is by no means divested of her worth. Status, dignity, acceptance and love are all hers, from a far more reliable source, if she wasn't blinded to it by *teshuqah*, her need for affection from a man who cannot give her what she wants. God never deserts her. Seeing that she is passed over and unloved, he blesses her with children, while her sister, who has the looks and love Leah wants, remains temporarily infertile.

Nothing makes quite such a pathetic statement about her relationship with Jacob than the names Leah gives her first three sons. Reuben means 'to see', and is a prayer that Jacob will sit up and take notice of her. Simeon means 'heard', for now that she has given him another son, perhaps Jacob will not ignore her any longer. Levi, meaning 'joined' or 'attached', is a plea to Jacob to be part of her life and to love, not use, her.

With Judah, her fourth son, called 'praise' or 'worship', her focus seems to be shifting at last. Self-pity has given way to a glimmer of recognition that there are alternative blessings to be had that fill the void where Jacob's love should be and replace the pain and humiliation of his neglect. She is given the significance her marriage has denied her. Even so, her obvious material success in biblical terms is not enough to stop her trying to manipulate Jacob back into her bed. She exchanges a night with him for mandrakes, thought to be a fertility drug, an arrangement made with an ever more desperate Rachel. Leah still needs human arms, human warmth, and God doesn't condemn her for that, for she has three more children while Rachel has none, despite the mandrakes.

Eventually God remembers the oh-so-superior Rachel, and her two boys soon overtake Leah's children in their father's popularity stakes. Leah must have seethed with self-righteous anger when she saw little Joseph being treated as the firstborn. Unfortunately, it's an emotion she communicates to her hapless boys, whose jealousy of their two half-brothers eventually leads them into all kinds of murderous intentions.

But whether the actors see it or not, God's great historical drama is being played out and supersedes these minor domestic difficulties. Unlike Mary, mother of Jesus, Leah never grasps the great truth that it is the despised, not the overtly successful, who are exalted in God's great scheme. It is she who becomes the mother of priestly and kingly tribes. Jesus is descended from Leah, not from Rachel.

On the official Guinness family tree and pedigree, a strange upside-down triangle emanates from every married Guinness woman. They have progeny, but the tree doesn't say who and how many. Mothers and daughters are irrelevant. The women's line of descent simply dies out, whether their descendants were more interesting than those of their male counterparts or not. Not so in Judaism, which is essentially matriarchal. Jewish identity is passed on through the mother's line. The four great matriarchs of Israel have a vital part to play in the history of the people of faith.

Whatever their failings and weaknesses, however manipulative, they were formidable women, loved and chosen by God, respected and valued by the generations to come. They could, however, have spared themselves and their offspring a great deal of *tzorus* (Hebrew for 'hassle') had they chosen to be less manipulative and more assertive. Perhaps there is also a challenge here for men, to live eyeball to eyeball with the women in their orbit, welcoming honest comment and challenging any manipulative behaviour.

It was the 1980s before Anne Dickson and others took up Kathleen Bliss's call from the 1950s, and urged women of my generation to abandon their mothers' pattern and reject mere 'influence' for responsible power and assertiveness. In fact, this constituted a call from secular, not spiritual, sources for women to take up once more our God-given responsibility to speak love and life and truth. How often God has to bypass the Church to get his message across and empower his people! The biblical example of truly powerful womanhood has been there all the time. Within a few years of the death of the matriarchs there arose a number of women, equally courageous and strong, who gave us a rather better example of how to live.

Notes

1. Anne Dickson, *A Woman in Your Own Right – Assertiveness and You* (Quartet Books, 1982).
2. Kathleen Bliss, *The Service and Status of Women* (SCM, 1952), p. 183.

CHAPTER 3

The Assertive Woman

On a Friday evening in every Jewish home, when the family shares Kiddush, the traditional blessing of bread and wine, Jewish mothers pray for their daughters that they will grow up to be like Sarah, Rebecca, Leah and Rachel. Liberal rabbi Julia Neuberger, however, thinks the four women are so manipulative that she prays instead that her daughter will grow up to be as assertive as the five daughters of Zelophehad.

Admittedly, their story doesn't instantly spring to mind. I had to go and look them up. But there they are in Numbers 27 – Mahlah, Noah, Hoglah, Milcah and Tirzah – sounding a bit like an early biblical example of a girl band. The five sisters are indignant that, on the death of their father, tradition insists that they, as women, cannot inherit his estate, but that it must pass to a male cousin. These feisty women do not sit back passively bewailing their lot, or aggressively demand their rights, or wheedle some kind of financial deal out of their cousin. They air their case before Moses and the entire wilderness congregation, and demand their just and right inheritance.

It must have taken some courage to challenge the status quo. No doubt it raised a laugh or two in the men's club. 'Since when did a woman know anything about managing property? And just who do they think they are anyway?' As the sisters confronted the patriarchal system, they ran the risk of being seen as demanding, difficult, grasping and unfeminine. That could well have affected their chances in the marriage stakes. Yet Moses is forced to concede that they have a point. So does he rule in favour of tradition or justice? He's not very sure, and decides to consult a higher authority.

And God says, 'Moses, do me a favour, don't argue with assertive women like that!' or words to that effect. Justice must transcend tradition. Not only is their case upheld, but it sets a new precedent. From now on, Jewish women will have the right to inherit and own property, with all the freedom and status that implies. By the time the book of Proverbs is written, they are actively involved in running the family business and bartering for land.

Yet, for another 4,000 years, the non-Jewish nations in the West failed to recognize this essential, historical and biblical right. Everything a woman owned, earned or inherited belonged to her husband. In the event of a separation or divorce, even if it was happening as a result of his abuse, she had no means of supporting herself, no right of access to her children, no say in their upbringing, no possibility of custody. It was a nineteenth-century society beauty, Caroline Norton, forced to flee from an abusive marriage, who finally found the courage of the daughters of Zelophehad and, in a desperate attempt to gain access to her three children, challenged and changed the British legal system. It was a hard fight, lasting many years. She became the constant butt of public and private ridicule. Her reputation lay in shreds. But in 1839 a new Act of Parliament gave a mother custody of a child under the age of seven. In 1873 the age was raised to sixteen.

Another nineteenth-century woman recognized the importance of this issue. In 1867 Florence Nightingale, the doughty middle-class matron who made nursing an acceptable profession for respectable women and was so afraid of losing her independence that she never married, told the great reformer John Stuart Mill that she believed that owning property was more important for women than the right to vote. 'Till a married woman can be in possession of her own property there can be no love or justice.' In 1882 married women were at last granted that right.

It is the ineligibility of millions of women in developing countries to own land or have any share in their own homes that keeps them subjugated and subservient, and this was never the intention of a God who gave Eve equal rights with Adam over the whole of creation.[1]

Caroline Norton's continuation of the campaign initiated by Zelophehad's daughters illustrates another interesting point, namely that the struggles of biblical women were not so remote from ours. Time and time again, as we'll see, the trailblazers in ancient society had their historical and contemporary counterparts – women who picked up the baton where their Old Testament sisters left it lying, even if it was centuries later.

My own first triumph in assertiveness didn't quite challenge the status quo as the daughters of Zelophehad had done – but we all have to start somewhere. Acquaintances may find it hard to believe, but for many years I was a very passive person, a peace-loving pushover like my father, in fact. I never stood up to anyone, and my days were often filled with a feeling of unease and dissatisfaction rather than peace.

One day I bought an expensive coat at a local shop, but when I got home the family agreed that it made me look like a middle-aged mother trying to be a trendy student – an old marrow pretending it was a courgette. I returned to the shop and asked for my money back.

'We only give credit notes.'

I was about to creep out of the shop when Anne Dickson's words of wisdom – 'Repeat your wishes clearly and firmly' – resounded loudly in my mind, and I heard myself say, 'I don't really want a credit note. I'd like my money back.'

The owner was summoned, and she said without ceremony, 'We don't give money back. We give credit notes.'

Everything inside me urged me to take the credit note and run. 'This is a local shop in a small town. You may want to shop here again. Don't make a fuss.' But I knew that would be a humiliating defeat. It would be proof that all the lessons in assertiveness I was trying to learn didn't work. So, with my knees knocking below the counter, I took a deep breath and said firmly, 'I don't want a credit note. I'd like my money back.'

'We don't give money back, we give credit notes.'

Jesus, I reminded myself, had commended a woman for her persistence with an unrighteous adversary. So the ridiculous verbal ping-pong continued. Ignominiously, I couldn't think of anything more creative to say than, 'I want my money back.'

Eventually the owner turned away and ignored me, but I was determined not to be browbeaten, and when she turned back round I was still there, bleating politely, if feebly, 'I want my money back.'

'Oh, here it is,' she snapped, opening the till.

I was elated. Few transactions have ever given me such satisfaction, and as part of the discipline I have made myself shop there ever since. After ten years, I now get a grudging 'hello' from the owner when I walk through the door. This wasn't exactly a major victory as the world's great battles go, but I had taken my first faltering steps towards holding out for what mattered, and learned some tactics I have put to even greater effect in the rather more important and life-changing confrontations that have come my way. Assertiveness is a precondition for leadership.

Deborah, the judge, and Mary Slessor, her successor

Israel's first great female leader is not distracted by her own insecurities. To the Egyptians the name Deborah denoted regal power. Its Hebrew root, *davar*, means 'to speak', but it can also mean 'bee' or 'wasp'. This woman has the ability to sting her hearers into action. She is either married to, or comes from, *Lappidoth,* which means 'lightenings'. Was this a reference to her having divine enlightenment, or, as the rabbis believe, was she simply someone who had the menial task of attending to the lamps in the tabernacle?

Deborah manifestly led a very ordinary life before rising to be a judge. Her family were grown and departed, and her husband, if she still had one, doesn't seem to have had any objections to her new status. Would that workplaces and churches everywhere recognize the value of wisdom, age and experience! The ordinary organizational skills involved in running a home, a family or a voluntary group can be as good a preparation for management responsibility as any academic qualification.

I once heard a sermon to the effect that there were no suitable men available to lead Israel at the time, implying that poor old God, despairing of the weak, ineffectual male material at his disposal, was forced to scrape the barrel and appoint a woman. I defy anyone to justify that idea from the text in Judges 4. Deborah was leading Israel because she was the best man for the job. Her leadership qualities are plain to see. She gave people time – one of the greatest gifts we have to give in this frenetic world of ours. Every day she sat beneath a palm tree, listened to their worries and problems, and resolved their injustices. It may well have been unusual for a woman to have had such power, but it only takes one to break the mould. From this moment on, any imagined biblical justification for banning women from access to leadership is rendered null and void by biblical history.

Deborah never apologizes for her gender. She doesn't resort to passive tactics: 'Oh Barak, I'm only a weak and frail little woman, so you'll just have to come and help me out.' She isn't aggressive: 'Barak, get your butt over here now, before I kick you into action.' Nor is she manipulative: 'Barak, if you come and do this little job for me, I might be able to arrange that planning application for the new house you've been wanting.' Any of those approaches would have destroyed instantly any possibility of a positive relationship with the man chosen to work with her. She simply tells him what she believes God wants him to do – to deliver the people from their Canaanite oppressors – and leaves the door open for him to say 'no'. Unlike Sarah and Rebecca, who dare not risk the potential failure of their plans, Deborah rests in the certainty that God can bypass Barak, if it comes to it, and still achieve his goals. True visionaries know that no one is ever completely indispensable. There will always be an alternative way of achieving the necessary end. Prophets keep their perspective. They always have the wider picture in mind.

Barak agrees to her commission – but with one extraordinary condition. She must go into battle at his side. Soldiers have always resisted the idea of taking women to war, lest they be distracted by the need to protect their weaker, feebler colleagues. But Barak is no macho man. He's frightened enough, and honest enough, to admit that he cannot function without the authority, courage and confidence Deborah inspires in him.

This isn't exactly delegated leadership as Deborah intended it, and she warns Barak that it isn't the route to glory. In fact, the final victory will go to another woman. Her name is Jael and, according to Deborah, she is 'most blessed of tent-dwelling women'. The English translation is inadequate. The Hebrew actually means 'most blessed of women in the tent', or, as an early Hebrew version puts it, 'blessed like a woman who attends the house of study'. There was a tent adjoining the tabernacle that was used as a house of study, so it seems quite possible that from very early in Israel's history, some women, like Jael, dedicated themselves to theological and religious study.[2]

Yet despite Jael's slaughter of the enemy general as he sleeps, despite Deborah's leadership and initiative, it is Barak who ends up in the book of Hebrews as an example of faith in action. Once a task is handed over, when another takes up the responsibility for our ideas, we have to be prepared for the fact that they, not we, may get the kudos in posterity – however unjust that may seem.

Deborah was referred to affectionately as a 'Mother in Israel'. In the nineteenth century the Okoyong people of the Calabar in West Africa called Mary Slessor, their beloved missionary leader, the 'Great White Ma'. In many ways, her life was a mirror of Deborah's.

> So Ma became again the only woman judge in the Empire. The Court was held in a thatched building in Ikotobong. Ma sat at a small table, and around her were the chiefs getting their first lessons in acting justly and mercifully towards wrong doers. Often she had to keep them in order. They were very fond of talking, and if they did not hold their tongues she just rose and boxed their ears.
>
> She sat long days trying cases, her only food a cup of tea and a biscuit and a tin of sweets. She needed all her courage to get through, for the stories of sin and cruelty and shame poured into her ears were terrible for a white woman to hear. 'We do not know how she does it,' the other missionaries said. She could not have done it had it not been that she wanted to save her black sisters and the little children from the misery they suffered. She was like no other judge in the world, because she had no books to guide her in dealing with the cases, nothing but her knowledge of the laws and customs of the people and her own good sense.[3]

Born in Dundee in 1848, the daughter of a drunken Scottish shoemaker and a mother who supported the family as a weaver, Mary began work as a mill girl at the age of eleven. She used to tell her older brother Robert that one day she would go to Africa to work with a wild tribe of people who killed their own twin babies because they thought they were cursed. He only laughed at her and said, 'But you're only a girl, and girls can't be missionaries. *I'm* going to be one and you can come out with me, and if you're good I may let you up into my pulpit beside me.' But Mary had the last laugh, eventually becoming the first ever female vice-consul of the Calabar.

At the age of twenty-eight, she fulfilled her childhood ambition and went out to West Africa with the Scottish Presbyterian Mission to work in an isolated missionary station with the Okoyong people. There she openly challenged the prevailing cultural attitudes to human sacrifice, the killing of twin babies, and the drunkenness which was so familiar to her from her own home.

There was no end to her adventures. At one time she actually lived in a harem for a while, sharing tiny quarters with the chief and his head wife, about twenty or so lesser wives, slaves, two cows, goats, fowls, cats, rats, cockroaches and centipedes. Her own room was divided in two by a makeshift wall of boxes and furniture, so that three boys could sleep on one side of the partition and she and two girls in the other. Every night her belongings had to be taken outside to make room for them all. During the wet season they had to be dried out in the sun every morning before they could be taken back in. The idea of loneliness was unthinkable to an African, so good manners dictated that the wives follow her everywhere. They were always bickering with each other, and the slaves were persistently being flogged. There was never any peace, privacy or sleep. Perhaps that's why the alternative became so attractive – to live alone like a native deep in the jungle.

In her adopted homeland a chief could do with his wife whatsoever he pleased, even beat her to death if he chose. But if he died, one of the wives would be held responsible and would pay for it with her life. Mary Slessor's refusal to condone such behaviour, or to abide by any rules and regulations which went against the basics of human care, even if they were those of the mission or the ruling British government, ultimately earned her the undying love of the local people. It was the esteem in which she was so obviously held and her unique knowledge of local customs which encouraged the British Colonial Service to make her a government official in 1892. In the courts where she presided, women knew they were guaranteed a fair hearing and that rare and precious commodity – justice.

Ruth, Gladys Aylward
and adventures abroad

Throughout history God may have had to shake men like Barak, Gideon and even Moses into action, cajoling them out of their fears and inadequacies, dispensing with their unconvincing excuses. But the Bible is full of assertive, feisty women who jump to his command, ready to take risks and sacrifice their all if required – women like Ruth, the only non-Jewish heroine in the Old Testament, popular, I suspect, because of her sweet, humble, self-effacing, utterly feminine image. But to do what she did takes a great deal more than a passive, wishy-washy saccharine sweetness. It demands courage, daring and a toughness belied by the stereotype.

Of course, the cynical view of the story is that Naomi and Ruth are simply two gold-diggers out to stitch up some unsuspecting rich bloke. But let's assume that what actually happens is that Ruth sees that her mother-in-law is devastated by the death of her two boys, in desperate financial straits and unable to cope. Ruth cannot let an embittered, unhappy Naomi go back to Bethlehem alone to fend for herself, so she leaves her own family, friends, comfort and security, everything that is familiar to her, to accompany a lonely old woman.

'Where you go I will go, and where you stay I will stay. Your people will be my people and your God my God' (Ruth 1:16). The text is often used at weddings and it sounds so wonderfully romantic, but the reality for Ruth was very different. She has no idea what she is letting herself in for. 'Where you die I will die, and there I will be buried,' she adds, and for all she knows of their future, given their destitute state and the unlikelihood of meeting a male provider, starvation could make death sooner rather than later.

Many of us have no idea what we're committing ourselves to, what the future holds, when we first say, 'Lord, I'll follow you anywhere, do anything you ask,' but unlike Ruth we tend to balk at the answer if it isn't as glamorous or as comfortable as we first expected. Ruth is prepared to do a dogsbody job. Gleaning, or picking up the leftover wheat after harvesting, was reserved for the beggars, the down-and-outs, the rejects of society. In almost every church it is always the same people who set out the chairs, pull the chewing gum off the floor, or take the tea towels home to be washed – the tasks no one else wants.

Not only that, but Ruth is the equivalent of an asylum seeker, foreign and vulnerable – subject to racist remarks, to accusations of 'taking our jobs', to acts of violence, even rape. Her courage and self-possession gain her the attention and protection of the landowner, Boaz, who turns out to be a relative. Now, as Naomi reflects on the possible ramifications of this extraordinary coincidence, it seems as if Ruth's humility has merely been a test of her readiness for the real challenge. Perhaps, for us, there can be no real test of our faith and courage, no major commission, until we have proved our faithfulness in the humdrum matters, in getting on with the tasks we resent the most, which bring us the least kudos and satisfaction.

Naomi suggests to Ruth that on the night of the harvest party she puts on her glad rags, her make-up and perfume, and, when Boaz is asleep, climbs into bed with him. This is not something a mother would usually ask of a daughter! If Boaz, finding a warm and willing woman at his feet, simply takes what's on offer – as many men would – without anticipating any further commitment in the cold light of day, she is destroyed. Her reputation will be in ruins and she will lose everything, including her means of earning a living, let alone her honour. It is an enormous, if calculated, risk.

Fortunately, Boaz's experience of Ruth's character alerts him to the cost and generosity of her gesture. He is touched that she has opted for an older man, not one of the handsome local lads. This is an offer he can't refuse and, as far as we know, the couple live happily ever after. The story with the happy ending is an object lesson in the benefits of rejecting current values – the need for personal significance and status, and a vain, self-seeking, selfish lifestyle.

Ruth becomes the mother of Obed, grandfather of King David, and in so doing earns herself a place in history as the only Gentile in the Messiah's family tree. Among Jesus' other improbable female ancestors are Rahab, a prostitute who hid the Israeli spies who had come to check out the Promised Land, Tamar, treated unjustly by a father-in-law she subsequently tricked into sleeping with her, and Bathsheba, who commited adultery with and subsequently married King David, but to the very end of her life was always referred to as 'the wife of Uriah the Hittite'. God, it seems, takes great pleasure in picking out the most unlikely candidates to fulfil his plans, particularly when it comes to women. Rabbi Julia Neuberger maintains that, although there appear to be few stories about women in the Hebrew Scriptures, we should dig into them when we find them, for we strike gold. These four women were all victims of their circumstances, but didn't allow it to cramp their style. They could have opted for a passive acceptance of their lot, but instead, they rose up and grabbed their destiny by the throat.

There were several extraordinary women in the latter half of the nineteenth century and early part of the twentieth century who, like Ruth, left familiar surroundings and loved ones, sacrificed their creature comforts and even the possibility of marriage and children, risked ill health, loneliness, danger and death, to serve an unknown people. The most famous, portrayed by Ingrid Bergman in a hyped-up Hollywood version of her life, was possibly the most modest. When Alan Burgess wrote the biography of Gladys Aylward (1902–70), the Edmonton parlourmaid who became a missionary to China and helped bring an end to foot binding, he could hardly believe how unassuming she was.

> 'But surely,' I said, 'in twenty years in China you must have had many strange experiences?'
> 'Oh yes,' said Gladys, 'but I'm sure people wouldn't be interested in them. Nothing very exciting happened.'

It was at least fifteen minutes before she confessed that she had once taken some children across the mountains.

The rest of the conversation went in this manner, a verbatim memory which I have never forgotten.

'Across the mountains? Where was that?'

'In Shansi in north China; we travelled from Yangcheng across the mountains to Cian.'

'I see. How long did it take you?'

'Oh, about a month.'

'Did you have any money?'

'Oh no, we didn't have any money.'

'I see. What about food? How did you get that?'

'The Mandarin gave us two basketfuls of grain, but we soon ate that up.'

'I see. How many children did you say there were?'

'Nearly one hundred.'

I became conscious that I was saying, 'I see', rather often, and actually I was not 'seeing' anything at all, except that I was on the brink of a tremendous story.

It was not mock modesty on the part of Gladys Aylward; the stories she had been telling were, to her, the greatest in the world taken straight from the pages of the New Testament; that her own adventures might be worth setting down, she had simply not considered...[4]

Gladys Aylward's rescue of a hundred children from the advancing Japanese in 1940 was merely the culmination of her remarkable achievements. At the age of fourteen she had left school to work in the Penny Bazaar, the precursor to Marks and Spencer. Although she applied to the China Inland Mission she found studying difficult, failed her Chinese exams and was turned down. In the end she saved up her meagre parlourmaid's wages and went under her own steam.

The journey was horrific. She was imprisoned in Germany, almost raped in Russia and ended up in Japan, but finally made her way to China, where she quickly learned to speak the language like a native by living and working with the people. She even destroyed her British passport and became a naturalized Chinese.

Foot binding for women had become a tradition because men preferred wives not to have the capacity to run away, but it left even little girls crippled and in great pain. The government found a ban almost impossible to impose, and invited Gladys to spread the message on their behalf. That meant challenging rigid male authority in every traditional, rural community – an enormous risk for a woman. But, like Ruth, Gladys had a manner and integrity that was both intriguing and irresistible – winning over even the all-powerful rulers of the provinces where she lived and worked.

> The friendship between the Mandarin of Yangcheng and the tiny ex-parlourmaid from Belgrave Square is probably one of the oddest in the entire history of Eastern and Western relationships. Although she spoke the language fluently it was years before she managed to dig down through the layers of his mind. He was enigmatic. He regarded her urbanely, his thin face, with its high cheekbones and thin, dark almond eyes, always impassive. A glossy pigtail drooped from under the round silk cap; the gowns he wore were embroidered in wide scrolls of many colours, inevitably, beautiful: scarlet, blue, green, gold. To Gladys, he always looked as if, by some miracle of time, he had just stepped down from an antique Chinese scroll. His was a feudal society. From his *yamen,* civic authority was administered in much the same manner as it had been dispensed at the time of Confucius. . .
>
> There is little doubt that at first, to the Mandarin of Yangcheng, Gladys Aylward was as alien a species as a creature from the moon. She was a female, which meant that in the eyes of man she was socially and intellectually less than dust. Nevertheless, as news of her exploits reached him, and as, over the months, she continually bombarded him with applications, supplications, admonitions and near-threats, she loomed as astonishingly as a new planet thrust into his orbit. Indeed, as their contacts and acquaintanceship increased, not only was she becoming an adviser of sorts, but also a friend.[5]

And, like Ruth, Gladys achieved her objectives. In the end the Mandarin's profound admiration for this exceptional, assertive woman persuaded him to change the local laws.

Gladys was bemused and somewhat bewildered by the glamorized movie version of her life in *The Inn of the Sixth Happiness*. In today's world, so dominated by political correctness that women can be expected to live with appalling abuses of their rights in the name of cultural tolerance, where celebrity status depends more on looks, riches and a good spin doctor than on character or self-sacrifice, Gladys Aylward's achievements might have passed unnoticed. She might even have been accused of being patronizing or colonial. But it wouldn't have held her back. The lives of the little nobodies who risk their all to make their world a better place make a mockery of those who criticize from the safety of the sidelines.

Esther and Josephine Butler, risking their all

The greatest of all the Jewish heroines is a nobody plucked from obscurity. Esther's background is neither impressive nor devout. By the time of her birth, most serious Jews had been only too glad to leave their place of exile behind and return from Persia to Jerusalem, where they rebuilt the precious temple. A few, like Esther's relations, stayed behind, presumably because they were comfortable, happily assimilated into Babylonian society – much like the Jews of Austria and Germany in the 1930s, who dominated the professions and the arts, and thought they were safe. In other words, God doesn't choose Esther to play a leading role in saving his people because she has a pious pedigree or is outstandingly holy herself. Yet we often resist our own calling because we think there must be a more spiritual person sitting in a pew nearby.

She even uses a Persian name – Esther means 'Planet Venus' – rather than her Hebrew name, Hadassah, or 'palm tree'. True to her Babylonian identity, she wins a beauty competition and finds herself with the booby prize – the king himself. King Ahasuerus's first wife, Vashti, has been too busy at her own banquet to turn up for his, so he decides to find a replacement in this less-than-intelligent, but fairly twenty-first-century manner.

This is no heart-warming, Cinderella, rags-to-riches story. Esther is a prisoner in a harem, with at least twenty other women all suffering at various times from nerves, boredom and premenstrual tension. She probably cries at night with home-sickness for her family, or for the local boy she loves and might have married. But there is no indication that she goes on lamenting the life she might have had, no evidence of self-pity or complaint. She makes the best of a difficult situation and earns the approval of Hegai, the eunuch in charge. She could have stayed on her dignity and said, 'Actually I'm Jewish. We don't believe in making eunuchs.' But instead, with real humility, she asks him to teach her about her new culture, and finds it pays dividends in the long run.

So Esther submits herself to the regulatory aromatherapy, six months with myrrh, and six with oil and spices. In the Bible myrrh represents suffering and death, and oil is a symbol of the Holy Spirit. This lengthy procedure is repeated over and over again, until scent oozes from every pore of her body, and its fragrance trails after her wherever she goes. It could be a parable of the life of any human being who intends to live side by side with the King of Kings. There are no short cuts to being properly prepared and equipped.

Five years after her marriage – five years of life in the palace, treading water – Esther's moment finally comes. One day she finds her Uncle Mordecai sitting in sackcloth, weeping at the palace gate. Haman, the most senior politician in the land, doesn't like immigrants (what's new?) and has persuaded the king to issue an edict to destroy all the Jews. He has no idea that Esther is Jewish. She has kept her faith a secret, choosing to live it rather than shout about it.

Uncle Mordecai exhorts his niece to appeal to her husband and save her people. This is more difficult than it may appear.

An uninvited approach to the king risks the death penalty. But then, 'Don't think you'll escape if your people are destroyed,' Mordecai tells her. 'If you keep quiet, help will come from elsewhere.' God is not so dependent on one human being that an individual's refusal will thwart his entire plan. Esther is absolutely free to say, 'Not likely, Uncle. The king doesn't know I'm Jewish. Why should I risk my neck when I've got this far?' But she doesn't. She decides instead to risk her all – position, status, reputation, and even says, 'If I die for it, I die for it.'

The decision heralds a dramatic change in Esther. Previously a fairly passive young woman at everyone else's beck and call, she now begins to take control of the situation. She sends Mordecai to declare a fast, and to tell the people to pray for her. He does as he is told without question or argument, responding to a new authority in her voice. Traditionally, the Church has equated passivity with femininity. Being 'nice', or compliant, can seem to be one of the cardinal virtues of a Christian woman. But to do what is required of us, we may, like Esther, have to adopt a different, more assertive approach. The Holy Spirit strengthens rather than stifles us.

Esther faces the king and his possible wrath with her head held high, confident in the God of her people. She doesn't flutter her eyelashes, flirt, flatter or apologize for disturbing him. She is now Hadassah, as stately and dignified as a palm tree. The king is impressed and listens to her plea. The Jewish people are saved from annihilation. Haman ends up on the gallows he has built for Mordecai and, in a nice twist at the end of the tale, Mordecai is made prime minister.

Like Esther, we all have to decide who has the ultimate control of our destiny and the destiny of the world in which we live. Mordecai says to his niece, 'Who knows whether you have not come to the kingdom for such a time as this?' (Esther 4:14 RSV). In a world filled with suffering, alienation and injustice, even on our own doorstep, the challenge to give our all for such a time as this has never seemed more apposite. Yet we often hold back from making a stand. There is too much to lose – our reputation, popularity, status, financial security, goals and ambitions. We fear making a fool of ourselves, making enemies, or not having the energy to see a project through. We tend to be so much more self-conscious than God-conscious, and it costs us our determination to take an assertive stance, to follow our calling, whatever the cost. Jesus urged his disciples, 'Don't be afraid of those who kill the body, but can't kill the soul. Instead, be afraid of the One who can kill the soul and the body in hell.'[6]

By the middle of the nineteenth century it was becoming acceptable, if not exactly desirable, for middle-class women to fight for higher education, better employment and more protection at law, but it was still unthinkable to stand up for the rights of those who were regarded as society's untouchables. Yet one woman dared to speak out against the wholesale abuse of the most dispossessed of her gender.

In the 1860s the Contagious Disease Acts gave the police the power to drag any lone woman suspected of prostitution off the streets, so that they could subject her to the most brutal internal examination to check for signs of venereal disease. In reality, only a working woman went out on her own, so only a woman of that particular class, whether a prostitute or an innocent abroad, could be subjected to this flagrant denial of her rights. She was held down on a surgical couch with her legs strapped apart, while instruments lifted out of boiling water were immediately inserted inside her. If she turned out to be a virgin and her hymen was ruptured, she would be told she was a good girl and given five shillings for a hot dinner. Some women miscarried. Others experienced permanent internal damage.

When the respectable vicar's wife Josephine Butler (1828–1906) began her twenty-year fight to have the Acts repealed, she provoked a furore which cost her her health, her reputation, her privacy and precious leisure time with the husband and children she adored.

Josephine never questioned whether her campaign merited such a sacrifice. Her belief in a loving God simply would not let her remain silent in the face of such injustice. She saw only too well that the law was a thinly disguised form of persecution, enabling men to project their sense of self-loathing and disgust onto the victims of their lust. Josephine's crime was to say so in public. She dared to say that a woman could not pick up a sexual disease without the help of a man, and that he was more guilty than any prostitute he had used, for he had money, power and respectability on his side. Furthermore, she said it in sexually explicit language, exposing the hidden, shadowy side of upright male society and the hypocrisy of much Victorian morality. Josephine Butler's honesty made her intolerable.

Raised in a loving, stimulating home where she was not penalized intellectually for being a girl, Josephine was encouraged by her father not only to think for herself, but also to believe it was her Christian duty to improve the lot of the people in her orbit. She couldn't help but contrast her own comfortable, protected life with the appalling poverty and deprivation to be found elsewhere in her home county of Northumberland. At one point it filled her with doubts about the existence of a loving God. How could there be such huge inequalities? Why did God allow his creatures to suffer or tolerate such blatant abuses of power? Why was his Church so uncaring and ineffectual? She felt she was going mad and would shout out loud for him to come and deliver her, and demand that he show her what he wanted her to do. As she contemplated the future, she was terrified that being a woman would condemn her to a life of meaningless domesticity.

Fortunately, she met and married a man who not only shared her vision and her faith, but was way ahead of his time in his notions on the equality of women. George Butler was a gentle, likeable man, a clergyman and university tutor who was the perfect foil for the fiery Josephine. His fellow dons in Oxford were bemused at the way he encouraged his wife to take part in discussions on intellectual matters, expressing her own opinions. For her part, she found them pompous and stuffy and was glad when George took up the post of Vice-Principal of Cheltenham Boys' College.

It was in Cheltenham that the couple experienced the terrible tragedy that would change their lives for ever. One evening, as they returned from a dinner party, their fourth child, a much longed-for daughter after their three boys, rushed out of bed onto the landing to greet them. As their little one threw herself against the bannisters, they gave way and she fell to her death onto the tiled floor at their feet.

Josephine was devastated. At first she grieved alone. She couldn't believe that a man could suffer the loss of a child as intensely as a mother. Then one day, in her husband's study, she came across a scrap of paper on which he had written his thoughts about his beloved little girl. It had been hidden away with all the little presents, drawings, pressed flowers and bookmarks she had made for him. From that day they shared their sorrow, and it drew them into the deep and lasting bond that would keep their relationship strong and steady in the buffeting which lay ahead.

Memories of that dreadful night continued to haunt them and they were glad of the chance to move north, when George was appointed Principal of Liverpool College. George threw himself into his new job, but that only compounded Josephine's sense of emptiness. A wise old Quaker woman, realizing that Josephine needed some use for her pain, told her about the many young girls in Liverpool who needed, but had never known, the love Josephine felt for her little Eva. She encouraged Josephine to go with her to the local workhouse, where 4,000 destitute girls were housed in the most abysmal conditions.

It was by no means unknown for well-meaning women of Josephine's class to go into the workhouse to read the Bible and pray with the inmates. The difference was that, whereas few survived the ridicule and coarse language, it would have taken a great deal more than spittle running down the front of her dress to make Josephine Butler dissolve into tears. She not only weathered the initial rejection, but actually offered the girls physical contact, taking them into her arms as they poured out their problems. It was virtually unthinkable for someone as beautifully groomed and immaculately dressed as Josephine was to touch such dirty, ragged women, and it said more to them about the love of God than anything her words could convey. Their acceptance began to fill the aching void in her heart, and, as she listened to their desperate stories, she became convinced that prostitutes were not wicked, licentious women, but the victims of circumstances and of preying men.

When a government committee, set up to look into disease levels in the army and navy, led to the passing of the first Contagious Diseases Act in 1864, Josephine was horrified beyond belief and made her feelings public. Her crusading reputation was beginning to be well known, and with a sickening sense of inevitability she guessed it would only be a matter of time before she was approached and asked to lead a campaign. She was right. A small, predominantly male, protest group had been formed, but no man could fight for the rights of prostitutes or galvanize female opposition to the Act. That was a job for a woman, a respectable woman, a wife and mother, and Josephine was the perfect candidate.

She never doubted that the cost would be immense, and would have thought little of it had she been the only one with a price to pay. But George had been tipped for a shining career in the Church. He was in line to become a bishop, but not with a wife who publicly challenged the sexual status quo. Her three boys were now aged seventeen, fifteen and twelve, and very vulnerable to abuse from schoolmates. And then there were her family and friends. Anyone who had any connection with her would become a pariah. She agonized over the suffering she might cause, but in the end it was George who encouraged her to walk, in her words, 'straight into the jaws of hell'.

The cost turned out to be even greater than either had anticipated. In the first year alone she travelled 3,700 miles and spoke at 99 meetings. For the next few years she was constantly on the road. George ran the home and took care of the boys, an extraordinary achievement for a man of his time.

Josephine found public speaking an enormous strain, though her beauty, poise and pleasant voice enabled her to keep a large audience enthralled. Had she been a portly dowager she might have been left to have her say, but her striking appearance and understated sexuality seemed to incense her enemies as much as her message. She was constantly harangued and heckled, interrupted by rude innuendo, raucous laughter and vulgar abuse. Mobs were hired to pelt her with dirt and stones.

At home, George received obscene drawings of her through the post. He was howled down wherever he preached if he so much as touched on the subject of women's rights. Rumours suggested their marriage was in difficulty – a cruel experience for such a devoted couple. Both found the extended separations unbearable.

Yet one foggy night in April 1883, after years of persistent battling, Josephine, now a middle-aged woman, made her way to the Ladies' Gallery of the House of Commons to hear the reading of a Bill to repeal the pernicious Acts. Down the road, in the Westminster Palace Hotel, George and a motley band drawn from every class and status had gathered to pray. She joined them for a while, and it was a sight she would never forget.

> There were the poorest, most ragged and miserable women from the slums of Westminster on their knees before the God of Hosts with tears and groans, pouring out the burden of their sad hearts. He alone knew what their burden was. There were women who had lost daughters; there were sad-hearted women; and side by side with these poor souls, dear to God as we are, there were ladies of high rank, in their splendid dresses – Christian women of the upper classes kneeling and also weeping. I thank God for this wonderful solidarity of the women of the world before God. Women are called to be a great power in the future, and by this terrible blow which fell upon us forcing us to leave our privacy

and bind ourselves together with our less fortunate sisters, we have passed through an education – a noble education. God has prepared in us, in the women of the world, a force for all future causes which are great and just.[7]

At midnight she went back to the Commons, and she was in the gallery at 1.30 a.m. when a majority of seventy-two gave her the answer to those prayers.

She was too overwhelmed to go back to the hotel immediately, but went out onto the terrace overlooking the Thames. 'The fog had cleared away and it was very calm under the starlit sky. All the bustle of the city was stilled and the only sound was that of the dark water lapping against the buttresses of the broad stone terrace ... it almost seemed like a dream.'[8] They had done it. With God's help, and with a band of doughty supporters, she and George had made the world a kinder place for young women. But that was just a beginning.

> We shall not stop, our efforts will not cease when this particular struggle is at an end. God has called us out, and we must not go back from any warfare to which he will now call us in the future. We praise, we thank him for what he has done already for us, and for what he is going to do, for we shall one day have a complete victory. We can echo the words of that which is written, 'My soul magnifies the Lord, and my spirit rejoices in God my Saviour, for he has regarded the low estate of his handmaiden.' And remember, women, if we are faithful to death, henceforth all men shall call us blessed. Yes, generations to come, your children and your children's children will call you blessed because you have laboured for purer morals and for juster laws.[9]

Like Esther, Josephine Butler risked her all to save the young women she saw as her own people, her sisters.

There are other assertive women hidden like golden nuggets in the text of the Hebrew Scriptures: one is Hannah, who has fertility problems, but doesn't slink away in shame when she is accused of drunkenness as she weeps in despair in the temple, but gets the desire of her heart – a son, Samuel. Another is Abigail, the wise, who stands up to her fool of a husband, too mean to provide food for David and his men, and becomes David's wife when he is king. Still another is the unnamed woman in the book of Judges who drops a millstone from a high wall onto the leader of the army besieging her city. This really is strategic thinking. Since women don't have the brawn, they're forced to use their brain.

Whether women are key players or walk-on extras, they make their mark. They don't seem unduly concerned to discover God's will for their individual lives. Instead they ask, 'What is your will? And what is my part in it?' They have a vision of the wider canvas, the broader brush strokes used by the artist, and the importance of contributing carefully and accurately to the detail. They do what they know to be right and just, not what's expected of them, and that takes courage, self-sacrifice and a gentle but tenacious assertiveness. 'Unless a grain of wheat falls into the ground and dies, it remains alone; but if it dies, it bears much fruit' (John 12:24 RSV).

Notes

1. A World Bank report in 1993 concluded that promoting the rights and status of women would be a greater social investment in improving health in developing countries than pouring more money into health care.
2. See Professor Shmuel Safrai, 'The Place of Women in First-Century Synagogues', *Jerusalem Perspective,* September/October 1993. Shmuel Safrai is Professor of Jewish History of the Mishnaic and Talmudic Period at the Hebrew University of Jerusalem.
3. W.P. Livingstone, *The White Queen of Okoyong* (Hodder and Stoughton, n.d.), p. 148.
4. Alan Burgess, *The Small Woman* (The Reprint Society, 1959), pp. 254–55.
5. Ibid., pp. 110–11.
6. Matthew 10:28, *New Light Bible* (Hodder and Stoughton, 1998).
7. Joseph Williamson, *Josephine Butler – the Forgotten Saint* (The Faith Press, 1977), p. 97.
8. Josephine's letter to her sister Harriet, April 1883, quoted in Glen Petrie, *A Singular Iniquity* (Macmillan, 1971), p. 208.
9. Williamson, *Josephine Butler,* p. 97.

PART 2

The Christian Woman

A Liberating, Life-Changing
Inheritance

CHAPTER 4

A Woman of Little Status?

Jesus did not alter or override Old Testament theology. He interpreted it, enhanced it, divested it of the cultural flotsam and jetsam attached to it by the tide of time and human hypocrisy, and tempered it with mercy. This liberating, life-changing approach is particularly evident when he doesn't condemn the adulterous woman, but challenges her male accusers (who are indifferent to the fact that her partner in crime has done a vanishing act) to cast the first stone if they dare. Given the return of the fashion for stoning women, the story has a fresh poignancy today.

Nonetheless, I couldn't believe my eyes when I read in an article on the web that 'Jesus related to women as he did to any other outcasts'. Apart from the woman caught *in flagrante,* which of the Old Testament women we have met so far would answer to the name of outcast? Ruth, the asylum seeker, perhaps, but even she finds love, acceptance and respect.

To be fair, a great deal has been said and written through the centuries about how Jesus is supposed to have raised the status of the poor, excluded females who happened to fall across his path. Roman and Samaritan women, perhaps – but, knowing Jewish women as I do, I'm not convinced. Mary and Martha do not strike me as oppressed little creatures to whom

Jesus gallantly and condescendingly offered his friendship, publicly lifting them out of a life of seclusion and servitude. He simply enjoyed their company. He probably enjoyed the food Martha kept putting in front of him, too. I can almost hear her cutting into the flow of his stories with 'So eat, a growing boy needs his food', just as my Jewish great-grandmother used to do to her favourite visitors. And I expect he obeyed with a chuckle and tucked in with relish.

In fact, Jesus never seems to stop eating. In the gospels more of his sayings take place around the meal table than in the synagogue or temple. No wonder he made regular visits to that little house in Bethany. He wasn't trying to make a point. This was simply a chance to relax and unwind with special friends.

A number of the recent misunderstandings about the place of Jewish women at the time of Jesus seem to have filtered into Christian consciousness from the writings of a Dr Leonard Swidler, scholar of ancient Jewish texts.[1] Based on misogynist sayings in the oral Jewish law, Dr Swidler claims that Jewish women were uneducated, downtrodden, segregated, banished to their homes and generally abused. The evidence shows that this wasn't the case. Jewish biblical scholar Hyam Maccoby points out that, unlike a Roman woman, a Jewish woman did not forfeit her property rights when she married.[2] She could also initiate divorce – for ill treatment, incompatibility, an unsatisfactory sex life, or her husband's body odour, if it wasn't to her liking. Although her world revolved primarily around the home, she came and went as she pleased. Furthermore, like the superwoman in the book of Proverbs, she was honoured, respected, even revered by her man.

The hotchpotch of oral rabbinic instructions with their negative view of women were not formally transcribed into what became the Talmud for several centuries, and at the time of Jesus were only given credence by the most Pharisaic wing of Judaism. The Sadducees, who collaborated with the Romans and were part of the ruling classes, certainly didn't condemn women to a life in the shadows. In the Jewish quarter of Jerusalem, where a Sadducee house has been excavated and made into a museum, the personal belongings of the wife of the high priest are displayed in a glass cabinet – her jewellery, elaborate combs, lipstick and kohl pencil. In fact, her make-up collection looked very much like mine, and I certainly don't put on full war paint to sit at home and spin.

So, what was life really like for women at the time of Jesus and in the early days of his Church? And what impact did an encounter with this extraordinary man really have, not only on their lives, but on the lives of those who would come after them?

Banished to the gallery?

It now seems clear that women were once much more active in the religious life of the Jewish community than they are today.[3] In Judaism today a minimum of ten men must be present before corporate prayers can be said. That was a real trial when my father died and tradition required prayers in our family home morning and night for *shiva,* or seven days. We could guarantee a quorum every evening, but the early morning stint was another matter. My brother had to ring round all his friends to beg and bully enough men into calling in on their way to work, otherwise we would have had to do without a very meaningful ritual. But the idea that only ten males constitute a viable congregation isn't found in ancient sources until AD 500. Even as late as the twelfth century, rabbis agreed that a woman could count as one of the ten.

Participating in prayer was not the only privilege women shared with men at the time of Jesus. During my first visit to the ruins of an ancient synagogue in Israel, the guide asked the party where the women sat.

'In the gallery,' we all said immediately, in unison.

'Which gallery?' he persevered.

We looked up, and around, and our jaws, along with the penny, dropped. There was no gallery. No sitting up in the gods for the female members of this synagogue, ogling the talent below, as I did in my misspent youth. Galleries were not added until around the seventh century, possibly due to the influence of Islam.

One of the best-preserved ancient synagogues uncovered by archaeologists, at Dura Europos in the Syrian desert, dates from the third century. The congregation sat on two rows of plastered, tiered benches on all four sides of a rectangular assembly hall. There was no partition, no evidence of any seg-regation, either here or at the excavated first-century synagogue at Masada.

Not only did men and women sit together during syna-gogue worship, but recent excavations in Israel have unearthed large stones bearing inscriptions such as *archisynagogissa* – a female 'head of synagogue', and *presbytera* – a female elder, or council member.[4] No one is sure what these positions actually were. Inevitably, some scholars have tried to suggest they were merely honorary. That seems unlikely. From the time of Sarah there was always more than an 'honorary' hint of matriarchal power within the ranks of the Jewish people.

Banished to the women's court?

It now begins to look as if there was no segregation of male and female in the temple either. Most public assemblies, such as the reading of the Torah on the Day of Atonement, were held in an outer court where men and women mingled together. It became known as the Women's Court because the women tended to commandeer it, preferring to enjoy the girlie com-pany, rather than venture into the two more interior courts. It probably made it easier to nip out to breastfeed or drag out a screaming child. In the same way, the Israelites' or Men's Court got its name because the men from non-priestly families tended to congregate there, rather than in the Priests' Court. However, there was nothing to stop women walking through the Men's Court into the Priests' Court to offer sacrifices at the altar.

The only enforced separation in the temple was during the water-drawing ceremony at the Feast of Tabernacles. Men and women could worship together, but dancing together was a step too far.

Every night for six nights the priest would return from the Pool of Siloam carrying a golden pitcher full of water, which he would pour on the altar the following day, crying out for the latter rain. Rain is immensely important in a fairly arid climate. But these prayers were also symbolic, an outpouring of longing for the coming of the Messiah and the dawn of a new age.

For this one week the women were banished to a makeshift gallery erected above the Women's Court. Every evening the court, floodlit by four huge oil lamps, was filled with hundreds of men, awaiting the priest's return. A great shout would announce his arrival and the beginning of the dancing, which continued through the entire night, while the women sat above them in the shadows and watched the spectacle below.

This marathon of all-night knees-ups makes most Christian celebrations pale into insignificance. It was on the seventh day, the climax of the festival, as the water was poured over the altar and flowed through the elaborate drainage system from the temple into Jerusalem and eventually on into the Dead Sea, and the people called on the Messiah to come, that Jesus stood up in the Women's Court and said, 'Let anyone who is thirsty come to me and drink. Whoever believes in me . . . will have streams of living water flowing from within' (John 7:38 NIVI).

When it came to public worship, the only contribution allowed from someone who wasn't a priest was to read the Scriptures. Although it wasn't expressly forbidden, women were not exactly encouraged to put their name down for this particular rota. As late as the eleventh century a famous rabbinic scholar was asked whether a woman might be called up to read from the scrolls. Rabbi Solomon came to the convenient conclusion that according to the law she could, but 'out of respect for the congregation' she should not. It seems this was a polite way of saying, 'Sorry, girls, the men would find that just too threatening.'

No wonder the extraordinary events of Pentecost caused such a furore in the city. It seems quite possible that on that momentous Feast of Shavuot the disciples had gathered in a room at the 'house of the Lord' – the temple. Where else would a good Jewish boy be on such an important festival? Why else would they and the other female followers of Jesus have made the three-day trudge on foot from Galilee to Jerusalem? Jesus had told them to wait for 'power from on high'. They had no idea what he meant, but it was a tradition to count fifty days from the barley to the wheat harvest. Jesus had risen from the dead on the barley harvest, so it stood to reason that for his next supernatural intervention he would choose the wheat harvest. And they weren't going to miss it.

There in the crowded temple, as the traditional Scriptures rang out through the courts – the story of the giving of the Torah on Sinai when God appears in wind, noise and flames of fire – there was a simultaneous, audio-visual demonstration in an upper room. Men and women were filled with the Holy Spirit and began to worship God in unlearned foreign languages, and in public.

The Revised Standard Version of the Bible appears to dispute the idea that women were involved at all. Explaining the disciples' strange behaviour, the apostle Peter is supposed to have said, '*These men* are not drunk, as you suppose...' (Acts 2:15). But the King James Version's 'these' and the NIV Inclusive Edition's 'these people' translate the Greek accurately, because a male plural pronoun is used for a group of men *and* women. The same principle applies in French grammar, where four women in a car are referred to as *elles,* but if one mere man were to join them they would become *ils.*

It is because the Holy Spirit is poured out on men and women, both preaching about the mighty works of God, that

Peter makes the connection with the prophetic promise of Joel 2:28: 'I will pour out my Spirit on all people. Your sons and daughters will prophesy ... Even on my servants, both men and women ...' This, then, was one of the basic differences between the synagogue or temple and the brand-new Church. Women were given, by divine appointment, an active role in public worship. Pentecost is therefore the key to restoring the equality of men and women, lost at the beginning.

The Jesus women

The Jews always valued education and taught their girls to read. So even if Jewish women were denied the right to read the Scriptures in public, they read them in private. Jesus certainly expected women to know their Scriptures. His mother Mary, a peasant girl, not only knows Hannah's song of thanksgiving at the birth of Samuel, but has the insight to apply it prophetically to her own situation during her pregnancy. Did she often sing it to her boy at bedtime? I expect so. She would want him to know how special he was.

Martha and Mary revisited

Martha's education and intelligence are obvious when Jesus arrives at her home after her brother Lazarus has died. I love their relationship. It is wonderfully real and robust. While Mary sits quietly at home grieving, Martha marches out to confront Jesus about his failure to turn up in time. She's the assertive, combative type, and I reckon that when Jesus saw her coming, he knew he was in for a hard time.

'If you'd come when we first sent for you,' she snaps, 'my brother wouldn't have died.'

'Don't worry, Martha, Lazarus will rise,' Jesus reassures her.

Martha doesn't appear to have heard. She stands her ground.

'On the last day,' she retorts, referring to a verse in the book of Daniel,[5] with the unspoken but obvious implication, 'That's a fat lot of good to me, because meanwhile, Lazarus is dead and this isn't the last day.'

There is no sense here that Jesus treated Martha any differently from a man. She is no fading violet in his presence. She is a strong and sensible woman who isn't afraid to give him a piece of her mind, and he loves her for it. For now he tells her what he hasn't yet revealed to anyone else – that he is the resurrection and the life. And she responds exactly as he knew she would, in her usual straightforward way, becoming the first person to declare, 'Yes, Lord . . . I believe that you are the Messiah, the Son of God' (John 11:27).

Martha was so at ease with Jesus that she thought nothing of drawing him into a family tiff. She genuinely expected him to tell her sister off for sitting around while she did all the work. And he knew Martha well enough to know that she could take his criticism on the chest like a man, when instead he affirmed Mary for giving him the gift of her attention. Martha probably went on muttering to herself in the kitchen. She had given him the gift of her cordon bleu cuisine, but then he was a man, after all – what did he know about the grind of the kitchen sink? And he would have shaken his head and laughed. It would take more than his gentle word of rebuke to flatten Martha.

> I think I have never heard a sermon preached on the story of Martha and Mary which did not attempt, somehow, somewhere, to explain away its text. Mary's, of course, was the better part – the Lord said so, and we must not precisely contradict him. But we will be careful not to despise Martha. No doubt, he approved of her too. We could not get on without her, and indeed (having paid lip service to God's opinion) we must really admit that we greatly prefer her. For Martha was doing a really feminine job, whereas Mary was just behaving like any other disciple, male or female; and that is a hard pill to swallow.[6]

Dorothy L. Sayers (1893–1957), best-selling detective story writer and creator of the new, caring, gentle, upper-crust hero

Lord Peter Wimsey, could be as tart in her sayings as Martha. The only child of a clergyman, and a student of medieval French at Somerville College, Oxford, at a time when a woman wasn't entitled to a degree, Sayers continually prodded polite society, including the Church, over its attitude to women and begged for their gifts to be acknowledged. She lampooned the bishops and other male authority figures in her orbit who referred to 'the women, God help us!' or 'the ladies, God bless them!'

Jesus, she maintained in her most outspoken essay on the subject, *Are Women Human?* (first published in a volume knowingly called *Unpopular Opinions*), never mocked or patronized women because he had 'no axe to grind, no uneasy male dignity to defend'. He was completely relaxed, completely unselfconscious with them. No wonder they were 'first at the cradle, last at the cross' (she seems to have overlooked the fact that they were first at the resurrection as well). In the 1980s, nearly thirty years after her death, those words became the rallying cry of the Movement for the Ordination of Women in Britain. But even in her time she was a thorn in the side of the Church of England. 'It is necessary,' she wrote, 'from time to time, to speak plainly, perhaps even brutally, to the Church.'[7] Unfortunately for the Church, her popularity made her hard to ignore.

I love her description of the discomfort of preachers trying to handle the Mary and Martha story, forced against their better judgement to disagree with God because they cannot break out of the confines of their own cultural prejudices. In Dorothy Sayers' time, the late 1940s and 1950s, a 'kept' wife was a badge of status and success for a professional or businessman, aping his aristocratic superiors. Meanwhile, poor women did the domestic donkey work. No preacher balked at their peeling potatoes, blacking grates, polishing the brasses or scrubbing floors. I still remember the large, rough, calloused hands of our 'daily woman', as my mother called her, when I was a child. In the 1980s, when we arrived for Peter's curacy in a mining town in West Yorkshire, somebody said to me that you could tell I was middle class by the length of my nails.

For most of the twentieth century the Church was dominated by the middle classes and their cultural attitudes. On the positive side, there was an army of women who had the freedom to work on a voluntary basis for the Church. Their loss in recent times, as younger women rush back into the job market, has been incalculable. On the negative side – and this applied for centuries – women who went out to work, or who operated in any other than an unpaid domestic setting, were treated with suspicion, if not downright hostility, and felt there was no place for the likes of them in the Church.

Today, I still get speaking invitations that read, 'Dear Mrs Guinness, could you possibly come to speak at our women's group one afternoon? We realize you may be too busy what with running a busy home and a parish . . .' The home and parish are the least of my worries. In fact, they're my husband's. But my job could be a bit of a problem. Employers aren't too keen to give me leave to gad all over the country speaking at Christian meetings.

In Jesus' day, although Jewish women were educated, it was their duty to run the home. Theological study, to sit at the rabbi's feet and learn, was a male prerogative. In his affirmation of Mary's unconventional behaviour, particularly in the Middle Eastern setting where hospitality and good manners went hand in hand, Jesus is making an important point – women don't have to be condemned any longer to a life of domesticity or social entrapment. The prime role of any disciple, male or female, is to spend time with the Master. For Jesus, the kingdom supersedes the kitchen.

> It is strange, but it is true, that John Stuart Mill could not have written in Queen Victoria's day of the emancipation of women had it not been for this carpenter of thirty who told Martha, and no doubt certain listening disciples, that Mary had many gifts which must be given freedom to develop. The intellectual woman of every sort today, university graduate,

writer, artist, musician, social worker, world traveller, may feel she goes forward in her work with the approval of Jesus Christ; that he looks for her part as a thoughtful citizen of his kingdom, and would miss it, were she not to use her talents. He sat down gratefully to Martha's good meal; he also took joy in Mary's acceptance of his wisdom. His courtesy to women includes the liberty of the whole of the personality, the use of all the gifts with which God has endowed her. The parable of the talents is for her equally with man.[8]

The man who made women feel special

In his gospel, John tells us that it was Mary of Bethany who poured perfume all over Jesus and wiped his feet with her hair (John 12:1–8), possibly at the first ever 'rising-from-the-dead' party. What made Mary do such an extraordinary thing in public?

Luke describes a very similar event in his gospel (Luke 7:36–50), but says the woman in question had a reputation for having 'lived a sinful life'. Was this Mary of Bethany, or was this another occasion and another woman – Mary Magdalene, perhaps? One thing is sure: whoever she was, only a prostitute would let her hair hang loose outside the privacy of her own bedroom. This may have been a spontaneous act of gratitude for the fact that she was restored, whole and free, a declaration that she wasn't going to submit to a life of shame any more. Or perhaps it was an opportunity for the abused to show the abusers that she was no longer in their power. Bethany was a small place, and in that room there could well have been men who had known her in another context.

Having experienced the worst kind of subjection, she now knew the greatest kind of liberty. She was so caught up in her love for Jesus that she didn't give a fig for convention, or what anyone would think of her, but, like Ruth and Esther before her, she risked her reputation to do what she had to do.

It was an uncomfortable situation. Mary's striking behav-
-iour had rather erotic overtones, but Jesus was comfortable

enough with his own sexuality not to be disturbed by it. He didn't say, 'Stop making an exhibition of yourself, woman. You're embarrassing me!' Instead he saw the intention behind the gesture, and accepted it for what it was – an expression of pure love. Theirs was an intimate, yet utterly safe relationship. He welcomed the tears and kisses, the warm, physical display of affection. Then he said he only wished men would respond to him as freely.

All Jesus' relationships with women are characterized by that same easy, loving acceptance and rejection of stereotypes. He called a girl of twelve his 'little darling' when he raised her from the dead[9]; he singled out and healed a bent and broken old lady, crippled with osteoporosis or rheumatoid arthritis, too plain and poor to think that a dynamic young man would have any time for her; he never reproached the worn-out, anaemic, middle-aged woman who'd had menstrual problems for years and took an enormous risk when she pushed through the crowds and made a rabbi unclean by touching the *tzitzit,* the tassels of his tunic, but instead, he cut through the taboos of the time and commended her for her faith.

Was his extraordinary encounter with the Samaritan woman at the well remarkable because she was a woman, or because she was a member of a race treated in Israel like the untouchables in India? The Jewish people had a proverb at the time of Jesus that said, 'The daughters of the Samaritans are menstruants from the cradle.' But Jesus still does the unthinkable and shares her drinking cup. He sits and talks to her as if it's the most normal thing in the world for a Jewish man to do, leaving his disciples in a state of shock. She rushes back to her people and says, 'Come and see a man who told me everything I ever did.' All Jesus had actually done was to enumerate her partners. 'Everything I ever did' didn't really amount to much, and that makes this a very contemporary story. But the seventh man in her life forgives, liberates and transforms her – and the people of the village who respond to her words of life. She becomes, as Mark Stibbe pointed out to me, the first apostle in the gospels.[10]

Anyone who does his will is his brother, sister and mother, Jesus says, without gender distinction (Mark 3:35). He was quite comfortable having a large number of women as disciples and travelling companions, including Mary Magdalene, who had been healed of evil spirits, which meant she had probably shown all the signs of severe mental health problems and had been an object of ridicule and abuse for years. And, what's more, when they provided the financial support for his mission (Luke 8:2–3), possibly from the proceeds of their cottage industries, he didn't say, 'Just a minute girls, I'm the man, I need to be the breadwinner around here'.

Jesus doesn't only raise the status of women. He raises the status of all human beings by showing them what God intended them to be. The pouring out of the Holy Spirit on men and women alike at Pentecost after his ascension was the natural and logical conclusion of his earthly ministry. It is hardly surprising, then, that women played a key part in the early Church.

Prophets, apostles, deacons and fellow workhorses

The prophecy of Joel was more than adequately fulfilled in the apostle Philip's household, as he had four single daughters who were all prophets. That must have kept Daddy on his toes, especially when they were all at home together. Whenever he went on a mission, he had four possible assistants to call on. No wonder their reputation went before them.

The apostle Paul also experienced the new gifting of women at close quarters, and valued their hard work. The end of Romans must have one of the longest PS lists of any letter ever published, as Paul recalls, one by one – no doubt to a flagging amanuensis – all the friends and colleagues to whom he wants to say 'hello'. Ten of the twenty-nine people in his roll call of the great and good are women. Leading evangelical scholar Dick France points out that four of them – Mary, Tryphaena, Tryphosa and Persis – are described as having 'worked hard' for the kingdom of God, a translation of the verb *kopiao,* which Paul uses to describe his own and his other male colleagues' ministry in evangelism and church-building.[11]

Like Tryphaena and Tryphosa in Rome, Euodia and Syntyche, those two embattled dears in Philippi, and Priscilla of Corinth are all referred to by Paul as *synergos,* or co-workers. In other words, he regards them as having the same ministry as Timothy, Titus, Mark, Luke and Philemon – the big male guns in his apostolic mission.

The most interesting name on Paul's list in Romans is his fellow prisoner, Junia, because he actually calls her a leading apostle, or church-planter. Although contemporary translations refer to this person as Junias, no such male version of the name existed in Roman times. In his writings, Jerome, the foremost fifth-century Christian scholar, speaks about this 'leader among the apostles' as if she were a woman. In fact, Junia's gender went unquestioned until the thirteenth century, when Aegidus of Rome became the first commentator to describe her as a man. To give them the benefit of the doubt, the appearance of that definitive little 's' on the end might have been unintentional, since the medieval scribes simply couldn't conceive of a female apostle in the male-dominated Church of the time. On the other hand, they may have added it deliberately, because they wanted the Church to stay that way. Either way, medieval scribes were notoriously inaccurate.

Professor Richard Baukham of St Andrew's University thinks it possible that Junia may have been Joanna, the well-to-do wife of Herod's influential steward Chuza who is described in Luke's gospel as one of a number of female followers of Jesus. The defection of such a powerful courtier to the new religious movement must have sent shock waves through the society in which she lived, which may be why she took on a Latin version of her Hebrew name – to give her greater clout in spreading the word in the Romanized culture of her home town, Tiberias.[12]

It is a woman, Phoebe, who is entrusted to take Paul's precious letter to the church in Rome. She is a *diakonos,* the same word used for a male deacon, and a 'helper to many'. Helper here is a translation of *proistatis,* from the verb *proistemi,* 'to preside over or care for'. It means supervisor, protector or patron, someone who stands by their protégés when they get into scrapes. In other words, she had a prominent role in the church at Cenchreae. She may even have hosted it in her home, with all the implications of leadership that entails.

Priscilla and her husband Aquila, joint leaders of a church in their home in Corinth, left it to go with Paul on his missionary journeys. Priscilla is no back-up for her man, at his side though slightly behind him, making sure he goes out to preach in clean underwear and matching socks. Nothing suggests that, when they share a pulpit, he is the meat and two vegetables while she is the dessert. In fact, it seems that she took the lead in correcting the doctrine of the formidable Apollos. She manifestly had an outstanding and authoritative ministry in her own right. Contrary to even contemporary tradition, when Paul mentions the couple he often puts Priscilla's name first. It is believed that their powerful ministry came to an end in AD 98, when they were both beheaded.

One thing is sure – the first Christian women were not confined to domestic roles. Lydia was a successful businesswoman of Philippi who owned a large house and had her own slaves. Damaris, who was converted in Athens when she heard Paul preach at the Areopagus, was obviously an educated woman with a public role, possibly as a philosopher. Both used their influence to spread the Gospel. In fact, many well-heeled Roman matrons, such as Chloe in Corinth and Nympha in Colossae, used their wealth and standing in society to preach the Gospel and lead groups or churches in their own homes. Their evangelistic initiatives enabled Christianity to penetrate the upper classes.

Martyrs, missionaries and Montanists

By the middle of the second century the persecution of Christians has begun in earnest. But though women suffer alongside the men, though they are hung up by their hair and drowned, raped and ravaged, burned, beheaded and beaten, gored to death for sport by wild beasts, though they are forced to watch their children being killed for refusing to sacrifice to the Roman gods, they are now denied any leadership in the faith that costs them their lives.

For the first hundred years they were teachers, administrators, evangelists and prophets, but then the creeping tide of institutionalism pushed them from the centre to the periphery of church life, as the numerous house churches spread across the great cities were subjected to centralized control. The new structures that were introduced were based on the secular Roman model of civic government – in other words, a male, clerical ruling class and a subservient people of God. No Communion service could take place unless a bishop was present to officiate. The life began to be stifled out of the Church, and whoever dared to challenge the system was swiftly discredited.

God's Holy Spirit has never remained boxed and packaged for long, and in the latter half of the second century renewal broke out for the first time. It was led by a man called Montanus and two women, Maximilla and Prisca, and it spread like wildfire through the churches of Asia Minor. As the gifts of the Holy Spirit were restored, believers began to participate in services once again, and women were powerfully anointed to preach and exercise key leadership roles.

Terrified of losing control, the hierarchy of the official Church denounced Montanism as a form of paganism. Montanus was personally discredited, particularly for allowing women such prominence. Maximilla and Prisca were falsely accused of leaving their husbands and of prophesying for financial gain. In the name of order and common sense, the Holy Spirit and the ministry of women were effectively banned, and in many ways the Western Church never really recovered.

The masters of misogyny

Man is active, full of movement, creative in politics, business and culture. The male shapes and moulds society and the world. Woman, on the other hand, is passive. She stays at home, as is her nature. She is matter waiting to be formed by the active male principle. Of course the active elements are always higher on any scale and more divine. Man consequently plays a major part in reproduction; the woman is merely the passive incubator of his seed.

ARISTOTLE

It is evident, when he wrote these immortal words, that Aristotle had never been pregnant! Yet though he lived more than 300 years before Jesus Christ, though he had no knowledge of the Hebrew Scriptures, his views on women did more to shape the thinking of the Church than anything Jesus did or said, because of their influence on its founding fathers.

The Early Church Fathers, who lived between the third and fifth centuries, were the authority on what Christians should believe, but they appear to have worn mental, emotional and spiritual blinkers when it came to the place of women. Hostile to the Jews who had killed their Christ, steeped in the classical, Graeco-Roman mindset, and beset by struggles to come to terms with their own carefully controlled sexuality, their writings are a sorry catalogue of anti-female feeling. Yet these views seeped their way into the Church's conscious and subconscious thinking and influenced biblical exegesis for many centuries.

Tertullian (AD 160–240), the Father of Latin theology, who referred to women as 'the devil's gateway' because these sirens lured poor, unsuspecting men into sin, was the first to use the instruction 'let the women keep silence' in the letter to the

Corinthians as a justification to gag women completely. They were not to be allowed to pray, teach or even sing. Instead, they were to sit like dummies. Montanism helped modify his views, but the established Church chose to ignore what it regarded as his later aberration and clung instead to his pre-charismatic theology.

Clement of Alexandria (AD 150–220) insisted that women should wear an early Christian version of the *burqa*, lest they be a source of temptation to men.

Origen (AD 185–254) claimed that God didn't even lower himself to look at woman. For reproduction's sake they were evidently a necessary evil. He castrated himself.

Cyril of Alexandria (died AD 444) was so adamant that women were inferior and were not to teach men in any capacity that when a local woman, Hypatia, dared to contradict him and went on teaching maths and philosophy to her male students, he incited his monks to murder her and burn her flesh as they hacked it off the bone.

Augustine (AD 354–430), hailed as the greatest of all the Church Fathers, was an inveterate womanizer as a lad and despite, or perhaps because of his celibacy, appears to have lived with a perpetual bonfire under his loincloth. Augustine couldn't understand why he wasn't more holy and projected the blame for his sexual temptations onto the object of his fantasies. His self-disgust pokes through a thinly disguised veneer of hatred for women. 'Only man is fully created in the image of God,' he proclaimed. 'The female state is a deformity.' Eve was the great deceiver and seducer, the fount of all evil. 'The woman herself alone is not the image of God, whereas the man alone is the image of God as fully and completely as when the woman is joined with him.'

Jerome (AD 340–420) referred to women as 'miserable, sin-ridden wenches' and popularized the idea of Mary's perpetual virginity, while John Chrysostom (AD 347–407), the greatest preacher of the Greek Church, said, 'God maintained the order of each sex by dividing the business of human life into two parts and assigned the necessary and more beneficial aspects to the man, and the less important, inferior matters to the woman.' Some might be tempted to say that not a lot has changed in the Church in the sixteen centuries since Chrysostom's preaching.

However, the early centuries were not entirely bleak for Christian women. It would take more than the jaundiced pronouncements of a few theologians, even if they were the spiritual intelligentsia, to curb women's spirits and force them into subservience. Reluctantly, the Church had to recognize that, whatever the theory of the leaders, in practice women's capacity for holy living and godly service was as great as any man's. A truly spiritual woman was encouraged to pursue the monastic life, presumably because, if she took a vow of celibacy, she was no longer 'available' and a source of temptation. Religious communities gave any exceptional woman the chance to exercise authority and leadership gifts – particularly in Celtic Britain.

The Celts

While the women of the Roman Empire belonged to their husbands, along with any property they brought into the marriage, Celtic women were highly respected matriarchal figures with a great deal of freedom in their close-knit communities. Like Boudicca in AD 60, they could become a tribal chief, or even a military commander, leading their people into battle. The only drawback was that in an era when Britain was divided into many hostile, warring kingdoms, tribal lords seemed to have an unfortunate habit of marrying off virginal daughters, nieces and wards to suit their own expansionist urges.

For a Christian young woman, entering a religious community was one way of escaping the clutches of some powerful heathen brute. Not much of a choice, really, but if she became an abbess, she could do whatever she wanted with her land, exercise considerable organizational and managerial skills, and maintain a measure of independence. Furthermore, as communities were mixed, she ruled over men, taught them the Scriptures and trained them for ministry. The only thing she was not allowed to do, according to edicts from the traditionalist Roman Church, was to become a bishop and officiate at a Communion service. Nonetheless, Brigid of Ireland was consecrated bishop rather than abbess. No one knew for sure whether it was because the officiating Bishop of Kildare was so overwhelmed by the power of the Holy Spirit upon her that he could not countermand the instructions of God, or because he fell asleep during the service and didn't notice she was a woman.

The innate equality of men and women in Celtic society meant that leading churchmen like Patrick of Ireland don't appear to have been threatened by a powerful or clever member of the opposite sex. Since a religious community would require daily Communion, every abbess appropriated her own bishop, though there was never any question about who had the ultimate authority over the order. This led to many close, extremely fruitful partnerships – like Brigid and Conleath, who proved it was possible for single men and women to work closely together without sex getting in the way.

The most outstanding female Celtic Church leader after Brigid was Hilda of Whitby (AD 614–80). When Hilda was little, her mother dreamed that under her robes she discovered a valuable jewel, which, according to the Venerable Bede's history of the time, 'emitted such a brilliant light that all Britain was lit by its splendour'. The jewel was fulfilled in her daughter.

On a windswept peninsular high over the North Sea, at Streaneshalch, now Whitby, Hilda presided over one of the most exceptional communities of all time. Every member was committed to a disciplined life of study and prayer, and to working in whatever way they could to bring justice, mercy and peace to the world outside. Drawn by its reputation like moths to the light, people came to Whitby from miles around and every walk of life, for spiritual direction, counselling, support and prayer, to learn the creative arts such as poetry, music, writing and graphics, or to study the Scriptures, and, whoever they were, clerical or lay, noble or poor, they were shown the same attention and care. Caedmon, the first popular British poet, moved in permanently. Five of Hilda's students became bishops, including John of Beverley and Wilfred, who was to cause her the most searching of heart.

While the Whitby community flourished, the Church in Britain was becoming ever more deeply divided between the Celtic and the more formal Roman way. On a visit to Rome, Wilfred was very taken with the pomp and ceremony of the church hierarchy there, and was sent home on a mission to bring the Celtic Church to heel. The growing tensions came to a head at a national consultation on the future of the Church in AD 664, held, inevitably, at Whitby, with Hilda in the chair.

It is hard to imagine what she felt. The famous Synod must have been extremely difficult for her. She revered and respected the great Cuthbert, who defended the Celtic Church, with its commitment to equality, community and poverty. That was where her own personal inclination lay. But Wilfred had been her student and she was extremely fond of him. She must have used all her conciliatory powers to preserve the unity and integrity of the Church she loved. But in the end, conflict was contrary to Cuthbert's nature and he capitulated without a fight.

It must have grieved Hilda to witness the defeat of a way of life which was the very essence of her being, and at the hands of a past student she thought she knew and trusted. She may well have wondered how different things might have been had she abandoned her impartiality and offered Cuthbert more support. The Roman Church was so powerful that it would probably have dominated the British Church and imposed its rule in the end anyway. Yet Hilda and Cuthbert could have postponed that eventuality a while longer, and even preserved some of the traditions they loved, had she encouraged him to stand firm.

Perhaps she guessed eventually that compromise was bought at far too high a price, for, as far as female leadership was concerned, she effectively 'pulled up the ladder' behind her.

Churchwomen medieval and modern

In the centuries that followed, the attitude of most church leaders to women could be summarized in the words of the medieval monk and theologian, Thomas Aquinas (1225–74). Woman, he wrote, was 'defective and misbegotten ... biologically, spiritually and intellectually inferior.' As a concession he added, 'a necessary object, a woman, needed to preserve the species and provide food and drink'. This is about as far from God's intention at creation as it is possible to get – more Taliban than true Christianity.

Nonetheless, true to form, there arose from time to time a woman to prove him wrong – like Julian of Norwich, born around 1342, a great mystic, writer and counsellor, whose spiritual insights attracted visitors from miles around. A recluse, Mother Julian lived a life of prayer and self-denial in her hermit's cell, and was given no leadership in the church to which she was attached. Even so, she must have expected criticism, for she wrote in her *Revelations of Divine Love*, 'Because I am a woman, ought I therefore to believe that I should not tell you of the goodness of God, although I saw that it is His will that it be known?'

For Mother Julian, if God is total and complete he must be male and female, mother as well as father. Her distinctively obstetric language to describe the process of rebirth is fairly shocking today, let alone then. Jesus carries us within himself in love, she says. Inevitably, pregnancy leads to childbirth, so the pains of his death are really labour pains which bear us 'to joy and eternal life'. And then, just as a mother puts her child tenderly to her breast, 'our beloved Mother, Jesus, feeds us with himself', by his body and his blood. Not surprisingly, her writings fell from favour at the Reformation. Some found the imagery a little hard to stomach.

The great Spanish mystic Teresa of Avila (1515–82) was the first woman to be declared a doctor of the Church – but not until 1970. She founded and reformed Carmelite convents all over Spain, and gently but firmly challenged the established male authority of her time about its attitude to women. If the Spanish king could exalt and honour whomsoever he chose, without being constrained by lower officials, so the King of Kings, she said, could bypass the hierarchical structures of the Church and give special gifts to women, if he so chose. Even so, she envied men their freedom 'to cry out and spread the news abroad about who this great God of hosts is'.

In the nineteenth century, as women began to reappropriate that freedom in the name of social justice, as the revivalist power of the holiness movement gave them the courage to weather opposition and preach in public once again, the doors to ministry overseas swung wide open, and they proved on other continents what they might have been capable of doing at home, had they been given the chance. In foreign lands, where out of sight was out of mind as far as the Western Church hierarchy was concerned, they laid the foundations of churches that thrive today in Africa and Asia. They challenged, with some success, the cultural attitudes which denied women and children their basic rights. They built hospitals and clinics, opened schools and developed cottage industries. And as they took the message of Jesus' love for women to countries where women knew only oppression and abuse, as they proclaimed the freedom of the Gospel, they received a new freedom for themselves in leading, preaching and creating communities.

Amy Carmichael (1867–1951), a remarkable combination of Irish Protestant and mystic, was a thorn in the side of some other Western missionaries in India at the turn of the nineteeth/twentieth century in her outspoken refusal to submit to either imperialist tradition or the rigid caste system. She wore a sari, lived simply with a band of local women, and eventually founded a community of both men and women at Dohnavur as a refuge for hundreds of small girls who had been used as cult prostitutes in the Hindu temples – a practice later forbidden by the Indian government. Here Amma, or 'Mother', as Amy was known, watched over a 'Family' which lives to this day, a little like Hilda's Whitby community, in a kind of model village, with schools, workshops, weaving sheds, sewing rooms, hospital, chapel and farm, fruit and vegetable gardens. The aim was to demonstrate God's love in action, not just in teaching but also in serving the local area. And, like Whitby, Dohnavur became an oasis, not just for the girls, but for many travellers looking for spiritual truth, encouragement and comfort.

Several young Englishmen who went out to India, ostensibly to see her work and support her in it, challenged Amy Carmichael's authority. They couldn't cope with her distinctively female style of leadership with its team approach. Yet it was the emphasis Amy placed on right relationships that made Dohnavur unique. An older missionary had once told her that missionaries were always falling out and making up again. For Amy, that idea was intolerable, incompatible with Christ's Calvary, sacrificial love. Unity was paramount, and that meant establishing a firm discipline within her community, where each and every member was required to live a life of self-denial, mercy and forgiveness, always putting the other first. Her demanding rules for life, which she lived to her dying day, even when she was bedridden after an accident, fly in the face of every contemporary view of authority and success. But she was no ascetic. Children loved her because they saw the Irish mischief in her eyes.

Amy Carmichael never returned to Britain, but in the twentieth century, female missionaries who did go back, usually on furlough, often presented a problem for the Church. Many who were great leaders abroad were denied access to the pulpit at home. It was perfectly acceptable for natives, both male and female, to be the beneficiaries of their leading and preaching, but not so-called 'civilized' congregations. To get around these difficulties, missionary meetings were often held in an uncon-secrated building, preaching was called 'speaking' and a ser-mon referred to as 'an address'.

As Lavinia Byrne put it,[13] having challenged a world which had been established by men for the convenience and servicing of men, whatever the religious tradition – Islam, Hinduism or the African religions – missionary women suddenly discovered that the Church was found wanting too. It failed to offer them the freedoms of Christianity they were preaching abroad. They suddenly came face to face with the fact that their very success was a threat to the establishment at home. The irony was that they had seen first-hand that raising the status of women did not diminish men; rather, it raised their status too.

Yet the definitive history of missions, written in the 1960s by Bishop Stephen Neill, one of the young men who had seen the formidable Amy Carmichael at work and had struggled with her leadership, barely mentioned the extraordinary achievements of these remarkable women. Nor was there any recognition of the wives of the great pioneers, who either laboured at their husbands' sides, or let them go and lived alone, laying down their lives – literally or metaphorically – for the Gospel. They simply didn't count. But then, after almost nineteen centuries of women being overlooked and disdained, attitudes were not going to change overnight.

'It is extraordinary,' writes Hyam Maccoby, 'that it has so often been believed that in Pharisee law women had no rights, and that it was only the advent of Christianity that raised women to the status of legal personages. The historical fact is that the abolition of Pharisee law by the church led to the loss of much humane legislation and to a tragic lowering of the sta-tus of women.'[14]

How was that possible? Many would lay the blame squarely at the feet of the apostle Paul – but perhaps history has done him a great injustice too.

Notes

1. Dr Leonard Swidler, *Women in Judaism* (Scarecrow Press, 1976).
2. Hyam Maccoby, *Judaism in the First Century* (Sheldon Press, 1989).
3. Professor Shmuel Safrai, 'The Place of Women in First-Century Synagogues', *Jerusalem Perspective*, September/October 1993.
4. Maccoby, *Judaism in the First Century*, p. 61.
5. 'Multitudes who sleep in the dust of the earth will awake: some to everlasting life, others to shame and everlasting contempt' (Daniel 12:2).
6. Dorothy L. Sayers, *Are Women Human?* (Eerdmans, 1971).
7. Dorothy L. Sayers, *Unpopular Opinions* (Victor Gollancz, 1946), pp. 117–18.
8. Lady Dorothea Hosie, *Jesus and Women* (Hodder and Stoughton, 1946), p. 196, from *The Hidden Journey, Missionary Heroines in Many Lands*, ed. Lavinia Byrne (Triangle, 1993).
9. Mark 5:44.
10. Mark Stibbe, *John (Readings: A New Biblical Commentary)* (Sheffield Academic Press, 1993), pp. 66-68.
11. R.T. France, *A Slippery Slope? The Ordination of Women and Homosexual Practice – a Case Study in Biblical Interpretation* (Grove Books, 2000). France is a former principal of Wycliffe Theological College in Oxford.
12. On 6 July 2002, the religious correspondent of *The Times* announced that a paper by Professor Richard Baukham, containing evidence that Junia, the apostle, was a woman, was being studied by Church of England leaders debating whether women should be ordained bishops. 'The discovery suggests that society was far less patriarchal than previous research has shown ... The assumption that the leading apostles were all men has been one of the most unassailable arguments against the ordination of women bishops. If the claim that Joanna and Junia were the same person and that Junia was a woman and an Apostle is accepted, the argument for women bishops will have been all but won.'
13. Byrne, *The Hidden Journey*.
14. Maccoby, *Judaism in the First Century*, p. 56.

CHAPTER 5

The Silent Woman?

I brought up my children to believe there was nothing a woman couldn't do. Seeing my ineptitude at handling anything vaguely technical, Joel had one or two doubts about that in his boyhood, happily dispelled when he realized that his female classmates were not tyrannized by gadgetry and machinery the way his mother was. The new generation, like his sister, could change a plug without an immediate explosion, hang cupboards and shelves without them crashing to the floor, and change a flat tyre without the ignominy of having to flag down a male passer-by.

Joel's egalitarian convictions weren't challenged until he arrived at Oxford University. In his first term he was helping to arrange a special event for Jewish students on behalf of the Christian Union. There were problems in finding a suitable speaker.

'I suppose, if we were really stuck, my mum could do it,' he said.

The suggestion was greeted with an uncomfortable silence.

'Well, I know she's my mum, but that's not a problem, is it?'

'The fact that she's your mum isn't a problem,' one of the students explained. 'The fact that she's a woman is.'

Joel refrained from a sarcastic comment to the effect that he had noticed his mother was a woman. In many ways he was too staggered to respond at all. To cancel an opportunity to share the Christian faith because of rigid adherence to dogma – dubious dogma at that – was beyond the realms of both his experience and his comprehension.

He soon discovered that no woman was allowed to become the president of the Christian Union or speak at their main evening meetings. Notions of equality which, like most of his generation, he had taken for granted were being challenged in this microcosm of the Church, not by a brigade of traditional old boys, but by the so-called cream of society's bright-eyed, bushy-tailed intelligentsia. And all because of two verses in the Bible – one in the book of Corinthians that said women should keep silent, and one in the book of Timothy that said they shouldn't teach.

Joel tried to encourage his fellow students to see that in the not-too-distant future many would have female bosses with the authority to hire and fire them, so why impose a set of cultur-ally alien rules on themselves that might cause them a struggle later? His efforts were in vain. They saw no gaping chasm between the secular and sacred worlds in which they moved. They clung to one interpretation of these verses, blissfully unaware that, by inference, their message to Western society was that the Bible was out of date and irrelevant. Since that simply isn't the case, it's time to tackle some of those tricky texts head on.

Wrestling with the text

Anyone studying a passage of Scripture has to ask four basic questions. What did it mean in its original context? What do the words actually mean? How does it fit with other texts on the same or similar issues? What is its meaning for today? All traditions accept that this is a necessary process in biblical exegesis.

Among Christians there seems to be a deep-seated fear that to look at a passage in its cultural context must somehow reduce its relevance and contradict Paul's teaching that 'All Scripture is God-breathed and is useful for teaching, rebuking, correcting and training in righteousness' (2 Timothy 3:16). But Christians, unlike the Jewish people, often have only a remedial knowledge of their history. They have no sense of where they came from or how they got here. There seems to be an assumption that the Church simply landed one day, like a flying saucer, in its present form.

Far from reducing Paul's teaching, understanding the backdrop to his letters makes it more accessible and expands the potential breadth of its application. Once upon a time, when I arrived at Paul's letters in my daily readings, I would feel the muscles in my stomach knot. How could such a great and godly man be so dismissive of half the human race? Gradually, as I developed a feeling for the world in which he lived and came to understand why he said what he said, I found I could face him with equanimity and even excitement, and positively dispute any suggestion that he was a misogynist. It is ignorance that has earned him such a bad press.

Delving into the original meaning of the words used in the text, matching them with the same or similar words used elsewhere, and analysing the choice of language can be a fun piece of detective work. Is the translation accurate? Does the grammatical construction of the sentence have any significance? The use of different words in different translations for the original Hebrew or Greek can even produce conflicting interpretations of the text.

Being Jewish does not make me an expert in ancient Hebrew. Despite years of instruction – two hours of classes every Sunday morning and one hour after school three days a week – my Hebrew is fairly rudimentary. I was taught to read Hebrew fluently so that I wouldn't look silly in the synagogue on Sabbath or festivals, but no translation was ever forthcoming. We simply learned to translate the Torah by rote, and it was so painfully slow that by the time my education was deemed complete, the Children of Israel still hadn't managed to get out of the desert. But I was left with a basic knowledge of how the words were put together, the difference made to the root by adding suffixes and prefixes, or those mysterious hieroglyphics that are the vowels.

If the Bible is inspired, which of the many translations over the past 2,000 years is the most inspired, and how might the variations affect our perceptions? We saw in Chapter 2 how two contrasting translations of the word *tsachaq* can alter our opinion of Sarah. Or what about the subtleties surrounding Priscilla in the story in Acts where she and her husband put Apollos straight? In the original Greek Priscilla is named before her husband, which suggests that on this occasion at least she took the lead in the partnership (Acts 18:26). In the English translation authorized by King James I in 1611, however, the order is reversed and Aquila is mentioned first, a sign of traditional deference to the male. Or take another example. In the original Greek, Paul's buddies, Timothy, Epaphras, Tychicus, Apollos and Phoebe, are all referred to in various letters as *diakonos*, translated as 'minister' in the King James Version – with one exception. The only woman *diakonos*, Phoebe, is called a 'servant'.[1]

Is it pure coincidence that King James I was one of the most misogynist monarchs ever to mount the British throne? He refused to allow the improvement of education for women on the grounds that 'to make women learned and foxes tame has the same effect: to make them more cunning'.[2] He believed women were all like Eve, highly susceptible to demonic influence. Witchcraft was punishable by hanging. Guilt could be established on hearsay without recourse to the normal system of justice. Anyone who disliked or resented a female neighbour, or found her just a little bit strange, could report her to the authorities – and they did. Isn't it possible that the rather bigoted culture of the time could have coloured the first English translation of the Bible?[3]

Comparing texts on any one issue, taking the whole range together, gives an overall perspective which extracting lone verses out of context can never do. In fact, lone verses can lead us up blind alleys. Some have used the verse 'The blessing of the Lord makes rich, and he adds no sorrow with it' (Proverbs 10:22 RSV) to justify having health and wealth, even if the reality of life in developing countries tells a different story. Jesus, in fact, extolled and lived a life of poverty, but that's a harder path to follow.

The power on the platform

Whether we justify our position from the texts, like many evangelicals, or from history, like the Catholic wing of the Church, the status of women is such an emotive issue that it almost always reaches us in a pre-packaged state. We come to it with a host of preconceived ideas, wearing sunglasses tinted by our background, culture, personal preferences, and negative or positive experiences of women in authority – including mothers and teachers – that filter out whatever we find uncomfortable.

Male fear of losing power and domain in this one last, safe bastion of supremacy can be very real, and that's understandable – but it isn't only men who are opposed to women preachers or leaders. Women can be equally vehement in their objections, which is more surprising. In her study of the differing communication styles of men and women, Deborah Tannen, Professor of Linguistics at Georgetown University, explains that 'men and women who do not conform to the expectations for their own gender may not be liked', particularly by members of their own gender.[4] Women can fear that, when some of our species break rank and behave in a way that is deemed unfeminine, we will all forfeit male approval and our *teshuqah*, that instinctive need for a dominant male, wants to prevent that happening at any cost.

Whatever the arguments for and against female leadership in the Church, they are often far less rational and far more emotional than they may first appear.

There was a student in our church called Chris who came from a background where the very idea of a woman speaking from the pew, let alone the pulpit, was anathema. He struggled with the way women were allowed to preach in our church, especially Ruth, our young people's worker. His real difficulty was that he admired and respected her, and was forced to admit that there were few people from whom he had learned more about what it meant to be a disciple.

'So what's the difference between my sitting next to you here in a pew, sharing something I think I've learned from the Bible, and my sharing it with the entire congregation from the front?' Ruth asked one Sunday night, exasperated by the inconsistency of his arguments and in fighting mood.

'That's different!' he insisted.

'Only geography. You have no objections to my teaching strapping great teenage lads in the Sunday school.'

Peter watched the interaction with some trepidation, and not a little admiration for Ruth's assertive powers.

'Look,' she said to Chris, when she saw he was refusing to give an inch, 'why don't you use your imagination and try to think your way into how God feels when he sees me up there. What does he say? "How dare she! Doesn't she know she's only a woman?"'

'No,' Chris admitted reluctantly, 'I suppose he thinks it's great.'

Instinctively, Ruth felt the issue was about power, the perception of the person who stood a mere six inches up on the platform.

'Then I tell you what,' she said, taking the kind of risk that Peter admitted later he would never have taken himself, 'you go away this week and think about it, and if you really believe that it's a sin for me to preach, it's your Christian duty to tell me so and I'll resign.'

'You can't do that!' Chris gulped, shrinking a little from the petite, almost delicate-looking woman who held his gaze throughout. 'You're . . . you're just such an amazing person.'

'Yes, and I've felt called to teach the Bible since I was a child.'

Chris looked completely bewildered. It had never occurred to him that a woman might have a sense of calling.

'So if I've been wrong all these years, it's your responsibility to tell me, and I'll resign.'

What Chris and many others would like are black-and-white answers, which are so much easier than facing up to the apparent contradictions in the text. Yet we have no choice. Our knowledge of remarkable female church leaders from the last century or so confronts us with the issue head on. Some would say, of course, that we cannot base Church doctrine on experience. But the early Church developed its doctrine by reflecting on experience and applying theological principles to it. Gentiles were only accepted into membership because they had been filled with the Holy Spirit as the Jewish Christians were. Such had been his mindset against that possibility that the apostle Peter had needed a special revelation to convince him that non-Jews could be kosher.

So would the apostle Paul really have disapproved of female preachers and teachers? Would he have deplored the actions of Corrie ten Boom, the elderly Dutchwoman imprisoned in a concentration camp by the Nazis for rescuing Jews, who, after her release, travelled the world urging Christians to rediscover the gift of forgiveness? Or Kathryn Kuhlman, with her dramatic gift of healing, who drew thousands to her evangelistic crusades in the 1950s and '60s? Or Jackie Pullinger, the Englishwoman who gave her life to working among the triads and drug gangs of Hong Kong and whose unique success earned her the financial backing of the Hong Kong government? It hardly seems likely.

How did Paul really relate to women?

The letters of Paul say three things: love God, love your neighbour, and you women caused all the trouble in the world, so just sit still and keep quiet.

THE REDUCED SHAKESPEARE COMPANY
IN *THE REDUCED BIBLE*

The equality of men and women may no longer be an issue in Western society, but the fact that the secular world believes the Bible has a down on women is. When the Reduced Shakespeare Company toured the country with their 90-minute version of the Word of God, their three-point summary of Paul's letters raised many a knowing laugh. Yet throughout his descriptions of his adventures and escapades, there is never any suggestion that the apostle had an aversion to females or their ministry, or that he deliberately steered clear of their company. On the contrary, he appears to have positively welcomed their partnership in his work, and even targeted them in his evangelistic strategy.

Luke, the doctor, an eyewitness to the events of Pentecost and, of all the New Testament writers, the most sensitive to the key role women had to play, describes how he and Paul went down to the river on the Sabbath to find a place of prayer and sat among the women who had gathered there (Acts 16:13). This supports the idea that, far from being outcasts, Jewish women were already playing a full part in religious life. If Christianity is truly liberating, it seems unreasonable that Paul would seek to diminish rather than enhance their role. In fact, Lydia, who is converted there and then, persuades Paul to use her home as his base whenever he is in Philippi.

Not only does Paul refer to women as full colleagues, patrons and friends, but when he describes the sacrifice his missionary travels entail, he says rather wistfully, 'Don't we have the right to take a believing wife along with us, as do the other apostles and the Lord's brothers and Peter?' (1 Corinthians 9:5). There were obviously moments when he would have loved to have had one special woman in his life. This doesn't sound like a woman-hater. Since he was a Pharisee, and Pharisees always married, he may well have been a widower.

Paul's most all-encompassing statement of egalitarianism is in his letter to the Galatians, a predominantly Jewish church, where he says that once a person belongs to Jesus Christ there is no Jew or Greek, slave or free, male or female (Galatians 3:28). In the Gospel there is no room for superiority, posturing or domination. Admittedly, the context is salvation, but Paul is saying that all the old man-made distinctions created by race, status and gender have been broken down by the cross and resurrection. Hierarchy has been dismantled, exclusion is not an option. A new order has come into being, and the proof of it is Pentecost. The Holy Spirit was not and is not discriminatory. So Jewish men can stop thanking God they're not a woman.

When Paul talks about gifts and ministries of the Holy Spirit in 1 Corinthians 12, he does not say evangelism is for men, embroidery is for women; teaching is for men, typing is for women; prophecy is for men, praying at home is for women; leading is for men, knitting is for women. He says, 'All these [gifts] are the work of one and the same Spirit, and he gives them to each one, just as he determines' (v. 11). So why would he then urge women to keep silence in services? It doesn't appear to make sense.

Let the women keep silent

As in all the congregations of the saints, women should remain silent in the churches. They are not allowed to speak, but must be in submission, as the Law says. If they want to enquire about something, they should ask their own husbands at home; for it is disgraceful for a woman to speak in the church.

1 CORINTHIANS 14:34–5

Taken at face value, it would appear that women are condemned to sitting through every act of worship like stuffed
dummies, unable to read a lesson or join in the singing, let
alone pray or preach. I did hear recently of a church where
women were not allowed to ask a question or make a comment in a Bible study, but had to write it down and hand it to
the nearest male. That really is extreme, for only slightly earlier in the same letter, speaking about propriety in worship,
Paul says that any woman who prays or prophesies in public
must cover her head. There will be more on head-covering in
a later chapter, but for the moment it appears that we are left
with a complete contradiction. If a prophetic ministry was an
essential vehicle for encouraging and empowering congregations, a means of sharing a vision for God's wider plans and
intentions, if it was a call to integrity, authenticity and radical
lifestyle, it must have involved a measure of preaching and
required a certain amount of authority. So in what situation
should a woman be silent and submissive? Why might her
speaking be a disgrace?

I have five possible interpretations of these two verses, but
there are probably many more.

The respectful worshipper theory

Predominantly Greek and Gentile, the Christians in Corinth
were a remarkable collection of trophies. 'Do not be deceived,'
Paul reminds them, 'neither the immoral, nor idolaters, nor
adulterers, nor sexual perverts, nor thieves, nor the greedy, nor
drunkards ... will inherit the kingdom of God. And such were
some of you' (1 Corinthians 6:9 RSV). There was certainly a
history of 'sexual irregularities', as Dr Stephen Travis, Vice
Principal of St John's Theological College in Nottingham, so
delicately put it when he explained the background to me.

Orgies and gorgies had once been the order of the day, and
they were not finding it easy to change the habit of a lifetime.
'The Lord's Supper', which included a full meal, had descended

into an undignified, disorderly bun fight. Participants tucked in on a first-come-first-served basis. Some, predominantly the poor who couldn't afford to bring food, were left without any, while others stuffed their faces or were rolling drunk. There was also disruptive behaviour during worship – women leaving their hair uncovered like prostitutes, people speaking out in tongues without waiting for an interpretation, others competing to get their prophecy heard.

Paul tells them in no uncertain terms that God is not a God of disorder but of peace (1 Corinthians 14:33). He is at pains to emphasize that outsiders shouldn't be tempted to think that Christianity is just another pagan cult with the followers in a permanent state of inebriation, sexual licence or spiritual ecstasy. Instead, it must be obvious from the way they live that they care for each other.

This is the context for the greatest treatise on love ever written: 1 Corinthians 13, so often read at weddings, is actually about *agape* – an extraordinary quality that should be the hallmark of any Christian community. Without it, the spiritual gifts are little more than a cacophony of discordant sounds. Love isn't rude, pushy or self-seeking. It puts the other person first. In other words, it actively chooses to be submissive.

According to Dwight Prior of the Center for Judaic-Christian Studies in Dayton, Ohio, the ex-prostitutes in the congregation had a particular little call they used to attract the men, which would no doubt have added to the general din and disturbance in the meetings. The Greek word translated as 'silent' is *sigao*. Here, it could mean to be quiet when someone else is speaking, to behave, or to pay attention. It is possible that these women are being told to stop disrupting the services and to show submission, or courtesy – not just to the prophet or preacher, but to God himself.

Rather than robbing these verses of their contemporary significance, putting them into historical context enhances their relevance. In our church, when Peter finishes his introduction to the Communion service and members begin to move out of their seats, it seems to be some kind of signal for a general hullabaloo. Instead of using the opportunity for quiet reflection, everyone exits for the loo or catches up on the week's gossip. Whenever he challenges the congregation about it, they blame the children. But actually, it's the adults, not the children, who are making a din. In fact, much as it sticks in my throat to admit it, the chit-chat does tend to be the domain of the women.

The respectful partner theory

A second possible interpretation revolves around the Greek word *gyne*, which can mean woman or wife – a source of some confusion in many texts. Paul has just finished speaking about prophecy, concluding that 'those who prophesy can take it in turns. Others should then decide if what they are saying is true.' If 'women' in fact means 'wives' in this context, then Paul could be telling the wives of any men who have just prophesied that they should refrain from evaluating, criticizing or challenging their husbands in public. They can wait until they get home instead. After all, it is only the common courtesy there should be in every marriage.

Although Paul was radical for his time, if social structures were not in conflict with Christian teaching, he didn't set out to challenge them. The Graeco-Roman household, classically defined by the philosopher Aristotle, was the basic unit of the state. Civic order demanded that a Roman man's powers were absolute.

The women in the church at Corinth appear to have been very excited by the new freedoms Christianity had given them, particularly full participation in worship, and were throwing off many traditional restraints and conventions, such as the requirement to cover their heads. Paul seems to be anxious that the husband's authority isn't undermined simply for the sake of it, throwing home life into disarray and causing disorder in the church community.

I have seen many women reduce their husbands to the size of a flea in public. The male ego may well be rather fragile, but that does not give women a licence to flatten it with a few well chosen words. It doesn't encourage respect for either of them.

I don't agree with every decision my husband makes in his capacity as a church minister. In fact, I often give him a hard time when he gets home. But it would not be appropriate for me to do so in public. It would embarrass the observers, as well as humiliating him. Peter and I still remember the excruciating, hot-under-the-collar feeling of witnessing a minister's wife challenge her husband's decision at a full church meeting. It silenced any debate, and I decided that even if I drew blood, I would bite my lip rather than put Peter in that position. Effectively, then, I am the only church member gagged at annual general meetings, and no matter how hard it is at times to keep my thoughts to myself, that is only right and proper.

The respectful disciple theory

The third possible interpretation follows on from the second. Debate was central to the rabbinic teaching method of the time – known as *remesh*. It would often involve asking apposite questions, a technique Jesus used to great effect when he was under siege from the Pharisees, or when he refused to let the disciples off the hook. 'Who do men say that I am? But who do you say that I am?' It was part of an ongoing, deepening teaching process.

In first-century synagogues it was traditional to follow the reading of the Scriptures with a lesson or sermon that basically consisted of a question-and-answer session. Prophecy, it seems, was to be subject to the same discussion. Professor Safrai of the Hebrew University of Jerusalem, an expert on Judaism at the time of Christ, says it was considered indecorous for a woman to question a man in public, though she could do so at home.[5] She was also allowed to debate the Scriptures in a women-only study group, of which there were many at the time. It may simply be that Paul is re-emphasizing the accepted behaviour of the time, though he must have known that Jesus never castigated, but actually affirmed Mary for sitting at his feet in the traditional position of a student or disciple.

The repeat of the question theory

Part of Paul's letter to the Corinthian church is a reply to questions they have put to him. They are still terribly confused about sexual ethics, and want to know whether a Greek man needs to be circumcised, and whether they should eat food offered to idols. Paul helpfully repeats some of the queries, introducing his response with words such as, 'Now, with reference to what you were asking about staying single ...'

Given both the Greek and Jewish traditions of members of the congregation, it is highly likely that there were some who would have preferred women to stay silent in the public meetings. One interpretation of these verses is that Paul was merely repeating something the Corinthians had written to him, so that he could then quash it completely with his explosion of exasperation in 14:36, 'Did the word of God originate with you? Or are you the only people it has reached?' In other words, are you arrogant enough to think that you alone have a monopoly on correct dogma?

The naughty scribe theory

The most controversial, but thought-provoking, interpretation belongs to American evangelical theologian Gordon Fee.[6] He claims that there are many strange features about these two particular verses, the opening phrase, 'As in all the churches ...' (RSV), for a start. We know for a fact that women were not silent in all the churches. From the time of Pentecost at least, they took an active part in worship. Then there are the words 'as the Law says ...' But as we have already seen, the Torah, or written law, never suggested that a woman should be silent in services. According to the historian Josephus, oral tradition stated, 'The woman, as the law says, is in all things inferior to the man', but never, in any of his letters elsewhere, does Paul give any weight to the Jewish oral law. Furthermore, when Paul does expound the Torah, he normally gives text and verse. Not here.

Fee also makes the point that the sentiments of the two verses do not fit in with Paul's overall attitude to the role of women, particularly since he describes so many of them as his fellow workers, and claims to the Galatians that the distinction between male and female has been done away with by the cross.

Fee therefore comes to the conclusion that some rogue scribe – a traditional, orthodox Jew, who was unhappy with the new freedoms given to women – took his chance and added the verses at some later date. Furthermore, the whole passage reads more easily and makes a great deal more sense without the interpolation of these two odd verses in the middle.

Some may find Fee hard to swallow on this particular point and may wonder how many more texts he explains away. He is, in fact, entirely orthodox in the rest of his approach to Scripture, and knowing what we now know, that key texts were occasionally tampered with to support a writer's prejudice,[7] means he has a very convincing argument.

In the end, we have to admit we do not know exactly what Paul meant, and can take our pick from a host of possibilities. In his commentary on 1 Corinthians, William Barclay says, 'In all likelihood what was uppermost in Paul's mind was the lax moral state of Corinth, and the feeling that nothing, absolutely nothing, must be done which would bring upon the infant church the faintest suspicion of immodesty. It would certainly be very wrong to take these words of Paul out of the context for which they were written.'[8]

But if women were not banned from taking part in worship, what about the vexing issue of authority?

I do not permit a woman to teach

A woman should learn in quietness and full submission. I do not permit a woman to teach or to have authority over a man; she must be silent. For Adam was formed first, then Eve. And Adam was not the one deceived; it was the woman who was deceived and became a sinner. But women will be saved through childbearing – if they continue in faith, love and holiness with propriety.

1 TIMOTHY 2:11–15

After I had spoken in Cape Town, urging women to go out and conquer the world for Christ, I was approached by an attractive young ordinand who told me with immense pain in her eyes that her fellow students, all men, regularly hit her over the head with these verses, and informed her that her place was in the kitchen, not at theological college. She knew her calling was to the pulpit, but to gain any headway she desperately needed to be able to stand her theological ground. At the time I didn't know how to help her. I hadn't taken the verses seriously enough or studied them in any depth. Now I have, and I'm so sorry that I let her down.

In fact, I think that for many years I was simply an ostrich, shutting out what I didn't want to face. Paul's first letter to young Timothy always left me feeling put down, patronized and very confused. I didn't want to be antagonistic to Paul. If I were in prison, would I write with so little self-pity or complaint, so full of concern for everyone else? But then how, having worked so closely with women, could he suddenly be two-faced enough to forbid them a teaching role?

Once I began to dig into the text with the help of impressive theologians and Greek scholars like Richard and Catherine Clark Kroeger, who wrote an entire book on these few difficult verses,[9] and once I began to follow my hunches, I began to see what I had never seen before. Paul was no chauvinist. He was a father figure, as concerned for the integrity of the church in

Ephesus as he was for the church in Corinth, and even more concerned for Timothy, the young man he had mentored as if he were his own son, and had sent into such a hotbed of sexual high jinks.

Timothy was raised and taught the faith by two women – Eunice, his mother, and Lois, his grandmother. He served his apprenticeship as an evangelist at Corinth, where Paul was ministering in partnership with Priscilla and Aquila. Priscilla and Aquila had also accompanied Paul to Ephesus, so the young Timothy had seen a formidable Christian woman in action, in two different settings, at a very formative time in his ministry. No doubt he learned a great deal from the fearless, outstanding women in his life. So it seems highly unlikely that Paul would suddenly instruct this young minister to deny his upbringing and adopt a universal prohibition on women preachers.

It must be the context here that is crucial to any real understanding of the text.

The sex symbols of Ephesus

Ephesus was a thriving trade port. Carved into the pavement was the figure of a woman with a sign across her chest reading 'Follow me', and next to it a foot pointing the men leaving the ships to the local brothel. In this lively, bustling Gentile metropolis, where there were many converts from paganism, some, it appears, were loath to let go of their more libertine traditions. Paul left Timothy in Ephesus expressly to put a stop to syncretism – the confusion of Greek mythology with the true Gospel that he had preached to them. He could see that, left unchecked, the false teaching would destroy the infant church.

When I was at primary school we had one rather eccentric, elderly teacher called Miss Davies, so obsessed with the myths of the Greek and Roman heroes and heroines that she neglected arithmetic and spelling. I didn't mind – I was fascinated by her stories. I knew the names of all the gods and goddesses, major and minor, both Greek and Roman, and their specific roles and preoccupations: Zeus or Jupiter, temperamental father of them all, teasing mortals and sending ineffectual thunderbolts from heaven to bring them into line; Aphrodite or Venus, charming yet cruel, enticing humans into hopeless, amorous entanglements; and then, of course, there was Artemis or Diana, patron of archery and hunting, stalking the countryside in search of sport, a strong, macho goddess. For years I never appreciated the benefits of this precocious wisdom. After all, I was Jewish. It wasn't my history or my culture, and it wasn't even real. Then one day I suddenly realized that this was part of the backdrop to the early Church, the context in which it was born and grew, the key to understanding Paul's epistles. Thank you, Miss Davies.

The most important deities in Asia Minor were often female, direct descendants from their ancient pagan counterparts. 'The Great Mother', as she was known, had different names at different times and in different places. In the Old Testament she was Ashtoreth. Elsewhere she was Demeter or Cybele, but whatever her name, this goddess had one universal attribute – she was the initiator of all creation. All life came from and returned to her womb. She could reproduce without needing a male.

Ephesus housed the most famous shrine ever built to the great earth mother, and it did wonders for the tourist trade. They called her Artemis, and her magnificent temple attracted thousands of worshippers from far and wide every day. Supported on a hundred massive columns, it was one of the seven wonders of the world. I saw the remains of some of those columns on a day trip to Ephesus as part of a package tour to Turkey, a welcome relief from lying on a beach in rows with hundreds of other British tourists. Judging by the massive bits and pieces still remaining, the temple must have been quite breathtaking – a vast, ornate building that seemed to reach up to the heavens. But to be honest, my main memory of Ephesus is of the ancient toilets, a long public bench with holes gouged out at regular intervals, where men would sit in rows and chat or read while they performed the necessary. A whistle would signal the end of the session and an opportunity for the women to take their turn. Heaven knows what happened to those with constipation, or an upset stomach.

Halfway up the main street our Muslim guide pointed out a small fish symbol carved into the pavement outside one particular house. It was almost invisible, a sign to those who recognized it that members of the new Christian cult lived there. I suddenly realized how oppressive and overpowering the dominant Graeco-Roman culture must have felt to the people who slipped in and out of that little house, dwarfed as it was by the magnificent buildings that surrounded it, symbols of prosperity and worldly success – particularly the temple of Artemis with its endless procession of visitors tramping past the door.

Inside the temple stood a huge statue of the goddess. She wore a high crown, representing the walls of a city, built on her benevolence. The top half of her body was covered in multiple egg-shaped breasts. Three rows of stags ran down her narrow skirt from her waist to her feet. Reliefs of bees, rams, bulls, crabs and griffins covered the rest of her, for she was responsible for all fertility, both animal and human. In cities other than Ephesus her devotees praised her perpetual chastity. In Ephesus they worshipped her for her surrender to love without restraint – no doubt a more attractive option for pilgrims. Sexual ecstasy was a means of direct contact with the deity herself.

This, then, was the Blackpool of Asia Minor. Trippers came from far and wide looking for a good time. Unlike Blackpool, however, Ephesus's tourist industry and healthy economy enabled it to become the richest province in the Roman Empire, a banking centre for the whole of Asia. Inevitably, Ephesian dignitaries were hardly pleased when the apostle Paul preached the Gospel with such power that some of the locals burned their magic books. Christianity was not good for business. The silversmiths who made high-class tourist tat – miniature statues for personal use, so that Artemis could be worshipped in living rooms and bedrooms everywhere – instigated a riot. For two solid hours a frenzied crowd screamed, 'Great is Artemis of the Ephesians!' (Acts 19:28, 34). The silversmiths lost their business, but the pharmacists can't have done a bad trade in throat lozenges.

In attacking the whole idea of the goddess mother, Paul had undermined the very economical and social ideologies that were at the heart of Ephesus's reputation and success. Without Artemis, what would Ephesus have left? Besides, a fertility goddess represented a great deal of easily available how's-your-father. Its champions, like today's advocates of free sex and accessible porn, were not going to allow any incursion into their liberties without a fight.

Seduction and syncretism slips into the Church

Living in such an eroticized culture, it is easy to see how some of the church members might have confused ancient mythology with Christian doctrine, Artemis with Eve, the first mother. Whatever their heresy, it seems clear in Paul's letter to Timothy that it was being preached by none other than the church leaders or teachers (1 Timothy 1:3, 7), and that their greatest fans were a number of women who had not only opened their homes to them, but were now actively involved in propagating their ideas themselves. Presumably this particular group included a number of young widows. In 1 Timothy 5, Paul appears to imply that young widows are universally wanton gadabouts, idle busybodies and gossips. It's not really likely, however, that Paul thought all young widows everywhere were morally suspect.

He calls these particular widows 'gossips' and 'busybodies' (1 Timothy 5:13). The Greek for 'gossips', *phlyaroi,* has nothing to do with passing on tasty titbits of information. It means to talk nonsense or untruthfulness. The actual translation of 'busybodies', or *periergoi,* is 'workers of magic'. In other words, he describes these particular widows in the same terms as the false teachers – foolish, empty headed (1 Timothy 6:20), and following 'deceitful spirits and doctrines of demons' (1 Timothy 4:1). They had been seduced by an early form of gnostic heresy which turned Christian truth on its head. According to the Clark Kroegers this heresy said that the Creator, the God of the Bible, was evil because he had made the material world. The serpent brought salvation by helping human beings to shake off the deception and Eve, who brought this secret knowledge into the world when she ate from the tree, was the mediator between human beings and Satan. Sexual licence was therefore a religious experience, an acceptable way of connecting human flesh with Eve, the divine mother figure.

It's hardly surprising that Paul is outspoken in this letter to the young pastor he has so carefully mentored. The evils of our society were all there in Ephesus, and they cannot be allowed to encroach on the Church. *Authentein,* the word translated as 'authority' in the sentence 'I do not permit a woman ... to have authority over a man', is particularly strong. It isn't used anywhere else in the entire New Testament, so there is no way of cross-checking Paul's meaning. In fact, it had no suggestion of usurping authority until the third or fourth century. In their intensive study of the verse, Richard and Catherine Clark Kroeger were forced to turn to Greek drama for clues to its original meaning. They concluded that *authentein* was in fact an extremely rare verb. Its literal meaning was 'to thrust', presumably with a sword, and it was used by Greek dramatists to refer to murder or suicide.[10] In Greek mythology there was a close association between sex and death. Death was often the fate of the poor, benighted human who dared to mate with a goddess. The sword was also a phallic symbol, which gave *authentein* a slang meaning at the time of Paul. It was, in fact, a rather coarse word for sexual relations. Now why would a nice Jewish boy like Paul, a rabbi at that, resort to such strong language? It would appear that these women in Ephesus were using their sexual charms to seduce and ensnare susceptible men, to entice them in as new followers of their heresy. This was not just erroneous. It was downright evil.

'For Adam was formed first, then Eve,' Paul continues. 'And Adam was not the one deceived; it was the woman who was deceived and became a sinner.' This has nothing whatsoever to do with superior male intellect or moral judgement. Nor is Paul suggesting that woman is more vulnerable or susceptible to sin. In fact, in his letter to the Corinthian church, Paul lays the blame for the fall firmly at Adam's door. 'For as in Adam all die, so in Christ all will be made alive' (1 Corinthians 15:22). Nor is Paul establishing a hierarchical order in creation. That would be a denial of the God-given equality of all human beings, irrespective of race or gender. Rather, Paul is issuing an out-and-out challenge to the way certain women in Ephesus were manipulating the Genesis story. He had to explain to them that Eve was not the earth goddess, and couldn't reproduce without a relationship with Adam. At creation men were not given authority over women, nor were women given authority over men. Women were never intended to use their sexuality to control, subvert, manipulate or dominate men. Paul was setting the record absolutely straight. It is hardly surprising, therefore, that he told Timothy to silence this pernicious little group.

According to Gordon Fee, the Greek present tense 'I do not permit' may be more accurately translated in this context as 'I am not permitting here and now', supporting the view that the verb is specific to the situation rather than a generalization. A woman is to 'learn in quietness', which Fee says doesn't mean 'not speaking', for then no woman would ever be allowed to participate in worship at all, but rather, it means 'with a quiet demeanour'.

Carefully translated in context, the verse begins to look like this: 'I am not permitting these women to teach while they seduce men and claim they are the author of man. Instead they are to learn with humility, for Adam was created first, then Eve.' In other words, they were not to be given a platform until they could prove they had learned the basics of true Christian doctrine and were disabused of their subversive, dangerous ideas. There would be no more revealing clothes, no more eyeing up anything in a toga, no more flirting or suggestive behaviour, all condemned by Paul in the strongest terms (1 Timothy 2:9). Instead, they would submit to learning a greater wisdom and truth.

Saved through childbearing?

But how will Timothy know for certain that these women have undergone a genuine transformation? 'They will be saved through childbearing,' says Paul. Does he mean that there is an alternative to salvation through the blood of Christ and his death on the cross? That cannot be reconciled with the rest of his theology. Does he mean that their life will be spared in childbirth, as some theologians suggest? From the beginning of time Christian women have died in childbirth like any others – many today in developing countries where there is no access to basic health care. Was Paul suggesting that mothering was the highest role for a woman and had some kind of redemptive function – easy to say for a busy man who had no children himself? If that were the case, why, in his letter to the Corinthian church, does he spell out the advantages of staying single?

The key here is the Greek word for 'saved', *sozo*, which can also mean 'restored'. These Ephesian women will demonstrate their restoration from deception only when they become model, godly women, bringing up children, running a home and doing good in the community. Even then, only when this new life of 'faith, love and holiness with propriety' is ongoing can Timothy be sure that their redemption is complete.

In marked contrast to the women denounced here as false teachers are the deaconesses or women ministers whose attributes Paul goes on to describe in the next chapter (1 Timothy 3:11). Because of the confusion caused by that little word *gyne*, some translations suggest that he is referring to the wives of deacons, but Fee and others think that if that were the case, he would have said 'their wives' and not 'the women'. It is more likely that he was speaking about women ministers, who are to earn respect by being reliable, not malicious, nor partial to a drink or two too many. In other words, they will have the same qualities he commends for any male leader.

Does it matter whether women are allowed to preach?

At the end of the day, what difference does it make whether women are allowed to preach or not? Shouldn't we be prepared to give up our right to the pulpit, our right to be leaders or even bishops in the Church of England, for the sake of love and unity? There is an argument that says the debate over the role of women within the Church is far less important than preaching the Gospel, and since it's so contentious, let's just bury it. But that would be a denial of an essential part of God's good news for all people.

Furthermore, for the majority of young people in the West, the equality between men and women is so much the norm that the alternative looks like an unwelcome return to the dark ages. When they see overt sexism operating in the Church, it's small wonder that they caricature Christians as reactionary, out of touch and irrelevant, and turn away from the very truths we want to share.

This is particularly sad as the Gospel spells freedom, not restrictions, for all men and women. Perhaps this should be our guide in all those tricky issues where there seem to be conflicting views in Scripture: what is going to be the most challenging and liberating message for the society in which we live?

Dick France's short essay entitled *A Slippery Slope?* compares the ordination of women with homosexual practice. On the face of it, he says, one issue had little to do with the other, except that he constantly came across critics of his acceptance of women leaders who claimed that, 'if our hermeneutical principles can lead us so clearly to discard the plain injunctions of Scripture on this one issue, we are bound also to approve homosexual practice, since the same principles apply.'[11]

France sets out to show that this is not the case. It is clear from his letter to the Romans that Paul regarded female co-workers as equal. That has to be weighed against those other, apparently conflicting, verses that may, on the face of it, seem to suggest the opposite. In other words, since there are arguments for both views, Christians are free to make up their own minds on this issue, and even change them, as France himself did as he studied the texts. On homosexual practice, however, France says that Paul is unequivocal, as he is in all matters relating to sex outside marriage. There are no conflicting texts, no room for negotiation or change of mind, no alternative but to maintain a traditional Christian view.

Where there is room for a variety of opinions and views – on issues such as Sabbath observance, for example – Christians don't necessarily have to be guided either by contemporary or Church culture, but by what seems most in keeping with the spirit of the Gospel. 'The history of biblical interpretation is the story of new insights discovered often under the pressure of changing circumstances and of cultural shift – the eventual abolition of slavery is a celebrated example.'[12] In other words, the whole debate about the place of women in our society and in the Church has made us all go back to the scriptural drawing board, and that is a very good place to be.

For people like my husband Peter, who had always thought he was very egalitarian, but who slipped unconsciously from time to time into the superior male mode of his childhood upbringing, it was a revelation to discover from the book of Genesis that to live in denial of the equality and compatibility between men and women, forfeited at the fall, was to live without the redemption bought by Christ at the cross. The message of equality is a message of vibrant new life and freedom for a world where sexual exploitation is still rife, and women can be valued so much less than their male counterparts. To deny women the chance to share in every aspect of ministry alongside the men is a negation of the liberating, life-giving message of the Gospel.

The revivalist preachers

Throughout Christian history, times of spiritual awakening have been characterized by the appearance of powerful women in the pulpit.

In the seventeenth century, Quakerism produced some outstanding women preachers. On my first visit to our local castle in Lancaster I was very struck by the life-size dummy of a woman wearing an extraordinary contraption over her head and face – a sort of cap of iron bars, one of which covered her mouth completely. Apparently, the 'scold's bridle' was the standard form of punishment for any woman accused of being the village gossip, or even a shrewish, nagging wife. The bridle was locked onto her head, then she would be led out into the square and fastened into the stocks, where she was pelted with rotten fruit or more dangerous missiles that could do a great deal of damage.

Our guide asked us to notice that the woman was wearing Quaker dress. The Quakers were what he called a 'fundamentalist Christian sect', because they believed in the Bible, the work of the Holy Spirit and, worse, the equality of men and women. For that they were regarded as enemies of the state and many, including the outspoken local preacher Margaret Fell, who later married the Quaker leader George Fox himself, were imprisoned in the castle. A Quaker woman could find herself incarcerated in a dungeon or locked into the scold's bridle for no greater sin than leading the equivalent of an Alpha course – sharing the Gospel with her neighbours – for that was regarded as a hideously unfeminine thing to do. Yet, despite the possible consequences of their actions, Quaker women refused to be gagged and went on preaching both in private and in public.

As I stood looking at the model, I wondered what I would have done in that woman's place. There is no one to gag me today except me, and yet I so often succumb.

Between 1761 and 1791 John Wesley appointed many women as local preachers and itinerant ministers. His approval of their ministry, however reluctant, paved the way for the Wesleyan Holiness movement to thrust a host of remarkable Nonconformist women into the limelight.

The first was the remarkable Phoebe Palmer (1807–74), an American evangelist and preacher who became a major force behind the great American Revival of 1858, and who was the first to preach the baptism of the Holy Spirit in the United Kingdom. She was in such demand and away from home so often that her husband eventually retired from medicine so that he could support her ministry. The four years she spent in the UK laid the foundation of the Pentecostal and charismatic movements that would impact the Church for the next 150 years. Phoebe justified a woman's right to preach on the experience of Pentecost. If the Holy Spirit had fallen on women and men indiscriminately then, what was to stop him anointing women for ministry today?

It was on Pentecost Sunday morning in 1860 that Catherine Booth (1829–90) first rose from her pew and walked up into the pulpit of her husband's church to 'share a few thoughts'. The impact on the congregation was so great that her husband quickly pre-empted any attempt she might make to resist his encouragement to preach, as she usually did, and announced, 'My wife will complete her sermon at the evening service.' As the wife of William Booth, founder of the Salvation Army, Catherine had never felt any inclination to preach. She simply wanted to be a pastor's wife. Her William, she was sure, would see hundreds turn to Christ wherever and whenever he preached, and she would be right behind him, supporting him all the way. Sure enough, when William preached hundreds were converted – but when she began to preach, thousands responded.

Neither Phoebe Palmer nor Catherine Booth had sought the limelight. In fact, both were reluctant to take up a calling which would expose them to verbal and physical attack, public criticism and allegations of being unwomanly and even ungodly. But in the end, both felt that was a small price to pay for doing what God had asked of them. When breast cancer brought her remarkable ministry to a premature end, Catherine Booth whispered as she lay dying, 'What would I have said to my Maker if I had not been faithful to the heavenly vision? What would I have said to him for all that wasted fruit?'

Phoebe Palmer was convinced that it was simply a matter of time before the Church gave women preachers its blessing. Catherine agreed. Inequality was 'a remarkable device of the devil'. How could any army go to war with half its forces chained to the kitchen sink? Her close friend, the campaigner Josephine Butler, wrote in 1892, 'Women themselves have been very slavish. It is humiliating to see a gifted woman, with dignity enough for a Bishop or Prime Minister, putting herself willingly under the guidance of some inexperienced, not gifted clergy-boy.'[13] Nineteenth-century Christian women felt it was time to stop colluding with those who held them back, and prepare themselves for the host of new opportunities about to open up before them. It was as well they didn't know then just how long women would have to wait for the fulfilment of those dreams.

In 1901 Florence Barclay, whose novel *The Rosary* sold over a million copies, began a weekly women's Bible class in the Victoria Room in Leyton that attracted around 500 women. Once a year, on Good Fridays, the Bible class was thrown open to men and over a thousand people packed the hall. But with Florrie Barclay the tradition for high-profile, evangelical women preachers was coming to an end – in Britain at least. In the USA it continued sporadically through the twentieth century with women such as Maria Wedgeworth Etter, Aimee Semple McPherson and Kathryn Kuhlman holding huge campaigns with high drama, mass conversions and miraculous healings. Yet even they operated alone, despite rather than with the support of the Pentecostal tradition from which they came. Susan Hyatt concludes, 'As the Pentecostal Revival spread and diversified, equality waned,' and in their desire for acceptance – the old *teshuqah* – 'women tended to return to their socially acceptable place as subordinate partner. As the Holy Spirit's presence withdrew, the hierarchical social patterns of institutionalism, especially patriarchy, snuffed out the egalitarianism that had characterised the early revival period.'[14]

In the post-First World War cynicism and disillusionment of Great Britain, where evangelical certainty faded and faith was at a low ebb, there appeared instead a succession of remarkable Anglican laywomen in the gentler, more mystical tradition of Hilda of Whitby and Julian of Norwich.

Evelyn Underhill was the first woman to lecture in religion at Oxford University and to lead retreats in the Church of England. She didn't become a committed Anglican until later life, yet Michael Ramsey, Archbishop of Canterbury from 1961 to 1974, is reputed to have said that she, more than anyone else, was responsible for keeping spirituality alive and well in the Anglican Church in the period between the wars.

Like Mother Julian, she established a reputation as a spiritual counsellor and hundreds of people, both ordained and lay, flocked to the retreats she led at the Anglican Retreat Centre in Pleshey in Essex. Although the Anglo-Catholic clergy were opposed to the ordination of women, none seemed unduly averse to allowing Evelyn Underhill to instruct them in how to keep their spiritual life in good working order, when the very pressures of clerical life mitigated against it. In diocesan lectures she regularly challenged them to maintain a disciplined life of holiness and prayer, whatever the distractions and however great the demands of their congregation.

Evelyn Underhill never campaigned for women to become ministers of the Church, but many of her gifted Anglican colleagues did, including Maude Royden (1876–1956), who worked among the poor in Liverpool and became a fearsome campaigner for women's suffrage and the rights of the socially oppressed. In 1917, although she knew she had a call to minister in the Anglican Church, she accepted the offer of a post as assistant minister at the City Temple, a Congregationalist church. She wrote, 'The church will never believe that women have a religious message until some of them get, and take, the opportunity to prove that they have. My taking it in a nonconformist church will ultimately lead, I believe, to other women being given it in the Church of England.'[15] In the 1920s and '30s people travelled miles to hear her preach at the Guildhouse in Kensington.

Maude Royden, Dorothy Sayers and the host of other outspoken Anglican women preachers and broadcasters who, in the first half of the twentieth century, often used the equivalent of the BBC's *Thought for the Day* as an opportunity to express their demands for equality, would have been horrified to see the advert which appeared in the *Church of England Newspaper* in the first year of the twenty-first century. A church which had passed Resolution B (exempting them from having a woman vicar) was looking for 'a mature, dedicated, prayerful, Bible-based evangelical Christian. The focus will be teaching the Bible amongst women.' In other words, she would not be allowed to preach to the men.

Women and authority

Women who are called to the pulpit face some difficult decisions. If they preach confidently and boldly they run the risk of being called unfeminine, abrasive or even aggressive. They may find themselves a threat to men and a pariah to other women. But if they preach hesitantly and uncertainly, apologizing for their very existence, they are not likely to be asked again.

Our expectations for how a person in authority should behave are at odds with our expectations for how a woman should behave. If a woman talks in ways expected of women, she is more likely to be liked than respected. If she talks in ways expected of men, she is more likely to be respected than liked. It is particularly ironic that the risk of losing likeability is greater for women in authority, since evidence indicates that so many women care so much about whether or not they are liked.[16]

The old *teshuqah* clutches at our hearts again. But in the end, if women choose the pulpit, we must forgo our need to be liked and in the face of every difficulty and criticism find our own uniquely feminine way of preaching with power and love, confidence and gentleness. In many ways we have not come all that far in over a hundred years. We face the same criticisms and struggles as Phoebe Palmer, Catherine Booth and Josephine Butler, except that today more people recognize the importance of hearing a woman's voice.

Lavinia Abrol, a well-known preacher in Northern Ireland, where the Church can still be rigidly traditional, told me how one Mother's Day she had been invited to preach at a rural church some miles out of Belfast. During her sermon she told the story of how she had lost her lovely baby daughter. Afterwards the church treasurer came to her in the vestry, weeping. Only a year before, he had lost a son. 'Why is it when a man preaches,' he said to her through his tears, 'he never seems to touch another man's pain?'

Yet how, when the demands of public speaking go against the grain of what is acceptably feminine, shall we encourage more women to preach? The desire to do so does not necessarily constitute an anointing, and there is therefore a danger in tokenism. On the other hand, women need a great deal more encouragement than men if we are to take on leadership or authority roles. Part of the problem is that, before anyone is given an opportunity to lead, we tend to look for and expect signs of leader-like behaviour, but because one-upmanship is not a woman's way, she may not play the leader until she is given the part.

I have to admit that I cannot think of any good reason why on earth God would deny a woman the chance to teach or lead. It could only be because women were somehow morally inferior to men, and that strikes me as the start of a very slippery slope indeed. Nazism, which graded human beings into greater and lesser mortals, also promoted *Kinder und Küche* – children and kitchen – as appropriate tasks for women. In other words, their only value was in the bedroom and the kitchen.

When I spoke on women and authority at our church, a wonderful ninety-year-old saint called John Dart rose to his feet and said he couldn't understand why people got so het up about the subject of women in leadership. What was their problem? Had God not foreseen the freedoms women in the West would have today? Had it caught him unawares? Even if Paul in his time had not really approved of women in the pulpit, had God, who knew and saw all from the beginning to the end of time, not reserved for himself the right to change his mind? It was unthinkable that his word would ever be irrelevant or inappropriate for contemporary society. And anyway, what was lost if women did preach? 'Surely,' John said, with all the godly wisdom of his age and experience, 'there would be more to lose if they didn't, and a great deal to be gained if they did.'

Notes

1. See Romans 16:1. Alvera and Berkeley Mickelsen, 'Does Male Dominance Tarnish Our Translations?', *Christianity Today*, 5 October 1979, pp. 23–7.
2. Antonia Fraser, *The Weaker Vessel* (Knopf, 1984), p. 122, quoted in Susan C. Hyatt, *In the Spirit We Are Equal: The Spirit, the Bible and Women, a Revival Perspective* (Hyatt Press, 1998), p. 77.
3. Hyatt, ibid., p. 77.
4. Deborah Tannen, *Talking from 9 to 5, Women and Men at Work: Language, Sex and Power* (Virago, 1994), p. 196.
5. This view is also supported by James Moffatt in his commentary on 1 Corinthians, *The Moffatt New Testament Commentary* (Hodder and Stoughton, 1943). Calvin took a very similar line, though he managed to argue that, while it may be necessary for a woman to speak in public from time to time, it shouldn't be a regular feature of church services.
6. Gordon D. Fee, *The First Epistle to the Corinthians, The New International Commentary on the New Testament* (Eerdmans Publishing Co., 1987).
7. For example the alteration of Junia, which appeared in the original Greek manuscripts, to Junias in medieval translations, to make the apostle appear to be a male.
8. William Barclay, *Commentary on 1 Corinthians*, The Daily Bible Study (The Saint Andrew's Press, 1956).
9. Richard Clark Kroeger and Catherine Clark Kroeger, *I Suffer not a Woman: Rethinking 1 Timothy 2:11–15 in Light of Ancient Evidence* (Baker, 1992), is devoted entirely to these verses, and, because of their in-depth knowledge of classical Greek language and culture, is an invaluable study of the text.
10. Ibid. Interestingly, in his *Analytical Concordance to the Bible* (Lutterworth, 1879), Robert Young defined *authentein* as 'to use one's own armour'. *Strong's Lexicon* gives the primary meaning as 'one who with his own hand kills another or himself'.
11. France, *A Slippery Slope?*, p. 3.
12. Ibid., p. 22.
13. Josephine Butler, 'Woman's Place in the Church', *Review of the Churches*, February–April 1892, p. 343.
14. Hyatt, *In the Spirit We Are Equal*, p. 220.
15. Sheila Fletcher, *Maude Royden: A Life* (Basil Blackworth, 1989), p.162, quoted in Jill Evans, *Beloved and Chosen, Women of Faith* (The Canterbury Press, 1993).
16. Tannen, *Talking from 9 to 5*, p. 202.

CHAPTER 6

The Submissive Woman?

There were three mature, experienced ministers' wives – one would later become a bishop's wife – on the panel that evening as we rather nervous, soon-to-be-in-their-shoes young women who had accompanied our husbands to theological college waited in anticipation for the glimmers of wisdom which would light our pathway into an unknown and frightening future. The essence of each of the three pieces of advice was the same: 'Don't worry your husbands with your minor problems to do with running the home and the children. He is doing God's work. Release him to fulfil his ministry.'

It took me a few moments to register the implications of what they were saying, but by the third repeat I was up, almost involuntarily, on my feet. 'I didn't know we were called to be parish doormats,' I heard myself say in the uncomfortable hush. 'I thought marriage was about each releasing the other to fulfil our God-given calling and potential.' I can't recall the panel's exact, rather embarrassed response, only the dismissive reaction of the other student wives. 'We always knew you were a radical and a feminist.'

I wasn't conscious of being either. The two years I had spent as a youth worker before my marriage had certainly given me an awareness of the demoralizing effects of social deprivation,

167

and had left me feeling that any exploitation or diminishing of one human being at the cost of another was not the gospel of freedom Christ had preached. Otherwise, I was fairly conservative, the educated daughter of a traditional, well-heeled Jewish family.

As for women's issues, although they were exercising the minds of many of the female students in those heady days of the early 1980s as they fought for the right to be ordained, and although my instinctive sense of fairness placed me on their side, I hadn't even begun to think it through theologically. In fact, converted as a teenager, and a member of a free evangelical church for most of my early Christian life, I was fairly conservative in my views on women too. Six years earlier, when I had sat with Peter in a café in the middle of Manchester shortly before our marriage, the lovelight shining in my eyes, and told him I would happily be the conventional housewife whatever the cost financially, I meant every word of it.

Nonetheless, if the college wives thought I was out of order that night, several of the single women students thanked me for my contribution. I had wondered what they were doing at a wives' meeting – gaining some insights, I suspect, into how a female curate might handle that all-powerful force, the vicar's wife. They were deeply concerned that so many of the wives felt they had been called into the ministry with their husbands as a couple, even though he, not she, would have the job, the pay packet and, inevitably, the predominance. If the wife saw herself as the key partner in ministry and not just marriage, there was a great danger that her nose would be put out of joint when a paid female assistant appeared on the scene.

Even now, twenty years later, there is still a tradition in some quarters for ministering married couples, though it is not a standard biblical pattern. Despite the fact that a higher proportion of people were married in New Testament times, no married partnerships in ministry are mentioned other than Priscilla and Aquila. The apostle Peter had a wife, but we know nothing about her, not even her name. Little is said about the marital status of any of the early disciples, apostles and church leaders. They ministered as individuals and in partnerships, mainly with someone of the same gender, and not necessarily with their spouses.

I had unintentionally questioned the accepted contemporary Christian view, and threatened some of the student wives by challenging their perceptions of the role they hoped to play. It later became clear that two of the women on the panel virtually ran their husbands' churches – from behind. Yet a banker's wife would not expect to play a major part in her husband's professional life, any more than a plumber's wife would pick up his toolbag and respond to an emergency call to mend a leak. I could not see how our marriage would be different from anyone else's simply because God was the boss.

To be fair, in the past husbands have hardly encouraged their women to explore and follow their own calling, in the Church or anywhere else. Until recently it was culturally acceptable for a wife to be back-up, support, substitute and understudy, rather than a key player herself. As late as 1959, in his study of the wife with the 'meek and quiet spirit' in 1 Peter 3:2, the great Bible teacher Alan Stibbs wrote:

> Meek describes the way in which such a wife submits to her husband's demands and intrusions by docile and gentle cooperation. Quiet describes her complementary and constant attitude, and the character of her action or reaction towards her husband and towards life in general. She shows no sign of rebellion or resentment, fuss or flurry.[1]

I looked up 'docile' in the dictionary. It means 'domesticated' or 'easy to manage', rather like the family pet. 'No flurry' is all very well for a woman who is naturally phlegmatic, but when you are as sanguine as I am it may not be easy to live up to Stibbs' rather passive ideal. It certainly isn't acceptable any longer in Western culture. Yet it was supported for centuries by two New Testament concepts, which were used as a mandate for the subordination of women in general, and not just wives: headship and submission.

Does headship actually exist?

I want you to realise that the head of every man is Christ, and the head of the woman is man, and the head of Christ is God … A man ought not to cover his head [when he prays], since he is the image and glory of God; but the woman is the glory of man. For man did not come from woman, but woman from man; neither was man created for woman, but woman for man. For this reason, and because of the angels, the woman ought to have a sign of authority on her head.

In the Lord, however, woman is not independent of man, nor is man independent of woman. For as woman came from man, so also man is born of woman. But everything comes from God.

1 CORINTHIANS 11:3, 7–12

In the whole of the New Testament, there are only two references to man as a head, this one in Corinthians, and one in Ephesians 5 which we shall look at later. Both are in Paul's letters, written to predominantly Gentile churches about good order, rather than about salvation.

In 1 Corinthians 11 Paul is exploring the issue of whether men and women should cover their heads during public prayer. The Revised Standard Version translates 'men and women' as 'husbands and wives', as the Greek words are interchangeable, but the overall passage would seem to be about church members in general.

In the church in Corinth many of the old gender distinctions had disappeared. Women were free to participate in worship, and as they revelled in this new experience some appear to have wanted to go too far too fast. It was customary then, and for many years after, for a woman to wear a kind of loose covering over her head when she appeared in public. (For a man to cover his head, however, was a traditional sign of mourning.) Only temple prostitutes let their hair hang loose over their shoulders. As late as the fifth century, in the Byzantine era, St John Damascene was shocked at the impropriety he witnessed in the city of Constantinople and wrote disapprovingly that 'Constantinople was the setting of dances and jests . . . as well as of taverns, baths and brothels. Women went about with uncovered heads and moved their limbs in a provocative and deliberately sensuous way. Young men grew effeminate and let their hair grow long.'[2]

Paul was obviously taken aback by a growing gung-ho attitude in the Corinthian church to the normal cultural mores of decency. It was shameful that a Christian woman could be mistaken for a prostitute, and unhelpful to outsiders if her appearance suggested that the same kind of sexually ecstatic religious behaviour that went on in the pagan temple was taking place in the Church, for they might assume Christianity was simply another pagan cult. He argued therefore, first and foremost for the sake of decency, that a woman should cover her head or cut off her hair. It didn't leave them with much of a choice. Only women of dubious sexuality wore their hair short. On the other hand, if a man had long hair it also blurred the distinction between the sexes, and Paul wanted to avoid the kind of allegations to which that might lead.

The good reputation of the Church with Jews and Romans alike mattered to Paul enormously. He submitted to many of the social conventions of the day for the sake of winning favour for the Gospel, even to the point of having poor Timothy circumcised, so that the Jews could not dismiss his message on the grounds that he wasn't strictly kosher. Becoming a Christian was not a licence for a woman to overturn the accepted rules of propriety and behave as if she had no morals. The delicate balance and interdependency of relationships between the sexes was not to be sacrificed for the sake of individual freedom.

But Paul argues that women should cover their heads, not simply because it was proper behaviour, but also from creation – and that gives rise to the complexities of the question, and the Christian notion of 'headship'. Actually, no such word exists in the New Testament. There is a 'head', but no concept of headship. 'The head of woman is man, the head of man is Christ, and the head of Christ is God.' What does it mean for God to be the head of Christ? Is there a divine chain of command? Traditional Christian theology of the Trinity maintains that all the members of the Godhead are co-equal. To suggest from this verse that God is somehow superior to Christ or has authority over Christ erodes his divinity and is a heresy known as subordinationism. There cannot therefore be any suggestion of hierarchy in the text.

Immediately after his discussion on head-covering, Paul uses the metaphor of the human body with Christ as its head to describe the essential relationship of members of the Church. 'Though all its parts are many, they form one body ... those parts of the body that seem to be weaker are indispensable'. In fact, God has put the body together in such a way 'that there should be no division ... but that its parts should have equal concern for each other' (1 Corinthians 12:12, 22, 25). A disembodied head cannot function. It is an integral part of the rest of the body. The whole picture is about interdependency and unity, rather than authority.

A metaphor is a picture, a clever way of conveying a difficult, abstract concept in accessible, everyday language. In other words, it is a model and models can't be applied rigidly or made into doctrines, because ultimately they always break down. The problem once again is our contemporary cultural mindset, our Western tendency to think in structural pyramids and orders of importance. Today the word 'head' denotes authority, as in a headteacher, or the head of a company. But the Greek word used here for head is *kephale,* and it does not mean 'boss' or 'chief'. It can refer to the human head. Salome asks for the *kephale* of John the Baptist, knowing it won't be much use to her, just as the rest of his body won't be much use to him without it.

Dr Katherine Bushnell, whose experience as a missionary in developing countries made her determined to build a case for the equality of women, believed that the idea of Christ as head of the Church refers back to the verse in Psalm 118 which says, 'The stone which the builders rejected has become the head of the corner' (v. 22 RSV). The cornerstone gives support to a building, so Christ supports his Church and holds its members together in a cohesive unity.[3]

Since *kephale* also means 'source' – of life, or of a river – Paul's view of Christ as head in his letter to the Colossians appears to reflect Katherine Bushnell's interpretation. He says that Christ is 'before all things, and in him all things hold together . . . he is the head [the source] of the body, the church; he is the beginning. . .' (Colossians 1:17–18). In the next chapter he warns believers not to be diverted by strange teachings that would cut them off from their head, their source of life, 'from whom the whole body, supported and held together by its ligaments and sinews, grows as God causes it to grow' (Colossians 2:19).

Ultimately, this indivisible interdependency between Christ and his followers allows spiritual life to flow through the veins of the Church. Paul concludes his instructions to the Corinthians on head-covering by reminding them that man is born of woman: although man was the source of woman in creation, woman is the source of man in procreation, and Christ, who came from God, is the source of life for both of them.[4] Evidently the picture Paul has in mind is of a circle, not a pyramid.

When Paul does want to convey a sense of hierarchy he doesn't resort to the word *kephale,* he uses *archon,* which means 'chief' or 'ruler', and he uses *exousia* to refer to 'authority' (Romans 13:1–2). The Septuagint, or Greek translation of the Hebrew Scriptures, completed before the time of Christ, acts as a useful dictionary, helping us to understand the meaning of many New Testament words used by Jewish writers like Paul. The scholar S. Bedale pointed out in 1954 that the Hebrew word for head, *ro'sh*, appears 180 times in the Old Testament and is translated *archon* far more often than it is translated *kephale*. In fact, it appears that the Greek translators actually avoided using the word *kephale* if there was any sense of authority in the text.[5]

Up to the 1960s, apart from a theologian called S.T. Lowrie, who wrote what must have been a very controversial article in 1921 defending the idea that women were appointed as ruling elders in the early Church,[6] most theologians believed that the man being a head did imply some kind of male authority and female subordination. For centuries marriage had brought immense benefits to men, even if it hadn't always been quite so kind to women. But there was no reason for them to question whether long-established patterns of behaviour were actually biblical.

Changes in the status of women in the West, however, made a re-examination of the Scriptures imperative. Later theologians, including F.F. Bruce[7] and Gordon Fee, felt there was nothing in the passage to suggest any sense of hierarchy. The only occasion on which the word 'authority' *(exousia)* is used in the passage on head-covering refers not to the man's but to the woman's own authority.[8] Even Paul is so anxious that 'at first blush', as Fee puts it, these verses might look as if they indicate subordination, that he adds a rider at the end of his argument. Man is born of woman and is therefore as dependent on her as she is on him.

Paul's concern in 1 Corinthians is not with hierarchies, but with relationship. Men and women come from each other and were made for each other. To support his argument he goes back to the book of Genesis, where man is created for 'God's glory' and exists to bring his Maker praise and honour. But woman is God's crowning glory, for man is incomplete without her. She came from his side and is the one companion suitable for him. Nothing must be allowed to blur the boundaries between the genders, spoil that special relationship, or bring it into public disrepute. That was why head-covering was an important gesture at the time. As the great commentator Matthew Henry puts it in his own inimitable way:

> Man being the last of the creatures as the best and most excellent of all, puts an honour upon that sex as the glory of God. If man is the head, woman is the crown, a crown for her husband, the crown of visible creation. The man was dust refined, but the woman was dust double-refined, she was one step further removed from the earth.[9]

No woman could have put it better! Although the whole concept of head-covering is hard to understand, especially today when hats are out of fashion, it would seem that Paul is saying that a woman should have 'authority on her head', because an uncovered head might distract the congregation, or even the angels[10] who participate in worship, by emphasizing the glory of man, not God. So the covering is not a symbol of woman's subjection to man's authority, nor of her need for his protection. It was, in those days, a sign of her authority to minister.

So, after all that, does 'headship' have any place in a male–female relationship and, if it does, what is it? Women had always released and resourced their men; that was the way things were. But now it seems that Paul, in his own way, while demanding order and decency from the women, also managed to present the male with a new challenge. If man is a source of life rather than a dominant force, he has a particular responsibility to resource, release and empower a woman. 'Headship', as it has become known, seems to be about his accountability, not his authority. When we look at texts on marriage, all will become clear.

What is submission all about?

Submit to one another out of reverence for Christ. Wives, submit to your husbands as to the Lord. For the husband is the head of the wife as Christ is the head of the church, his body, of which he is the Saviour. Now as the church submits to Christ, so also wives should submit to their husbands in everything.

Husbands, love your wives, just as Christ loved the church and gave himself up for her ... In this same way, husbands ought to love their wives as their own bodies...

EPHESIANS 5:21–5, 28

Wives, submit to your husbands, as is fitting in the Lord.

Husbands, love your wives and do not be harsh [embittered] with them.

COLOSSIANS 3:18–19

Holy women of the past ... were submissive to their own husbands, like Sarah, who obeyed Abraham and called him her master.

1 PETER 3:5–6

Although some have tried over the years, there is no way these verses on submission can be stretched to apply to single men or women. They refer to marriage and have to be seen in that context alone.

Marriage, in the Graeco-Roman world of Paul, was hardly a wonderful deal for a woman. It had little in common with the Jewish culture, where women were treated with respect and monogamy was the order of the day. As we have seen already, Roman society was highly sexualized – not so different from our society today. But in those times it was an integral part of religious life. The gods were not averse to popping down from Mount Olympus for a little rumpy-pumpy with the mortals on earth.

This was a licence for free sex. Marriage was primarily contractual. A Roman woman had some status in society, but little love in the home. She had a right to property, but not to her husband's fidelity. He would rely on a cult prostitute – male or female – to satisfy his sexual needs. Plato actually believed that only a lesser mortal would waste his affection on a woman. The truly noble soul was masculine and would seek another male as the object of its love.[11] The leader of a debate shortly after the New Testament was written judged that the obligation to marry should be universal, 'but let the love of boys be reserved only for the wise, because perfect virtue flourishes least of all among women'.[12]

According to Aristotle, the founding father of Greek philosophy and politics, a man was intended by nature to rule as husband, father and master. More than that, to dispense with the natural order would be disaster, not just for the family but for the entire state. In other words, proper household management was a political issue. Any suggestion of overturning the accepted social hierarchy was seen as a threat to society as a whole. Religious groups, like the Christians, that attracted large numbers of women and allowed them to question the status quo were seen as subversive.

It is no surprise, then, that for the sake of the reputation of the infant Church, Paul submits to the view of his day and has a clear household structure in mind – but with a major difference. In his letter to the Ephesians he compares marriage to the sacred relationship between Christ and the Church, for salvation has brought a new reality of grace into every relationship. He now invests marriage with a status it never had in the Roman world, and issues men with a new challenge which must have left them reeling – but we shall come to that in good time.

The Greek word used for submission is *hypotasso*, which has several possible interpretations. First and foremost it means to behave in a responsible manner, to show respect and common courtesy. There is no suggestion in the text, as some churches imply, that the husband should make all the decisions, the key decisions, or the ultimate decision in an impasse, while the wife simply says, 'Yes, darling. You're always right, darling.

Whatever you say, darling.' One minister's wife once told me she had always practised submission and that her husband had only been wrong three times in their marriage. But who's counting? I certainly can't, as Peter and I make decisions together. It's the only way to live them out in harmony, without me hitting him over the head with the wonderful rolling pin of blame.

Besides, Paul tells the Christians in Ephesus to submit to one another, and there is certainly no sense in which we're meant to do what every other church member tells us. We'd end up in pieces, pulled apart in countless different directions. Since *hypotasso* can also be translated 'to unite one person with another', it could therefore, in the context of both marriage and the church community, actually refer to living in harmony, peace and oneness with each other.

Hypotasso can also mean 'to remain in another's sphere of influence'. In his gospel Luke tells how, unknown to his parents, the twelve-year-old Jesus stayed behind in the temple in Jerusalem to study the Scriptures. When they eventually caught up with him, they took him back to Nazareth, where he was 'subject to them'. From his Bar Mitzvah, at the age of twelve, a Jewish boy is regarded as an adult spiritually, and is responsible to God for his own good deeds or failures. Later stories of Jesus' dealings with his parents suggest that he did not necessarily do everything they said, but he lived happily within their sphere of influence and showed them the respect to which they were entitled.

In my dictionary 'respect' is defined as 'an attitude of deference, admiration, or esteem'. Personally, I don't find the idea of admiring or esteeming my husband all that difficult – but then, I was clever enough to marry a man with a deeper faith than mine, and I can't remember him ever persisting in anything that would seriously diminish my good opinion of him. But to judge by the success of Laura Doyle's book *The Surrendered Wife*, which took America by storm, it would appear that in this age of self-fulfilment and self-expression, respect in marriage is not intrinsic, nor courtesy all that common. It should be noted, however, that this new marriage guru lives in Los Angeles where a marriage lasts as long as a computer, and self-development is the only antidote for self-loathing. One of the three women who agreed to take part in her therapy group filmed for television was a Bible-reading, committed Christian, onto her third husband, and she wasn't too keen on him any more since he had put on a great deal of weight. It was imperative that she should learn to accept him as he was – but it didn't come naturally.

However much Laura Doyle may claim to have a new revelation, certain aspects of her concept of surrender have a ring of the New Testament. 'People often say submissive wife instead of surrendered wife,' she said on the television programme, 'but submissive has the sub word in it which means below, so that word doesn't fit with me.' 'Surrender', on the other hand, means to relinquish or to give up control.

It sounds as if language is getting in the way of communication again. I looked up 'submission' in *Roget's Thesaurus,* and it offered me words like 'yielding' and 'deference', so there really isn't such a chasm between submission and the way Jesus surrendered, yielded or gave himself to the will of the Father, without forgoing any of his inherent equality with the rest of the Godhead.

Hypotasso strikes at the heart of what ails us and diminishes so many of our relationships – the big 'c', that need for control. It urges us instead to let go, give way and value our partner's opinion as much as our own. With apologies to Laura Doyle, there is a 'sub' word in there, a dying to our own selfish, demanding nature. It doesn't mean becoming a creeping Uriah Heep, but making a positive decision to acknowledge, appreciate or even embrace another person's perspective. Paul maintains that it should be the hallmark of every Christian relationship.

I asked a group of friends one evening if they thought they practised submitting to one another. Ruth, our youth worker, reflected, 'Well, there was that night we all went for an Indian when I really wanted a Chinese.' As the discussion went on, Ruth's words began to appear less trite. Friends who love and trust each other submit to each other almost without thinking. When we don't, it's probably an indication of how shallow those relationships really are.

As Christians we have the key to successful relationships – we simply don't recognize it for what it is and, as ever, leave it to someone outside the Church to appropriate our truths and then exaggerate, distort and popularize them. I tested some of Laura Doyle's philosophy against my own experience of marriage to see whether it worked. The surrendered wife, she says, relinquishes control ('I asked you to buy cabbages and you came back with chocolate biscuits instead. Well, what a lovely surprise, dearest!'), respects her man (Better not say, 'You lost it at the end of that sermon, my dear,' over Sunday lunch, and certainly not when guests are present.), receives his gifts graciously (What gifts? He says we're saving for retirement.), expresses vulnerability ('I really would appreciate your help in the kitchen, darling, when you can drag yourself away from your work.'), admits when she needs help ('There's no need to lose your rag just because I've lost the tool bar – again!'), and takes good care of herself (I do step aerobics once a week, does that count?).

'It doesn't work for you,' Abby explained, when I asked her whether she thought I lived out Doyle's suggestions, 'because your relationship doesn't depend on instructions. When you love someone, respect and kindness are instinctive.'

Out of the mouths of babes! Encouraged, I asked her what she thought of the statement, 'For the greatest intimacy, agree with your husband's ideas even when it scares you.'

'That woman needs shooting,' she snapped.

'How belittling,' said my spouse. 'I married you because I knew you would stand up to me.'

When we first married I was disconcerted to find there was a right way for everything – even the arrangement of knives, forks and spoons in the cutlery drawer. I thought I must have

a disordered, disorganized mind and tended to accept everything my clever, highly organized husband said – until I realized
that his rationale was to do things exactly the way his mother
always had.

'The worm finally turned,' my mother said, watching me
with amusement when, along with reorganizing the kitchen
drawers and cupboards to suit my convenience, I began to challenge a number of his ideas.

It is unbelievably patronizing to suggest the male ego is so
fragile that disagreement of any kind will cause it to crumble
into so many pieces that we won't be able to sit Humpty
Dumpty back on his wall. Submission is not the same as relinquishing responsibility. If I took that idea to its logical conclusion, I'd never get a decent night's sleep. One of the greatest
areas of disparity of preference in our marriage is over the
sleeping arrangements. For some years I put up with a continental quilt when the truth is that I hate it. It's probably due to
some profound emotional damage done in babyhood, but I prefer being swaddled as tightly as possible in sheet and blankets.
We have finally reached a not-very-satisfactory compromise –
we have sheets, blankets and a quilt. A far better idea would be
single beds, but somehow I can't yield to that symbol of a sex-
less, truly English marriage. My friend Pat says she can't understand the way two completely different activities have become
so confused. 'Sleeping is one thing, and love-making entirely
another.' She has a point, but it is in fact much harder to let the
sun go down on your anger when your bodies are forced into
contact, albeit by the tangles in the sheet, than if you have the
means of preserving a glacial separateness.

One night I found Peter in bed with his computer. My submission was admirable. 'If that thing can do for you what I can,
then I shall take the hint and sleep elsewhere.' It went and I
stayed.

To be fair, friends plagued by the temptation to dominate
and manipulate their men, like Sarah and the matriarchs, tell me
they appreciate Laura Doyle's emphasis on wifely subservience.

And, after all, the apostle Peter says that Sarah called Abraham 'lord' and holds her up as an example of godly obedience for women with non-Christian husbands. Sarah, obedient? Since God resigned himself to telling Abraham to do whatever his wife suggested, it looks very much as if it was the other way round.

In fact, the Greek word for 'obey' used by Peter in his letter means 'to listen carefully or attentively', as Sarah does when she complies with Abraham's request to pose as his sister. But when King Abimelech makes off with her, God warns him, 'You are a dead man, because of the woman whom you have taken; for she is a man's wife' (Genesis 20:3 RSV). The normal Hebrew word for 'wife' is *ishah*, but for the one and only time in the whole of the Old Testament, the word translated here as 'wife' is *ba'al*, or 'lord and master'. In other words, Sarah is referred to as Abraham's lady, mistress or keeper.

The Greek word Peter uses for 'lord' is *kurios*, which also means 'sir' or 'master'. In New Testament times this was a common form of address, the equivalent of today's 'Dear Sir' at the top of a letter. It was a term of simple courtesy. As we have already seen, for good or ill, there was a great deal of mutuality about this marriage.

What struck me about the three women in Laura Doyle's televised therapy group was that they were not kind to their men. They nagged and criticized them for not being what they wanted them to be, basically because they weren't satisfied with themselves. It is to the Ephesians that Paul also says, 'Be kind and compassionate to one another, forgiving each other, just as in Christ God forgave you' (Ephesians 4:32). The measure of forgiveness we receive should be the measure we give, and, however hard it can be, a partner is not exempt. There is little as liberating for any human being than to be totally accepted by someone who knows us exactly as we are, warts and pimples, foibles and failures. That's marriage for you – a lifetime of sharing your dirty laundry and bad habits.

Sadly, however, down through the years, a number of Christian men have not been averse to using the teachings of

Paul to justify behaviour he would find totally unacceptable. No woman is required to surrender, submit or put up with any form of violence in the home. In fact, evidence suggests that removing herself from the situation altogether may be the only means to convince her husband to get the help and therapy he so badly needs.

Paul says that a wife has as much control over her husband's body as he has over hers – and that truly was a revolutionary concept in Roman society. She, like her husband, is entitled to regular, satisfactory and exclusive sexual relations. 'The wife's body does not belong to her alone but also to her husband. In the same way, the husband's body does not belong to him alone but also to his wife' (1 Corinthians 7:4). This is the only suggestion of authority or control in the marriage relationship, and it is mutual – a yielding in love of the most intimate part of one's being to the other.

And now for the men

A wife is lower than a slave, for a slave at least can be freed.

AQUINAS

It is obvious from the writings of St Thomas Aquinas, the Dominican monk and great teacher of Roman-style theology, that Roman thinking on marriage was alive and well in the medieval Church.

Yet subjugation is a pagan, not a Christian, concept. Paul himself tells the Philippians that Jesus chose to become a servant. He washed his disciples' feet. He told them not to lord it over one another, and said that a child was greatest in the kingdom. This is the context for Paul's teaching on all relationships. His master was radical, and, when it comes to marriage, so is Paul.

Imagine the faces of the Ephesians as his letter is read out. 'Wives, submit to your husbands ...' The men nod self-righteously in approval, and look at their women knowingly. There had to be a limit to these newfangled liberties their wives were now taking. Then suddenly the smile is wiped off their faces. 'Husbands, love your wives, just as Christ loved the Church and gave himself up for her ...' There was probably a stunned silence while the information was absorbed, then a gasp as the implications sank in. Paul is demanding a self-sacrifice of Christian men unparalleled in Roman or Jewish society.

Christ laid down his life to liberate and release his Church. He nourishes, feeds, enables and resources it. He is *kephale* – its source of life. This clarifies the concept of headship and puts it into a league of its own. Theologian Colin Brown puts it this way:

> The headship and lordship of Christ does not consist in authoritarianism. Rather it is expressed precisely in self-giving. Likewise, the husband's headship is to be exercised in the same self-giving in which he lives out his new nature in Christ. The headship consists in a renunciation of all authoritarianism; the only subjection that it is to demand is self-subjection for love of the wife.[13]

How could Paul intend a man to have absolute power, and his wife to be subject to him, when he has disempowered him so completely? A man cannot be domineering, for he is no better than his master, and Christ modelled a radical new way to live.

I asked Peter how he understood headship and he said, 'I felt it was my religious duty to chaplain my children – to read the Scriptures and pray with them – and also to ensure that you felt fulfilled, whether you chose to work in or out of the home. I still feel I am the breadwinner, but hope I wouldn't be thrown into a personal crisis if I became unemployed.'

Peter's role in helping our children to develop their own relationship with Christ was essential. I was always the sleeping partner. I just can't wake up in the morning, and took the stories and the prayers in our big double bed lying down. But when we sat down and discussed his feelings, we both had to admit that they were instinctive rather than theological, for nowhere does Paul actually refer to a man as the head of the family. That was an American idea from the 1960s, promoted by Larry Christenson in books like *The Christian Family,* a conservative backlash to the new phenomenon of women going out of the house to work. I found it interesting that Peter still sees himself as the breadwinner, since I actually earn more than he does (that's not difficult!), although his job is more secure than mine and I live in the tied house that comes with it.

We once watched a couple ride a tandem swiftly and gracefully up a steep, narrow, cobbled hill.

'Wow,' I said to Peter, 'isn't that a picture of the perfect marriage?'

'No good for you,' he said dismissively.

'Why not?'

'You'd hate always being on the back.'

Now why should he assume I would always be on the back, and not on the front? There is a danger in promoting our own cultural traditions, using the Bible to back them up. In today's society many men are not the major breadwinner; they may be unemployed. Nor is every woman called to be a mother; many are single or cannot have children.

The Bible, if it is truly inspired, must be relevant in every age, and Paul's teaching on marriage is an example of how timelessly apposite it can be. It is woman, the natural communicator, with the skills to reduce a man to pulp with a few well-chosen words, who is told to respect, and man, warned at the fall that his instinct will be to rule over women, who is told to love, nurture and cherish. One must relinquish control, the other must relinquish power.

Yet despite the fact that Paul entrusts the role of sacrificial self-giving to the man, in almost every age ever since it has been seen as the woman's obligation. It has been her job to be the skivvy, releasing him not just to be the hunter-gatherer, but to find self-fulfilment too. Throughout history marriage has rarely been as good for women as it has been for men, and even now, when I look at the marriages I know, in the great majority the wife makes most of the compromises. Men are so focused, whether it be on their career, hobbies or sport, that they unwittingly put themselves first.

One hot afternoon in Ibiza, during the ritual afternoon tea with my parents-in-law under the shady pine trees of their lovely retirement home, my mother-in-law began to speak of her misery when my father-in-law left his job in Geneva and took a parish in Ashton-under-Lyne. They exchanged a flat overlooking the lake for a monstrous Gothic vicarage that was impossible to heat. 'Paul was always busy,' she said. 'I never saw him. At one point I became suicidal.' This was as much a revelation for my father-in-law as it was for us. There was a long and awkward silence, until he interjected, suddenly and defensively, 'I had my work.'

Social attitudes have changed. While the Church is struggling to catch up, society is redefining what it means to be a man. Women's new independence has apparently lurched men into an identity crisis. Relinquishing power could in fact provide an unprecedented opportunity for them to lay down the burden of machoism, the pressure of playing the omnicompetent leader and breadwinner. Instead, they would be free to live in partnership with women, expressing their real fears and needs, sharing in the joys of raising the children. But I fear they have been conditioned to keep their emotions in check for so many generations, long before feminism threatened their social isolation, that it may take radical action – a marriage enrichment weekend, for a start – to get them sharing.

A few years back, reflecting on the demands on women to juggle home, career and church, I wrote a piece called 'The Quintessential New Christian Woman'. At a conference a short time ago I threw down the gauntlet to the men and asked them to write me a male equivalent. This is minister Dave Beale's contribution:

A Day in the Life of the Quintessential New Christian Man – Stud, Father, Breadcrumb-winner, Giant and Responsible Citizen!

The Quintessential New Christian Man passes round the quiche at the cell group's hospitality dinner, holding his baby in one arm, sporting just a suggestion of designer stubble and a whiff of Aramis aftershave. He recalls his day with thanks.

Having empathized prayerfully and tenderly with his breastfeeding wife at 2 a.m., 3.30 and 4.53, he rises at six to make a bottle for the baby, pleased to have avoided a Nestlé product and happy to give his wife a break; he rinses a few nappies (no ozone damaging paper disposables in his household!), puts out the rubbish, brings in the milk, pours himself a healthy O.J. and settles down to a biblically based Ignatian exercise in the lounge.

Precisely 75 seconds into meditation a six-year-old with a David Beckham T-shirt propels a football across the room and demands a game in the garden. Conscious of the horrendous under-fathering of boys, he reckons that Ignatius can work as well in the garden as elsewhere and joins his son in a rough and tumble before breakfast.

A run to the station and he's on his way to work where he prays for everyone in his carriage between getting himself fully informed with the front page, business news and sport sections of the *Independent*. Once settled at his desk, the firm's ethical investment policy is uppermost in his mind until a sudden reminder from his conscience makes him pick up the phone and ask Interflora to deliver flowers for his mother's birthday.

The game of squash at lunch proves to be a witnessing opportunity; losing 3–2 to Mahmoud from sales and marketing, he manages to mention while showering that his church is hosting a men's breakfast and golf day next Saturday. He blushes when Mahmoud replies that it's Ramadan, so he can't eat before sunset.

A note in the personal organizer to host a men's supper next year, he returns to the office for the afternoon policy meeting where it is pointed out that his ethical plans would put 4,000 Nigerians out of work and open up market opportunities for the competition. Agreeing to prepare a paper on 'Corporate partnerships for strategic growth', he runs once more for the train. Using his handy mobile phone, theatre tickets are booked for the wedding anniversary, and the vicar is reminded to publicize the golf day at PCC – in between further prayers for passengers.

On arriving home, David Beckham tugs with glee once again, while a sensitive, lingering peck is delivered on wife's cheek and tender, gooey noises caress the baby's ears. Ignoring ravenous hunger and eager desire for cold lager (wondering whatever happened to that eager desire to prophesy) he loses 6–0 to David Beckham before picking up the babysitter, packing up the car with wife, baby, infant car seat, nappies, keyboard and copious quantities of quiche to head off for the cell group's hospitality dinner.

Remembering to chat to both 'pre-Christians' present he supports his wife throughout the evening before she tearfully requests they go home because the baby won't settle. The car unpacked, the babysitter returned, he just catches the late news (must keep informed) and experiences a pang of romantic passion as he ponders the beauty of mother and baby silhouetted across the couch, but feels frustrated and rejected when his amorous approaches are met with a contented, obviously sleeping woman. Identifying his need for prayer ministry to deal with his lust problem, he knows nothing more until the sun rises and David Beckham is jumping all over him.

Dave Beales is rare indeed. A survey published in the first week of July 2001, the biggest study of 23.1 million British men,[14] showed that the new man does not actually exist. Men are still not sharing in the cooking and cleaning, or looking after the children. Personally, I think the family picnic on the beach is the giveaway. Who heaves the food hamper around, organizes the plastic plates and sandwiches, feeds the dog, wipes the children's noses and towels them down when they come out of the sea? Who has remembered a change of trunks and swimsuit? Where's Dad? Half a mile away, playing frisbee or organizing beach cricket. So which of the genders is the more organized, logical, rational?

Marriage is a challenge for men. It can demand a great deal of women. But our very differences make it an adventure. Paul stresses that Christian marriage is very special. It must be distinctive – to challenge the lifestyle of those around us, to combat immorality, to prove that Christianity is the most wholesome way to live. That's why he also warns those of us who have been entrusted with such a gift that it is our duty and our calling, in so far as we are able, to make it last.

Till death us do part

> Marriage should be honoured by all, and the marriage bed kept pure, for God will judge the adulterer and all the sexually immoral.
>
> HEBREWS 13:4

Society is obsessed with the notion that monogamy is monotony, and would like to believe that the trade-in of a tired relationship carries no consequences – but Paul couldn't be clearer about our responsibilities if he tried.

A recent Generation X lifestyle survey revealed that 84 per cent of non-Christian young people and 97 per cent of their Christian counterparts thought marriage should be for life.[15] So far so good. However, 68 per cent of non-Christians and 32 per cent of Christians then agreed that a marriage should only last as long as a couple loved each other, and that divorce is perfectly acceptable, demonstrating once again the wide chasm that exists between our ideologies and the reality of living them out. We now have consumer marriage. The relationship is entirely disposable, screwed up and flushed away when it becomes dull, boring or difficult, or there appears to be a better offer down the road.

But then, not many Generation Xers have lived with a model of a happy, long-term relationship. Few understand how good marriage can be, and why it might be worth every ounce of dedication a human being can muster.

Among Christians the divorce rate is as high as it is in the rest of society. Despite the consequences, spelt out as clearly as the apostle Paul knew how, adultery is endemic in the Church. There's an old Jewish saying, 'A sin repeated seems permitted'. Society's self-indulgence whittles away at our resistance. On several occasions my husband has been shocked to hear the perpetrator say he sees no reason why he should not bring his new partner to church, in full view of the deserted spouse and children. In the new era, sexual gratification is king and demands obedience. And, since toleration is seen as the highest virtue, there is no moral judgement or social ostricism for anyone who wilfully abandons hearth, home and the children for whom they are responsible.

Heaven help anyone who sits in judgement, for 'there but for the grace of God ...' and 'pride comes before a fall ...' and all the other proverbs and truisms have a terrible way of wreaking vengeance on those of us too arrogant to believe it could ever happen to us. Yet, on the other hand, those who suggest that couples who survive have some kind of innate luck and have never known temptation are living on another planet. I have crawled to the edge of that yawning abyss and peeped over, but, thank God, he has got hold of me by the scruff of the neck in no uncertain manner and yanked me back – just as, in his mercy, he dragged Lot unceremoniously out of Sodom and Gomorrah.

Peter and I have always made it a principle to tell each other when we're finding someone else attractive. It seems the most effective way of killing temptation quickly. The first time I dared mention it, Peter simply said, 'I thought you'd been a bit distracted. Don't worry. I know you love me.' And immediately I thought, 'Of course I love this wonderful man. Who wouldn't? What an idiot I am.' On reflection, I don't think I could hurt beyond reason a man who has only ever sought my best, or the children who expect my best, or the community to which I belong and which would be destroyed by my betrayal. But I hope to God it's never really put to the test.

The Hebrew word for 'marriage' is *kiddushim,* a plural variation of the word *kaddosh,* or 'holy'. 'Holy' for the Jew does not mean put on a pedestal or in a glass box, removed from the nitty-gritty of everyday life. On the contrary, 'holy' means special, a unique gift of God to be enjoyed and appreciated to the maximum by those to whom it is given. A marriage is not to be shared by anyone but the couple. Intruders tread on holy ground at their peril, and that includes parents and children, as well as the work colleague, neighbour and acquaintance on the number 42 bus.

It is a closeness that can feel claustrophobic. While women usually have a wide selection of female friends who meet a variety of their different needs, men tend to rely solely on their wives to fulfil all their needs for friendship and intimacy. Occasionally I have found myself longing for my own space – just for a while. A week, or even two, might be nice, as long as I know it is temporary. There are also times when marriage interferes with my choices and, selfish though it may be, the sacrifice seems hard.

I gave up a full-time career in the media when we moved to Lancaster ten years ago, and found myself instead, for a number of weeks, stripping wallpaper, polyfilling and painting almost twenty-four hours a day. Our large vicarage with its high ceilings had been replumbed and rewired, but left undecorated, a dank, dark shell of torn wallpaper and bare plaster. 'And we don't even own the blinking house!' I exploded one night, hurling my brush across the room.

My hands were rougher than sandpaper, my nails had broken off, there was paint in my hair and paste in my mouth. 'I've had enough. I'm going home.'

There is nothing like a good tantrum in a crisis.

But as I made for the door, I realized, feeling stupid, that I didn't know where home was any more. I had nowhere to go. So I sat in the middle of the floor, waiting for revelation. I had never felt so miserable in my life, so certain I wanted out – of marriage, motherhood and ministry. What had any of them done for me? One or two ideas of possible bolt-holes formed in my mind, friends who would have me for a week or two, perhaps longer.

I was on my way to the phone when I remembered the children sleeping upstairs. We had only just moved. They were disorientated as well. They needed me. So did Peter, even if he needed a painter and decorator more at that precise moment. I couldn't simply walk out on my responsibilities. Good, old-fashioned words like 'honour', 'loyalty', 'perseverance', 'for better, for worse' flooded into my mind, apparently from nowhere, and demanded acquiescence, even if it was through gritted teeth. I had the power to bring love, life and peace to the household – or I could smash it apart.

Reluctantly, I went in search of the turps. I still have a patch of hair about the size of a penny that turned white overnight with the stress of those first few weeks. In the end, however, I'm so glad I didn't run away. God is more interested in our will than our emotions, in what we do rather than what we feel, and the rewards have been immeasurable.

One of the most helpful things ever said to me was that we fall in and out of love many times in a marriage. On occasions the spark may seem too feeble to survive, then suddenly, in the right environment, it bursts into flame all over again. Woe betide any outsider who wilfully sets out to extinguish that spark when it may be at its weakest. But when a partner of more than twenty years still has the power to induce the most mind-blowing, stomach-lurching passion, then marriage is as God intended it – the most liberating, joyful relationship ever given to human beings. If it isn't like that, our expectations are just too low.

I am thankful I chose a truly monogamous man. I could never have trusted a womanizer and a flirt, a man who needed the adulation of the opposite sex to fill a deep hole in himself, who subjected his wife to the whispered sympathy and pity of all their acquaintances. Instead I have been given a man who truly tries to live out the apostle Paul's encouragement to love, nurture and encourage his wife as Christ loves the Church, who silently puts up with the dints and scratches on the back bumper of the car, valiantly corrects my manuscripts and endlessly sorts out my messes on the computer.

At our wedding, in the middle of the sermon, there was a prophecy. 'Partings there will be when the way of the cross demands it.'

'So,' I said in the car on the way to our honeymoon, 'you're going to have a travelling ministry.'

'No,' he said, and we promptly forgot about it in the excitement of other things.

No one could have been more surprised than I was when I began to get invitations to speak all over the country. So much for darning his socks and ironing his shirts. I was away from home almost every week. It wasn't easy for either of us. I took the babies with me and fed them in some very odd places. When they were too big to take I left them behind with Dad, who, they complained, fed them some very odd food. I hated leaving Peter to look after them and missed them terribly. I was consumed with guilt at times. But those words, blurted out so unthinkingly that evening at St John's Theological College, certainly came true in our experience. At different times our different ministries took priority. We were called to release each other. But as we did, an almost perverse spiritual law seemed to come into operation: the more we let go, the more we had. Our different worlds each enriched the other.

I know very little about a certain missionary wife called Madame Coillard, except this wonderful story that seems to capture the essence of what marital love can be. The Coillards were missionaries in South Africa and had apparently witnessed scenes of shocking barbarity during the Boer War. Their ministry required that they work apart for a great deal of the time, so any time together was a joyous, precious gift.

One particular year they agreed to meet up in their little hut in Leribe to celebrate the anniversary of their wedding day. She was at Harrysmith negotiating the purchase of wood for the mission buildings, he was on a missionary tour, and between them ran the treacherous waters of the River Caledon.

> When she reached the stream the waters were in high flood. It was reported to her that her husband had been swept away and drowned in trying to cross to her. This sounded quite probable, since drownings were a frequent occurrence in those days, but when she discovered this was a false tale she determined to cross the water to him. Two powerful Zulus took her, one by each arm, and swam across with her, other men swimming before and behind. The procession of swimmers fought the strong current resolutely and silently. From the opposite bank her husband watched this adventurous crossing. Only the head and shoulders of his wife appeared above the flood. At last they reached the shallows and Mme Coillard came out, drenched and exhausted, but triumphant, to change into a habit and ride with her husband to their little turf hut at Leribe.[16]

This must surely go down in history as one of the bravest, most determined attempts to celebrate a wedding anniversary, and I have no doubt it was worth it. If Madame Coillard is the practical embodiment of positive, wifely submission, I think I could live with it.

Notes

1. A.M. Stibbs, *1 Peter*, Tyndale NT Commentaries (IVP, 1959), p. 125.
2. William Dalrymple, *From the Holy Mountain* (Flamingo, 1998), p. 37.
3. Katherine C. Bushnell, 'Lesson 37: Headship in the New Testament', *God's Word to Women* (Ray B. Munsen, 1923), paragraphs 282–91.
4. Hyatt, *In the Spirit We Are Equal*, p. 247.
5. S. Bedale, 'The Meaning of Kephale in the Pauline Epistles', *Journal of Theological Studies 5*, 1954, pp. 211–15.
6. S.T. Lowrie, '1 Corinthians XI and the Ordination of Women as Ruling Elders', *Princeton Theological Review* 19, 1921, pp. 113ff.
7. F.F. Bruce, *1 and 2 Corinthians* (NCB, 1971).
8. Fee, *The First Epistle to the Corinthians*, p. 502. Both the RSV and NIV say that a woman should have a 'sign of authority' on her head, but the Greek simply says 'authority'. The Living Bible translation, 'a woman should wear a covering on her head as a sign she is under a man's authority', is completely erroneous.
9. *Matthew Henry's Commentary On The Whole Bible in One Volume*, eds. Lesley Church, Marshall, Morgan and Scott, Zondervan, 1961, pp. 4, 7.
10. The Greek word for 'angel' is the same as 'messenger', so it is just possible that Paul was referring to messengers from other churches, who might be so shocked to see a woman with her hair uncovered that they would be distracted from enjoying the benefits of her ministry during worship.
11. Plato, *Symposium,* 180, 192.
12. Lucian, *Erotes*, 51, cited by Hyatt, *In the Spirit We Are Equal*, p. 250.
13. *Dictionary of New Testament Theology*, Volume 3, ed. Colin Brown (Paternoster, 1978).
14. *Social Focus on Men*, carried out by Office for National Statistics.
15. The results of the survey, initiated by Joshua Generation and undertaken by Christian Research, were published in *Quadrant,* May 2001. 'Generation X' is the term used to describe the generation born between 1960 and 1985.
16. E.C. Dawson, *Missionary Heroines of the Cross* (Seeley, Service and Co., 1930), pp. 212–13, quoted in Byrne, *The Hidden Journey*.

PART

3

The Contemporary Woman

Living our Bequest
in Today's World

CHAPTER 7

The Sexual Woman

Now that we have established that woman's biblical inheritance is a full and free opportunity to speak life into the world, how can we live it out in our own contemporary corner, in our homes, roles, relationships and workplace?

First and foremost, to be truly liberated, we have to come to terms with one of our fiercest enemies and critics – ourselves. We have to make peace with our bodies, and that can be very difficult when we feel we're constantly being judged by sexual standards and found wanting.

> Probably no man has ever troubled to imagine how strange his life would appear to himself if it were unrelentingly assessed in terms of his maleness; if everything he wore, said or did had to be justified by reference to female approval; if he were compelled to regard himself, day in day out, not as a member of society, but merely as a virile member of society. If the centre of his dress-consciousness were the codpiece, his education directed to making him a spirited lover and meek paterfamilias; his interests held to be natural only in so far as they were sexual. If from school and lecture-room, press and pulpit, he heard the persistent outpouring of a shrill and scolding voice, bidding him remember his biological function. If he were vexed by continual advice how

to add a rough male touch to his typing, how to be learned without losing his masculine appeal, how to combine chemical research with seduction, how to play bridge without incurring the suspicion of impotence. If, instead of allowing with a smile that 'women prefer cavemen', he felt the unrelenting pressure of a whole social structure forcing him to order all his goings in conformity with that pronouncement.[1]

At first glance, Dorothy Sayers' plea in the 1940s for men to put themselves in a woman's shoes and realize how galling it is to be valued for one's sexual attractions alone sounds quaint and dated. On reflection, however, it is salutary to wonder how much has actually changed. After all, it was only in the 1980s, during the debate over the ordination of women, that one churchman actually argued, 'Women, unlike men, radiate sex and their temperament is inappropriate in church ... Their ordination would introduce distractions and earthiness into worship.'

A now-retired bishop told Sue Lawley on Radio 4 that he was very afraid that, if he saw a woman ministering the sacrament, he would be tempted to take her into his arms. At least he didn't make any pretence of a theological foundation for his arguments. It didn't seem to occur to him that he was demeaning most of his own sex, who are not so overcome by the presence of women in the workplace that they find themselves leaping on top of their colleagues several times a day. Nor was he apparently aware of the possibility that women have been finding the man in the dog collar sexually attractive for years, which was why some of his clergy turned up in the *News of the World*. The particular distractions that caught his fancy were dangly earrings. He could just as well have said fishnet tights and suspenders.

A few days after the first women were ordained the *Daily Mail* ran a feature on the Rev. Joy Carroll, upon whom the Vicar of Dibley was based, complete with a large photograph of her in a miniskirt, dark hair tumbling over her shoulders – and the inevitable large, swinging earrings. Her mail for the following few days was full, not of offers, which would have been bad enough, but of complaints – from both men and women. The reasons for their objections were not very clear. Like the early Church Fathers, and the twentieth-century bishop, they simply reflected the 2,000-year-old discomfort with any mix of body and spirit, secular and sacred – the dualism inherited from Greek and Roman philosophy, not New Testament theology, that did women so much damage. Here is Tertullian (AD 160–240):

> And do you not know that you are Eve?
> The sentence of God on this sex of yours lives in this age: the guilt must of necessity live too. You are the devil's gateway: you are the unsealer of that tree: you are the first deserter of the divine law: you are she who persuaded him whom the devil was not so valiant enough to attack. You destroyed so easily God's image, man. On account of your desert – that is, death – even the Son of God had to die. And yet you think of nothing but covering your gowns in jewellery? You should always go about in mourning and in rags.

Beset by temptation, Tertullian and his fellow fathers of the faith felt revulsion for their sexual fantasies, and projected their nausea onto the object of their desire. The early Fathers convinced themselves that women's sexuality was a magic power and they were merely its helpless victims. Woman is temptress, seductress and sorceress, responsible for all the misery in the world. Noble man, good and pure, created in God's image, has been deprived of his greatness and potential, not through his own sin, but through the sin of woman. He is tainted, demeaned and reduced merely by contact with her. In the third century Augustine spoke with disgust of the shame which attends all sexual intercourse. Jerome believed marriage was actually harmful.

Sadly, this negativity towards sexual feelings continued throughout the history of the Church. Even today many male ministers try to disguise their sexuality in black and grey, bland shirts, boring suits, unfortunate socks and shapeless haircuts.

The pressure on women ministers to do the same, to look as unattractive as possible, lest their looks lower the debate about whether they should be leaders in the Church, has exposed them to the criticism of not being real women. They are damned if they are sexy, and damned if they are not.

It is hardly surprising that this is the area of our lives where women are most vulnerable, most subject to abuse, most easily stripped of confidence. Over the centuries our sexuality has been used in a myriad of ways to deny us equality and keep us from smashing through the glass ceiling – in misconceptions about periods, incessant pregnancies, restrictive clothing and fashions, and accusations of either physical weakness or unfeminine, unattractive behaviour.

Male leaders of institutions, in industry, government, education, the NHS or even the Church, have sometimes handled their inability to cope with their own sexual feelings either by sheer hostility, denying women access to leadership roles, or by flirting with them to undermine their authority. To desexualize or oversexualize a woman has the same effect. It devalues and dehumanizes her.

We ourselves sometimes fall into the trap of misusing our sexuality. We can resort to using female wiles to achieve our own ends. There is a certain amount of innocent flirtation and play in most creative male–female relationships, but when sex becomes a weapon the game is over.

Alternatively, since it can be such a source of rejection and humiliation, we can be tempted to hack off our femininity altogether and become asexual. When, occasionally, I sit as the only woman in a room full of dog-collared males on some diocesan committee and my views are ignored, as if I wasn't there, then it feels as if that is what the Church would like us to do. But losing a limb is disabling, and it doesn't necessarily cause the pain to cease – and groups like that surely need my uniquely feminine perspective.

So, how do we find our way through the bewildering mixed messages that bombard us on every side, own our sexuality and rejoice in it? Until we do, we will not have the confidence and poise to speak God's message of freedom to the world.

It is a subject I have explored at length with my daughter Abby, throughout the long process of her emergence from the chrysalis of childhood into a new, womanly mind and body. It isn't easy for a young woman to be so gloriously assured of herself in today's society, so I asked her to contribute her reflections to this chapter, to help me clarify the essentials of true female sexual freedom.

Sex-obsessed or silent?

Society, said the previous Archbishop of Canterbury George Carey, is obsessed with sex. Society may be, but the Church certainly isn't. In fact, it stalwartly ignores the subject altogether. Apart from one or two unfortunate but delicate references in the marriage service, sex is never mentioned again in sermons or teaching programmes, and young people are left to assume they were found under the nearest gooseberry bush, or, if there was a moment of passion that led to their sitting in the pew, it was an unfortunate incident over and done with a long time ago. We expect them to pick up Christian morality and values by osmosis, but what they actually pick up are those subconscious, extremely negative vibes. One student at our church said recently, 'You tell us to wait, but never tell us if it's worth waiting for.' We never tell them why to wait, how to wait or what to enjoy about the wait – and we do them a great disservice.

Why are we so coy? Judging by the UK's teenage pregnancy rate (the highest in Europe), the ever-increasing waiting lists for psychosexual counselling in the NHS, for which I work, and the growing number of people who approach Peter for help with their sex lives, a society that is sated in sex and not just the Church, is actually more repressed than ever. In every magazine, on every billboard and in every part of the media, women are young and gorgeous, blemish and flab free. Men can be middle-aged, if they still have hair, no beer belly and a big wallet. Couples bonk almost on acquaintance and achieve simultaneous orgasm in five seconds. They have to. Programme makers have one aim – to stop us switching channels or reaching for the off button, and they know that if we were subjected to the realistic length of time decent foreplay takes, boredom would drive us to channel-hop before the heavy breathing even begins.

Yet despite the fact that being out of touch with reality is a recognized sign of mental health difficulties, most of us still swallow everything the media tells us. Admitting virginity or less than James Bond-standard sex isn't socially acceptable. So we take the easy option and don't talk about it at all.

I worked for about a year as a local communications lead with the national campaign to reduce teenage pregnancy by 50 per cent in the next 10 years. All the evidence shows that giving young people information actually delays their first sexual experience, yet the myth persists, often propagated by religious groups, that educating them will encourage promiscuity. In fact, the great majority of under-eighteens do not have a sexual relationship. The girls who do, given a rare opportunity to talk honestly, will admit there isn't much pleasure in being bounced against a wall like a rag doll for however long it takes for a young man to find satisfaction – fortunately, not very long. In areas of social exclusion, where teenage pregnancy rates are the highest, sex is the cheapest form of entertainment – unless it leads to infection, HIV or an unwanted baby. But when the realization dawns that it isn't quite the fun it's made out to be, who will tell these young women about pleasure as God intended it?

If sex is merely recreational, it is reduced to performance. In typical Western thinking, based on Greek philosophy, feeling, mind and body are three distinct parts of the human being and function separately. Emotion can be disengaged altogether, so the participant can also be a spectator, watching a piece of drama. But the mind can be the body's greatest critic, not its greatest fan. Mine keeps reminding me that I'm getting old, that the sags, folds, bulges and broken veins make me look like a page in a road atlas. Then it whispers that my man couldn't possibly still fancy me. He's probably fantasizing that he's with some delicious, leggy young blonde. And then the emotions come into play, and I feel a failure.

Our real obsession – to the point of neurosis – is with body image. Society whittles sex down to its lowest common denominator – whether we get it or not – and defines sexuality as the way in which we get it. Yet sexuality in its broadest sense is about how comfortable we feel in the skin God has created for us. And the truth is that we don't always like, let alone enjoy, what we are. That is the real reason why the subject is so loaded.

Our deep ambivalence about sexuality is reflected in the change in attitudes to women over the last fifty years. Before 1960 the ideal woman was plain, homely and nonsexual, a devoted mother and wifey. It was a wicked woman who was sexually appealing and free with her favours. After 1960 and the advent of the contraceptive pill, there was a complete reversal of standards. Today's ideal woman is beautiful, thin and sexually active, for she always gets any man she chooses. It's the inferior version who is ageing, unattractive, overweight and either nonsexual or stuck with one partner, which is almost as bad. Morecambe and Wise were once asked on radio about the secret of their relationship. 'It's just like a typical British marriage, without the sex,' Eric Morecambe said. There was a pause. 'In fact, it's just like a typical British marriage.'

Many people are not in a relationship and are not having sex. And some are more at ease with their sexuality than their married friends, who can use marriage as an excuse for not facing up to a negative self-image or an unsatisfying sex life. Their very celibacy forces them to confront who they are, how they feel about their bodies, and how they relate to the opposite sex. For me, one of the most inspirational writers on sexuality is the Roman Catholic priest Jean Vanier, who founded L'Arche communities for people with special needs. In *Man and Woman He Made Them,* he describes the wonder and healing of both the sexual love between two people with special needs and the platonic love between celibate individuals living in a close community. He believes society's unhealthy emphasis on what he calls 'genital sexuality' is due to the disappearance of community life and the ties of true friendship.

> Forbidding genital sexuality outside marriage will not remedy the situation. What is needed is the creation of communities where people love each other deeply, and where there is an authentic covenant relationship between them, celebrated with joy, enthusiasm and creativity. A world without joy and celebration of this kind will necessarily engender superficial sexuality. When sexual relations between a man and a woman involve neither love nor celebration . . . they cannot bring true joy. They are rather the fruit of anguish and come from fear of isolation.[2]

Here is the real challenge for the Church – to provide loving, joyful, colourful communities where women and men can come to terms with their sexuality in its widest sense. For if sexuality is about self-acceptance at its deepest level, integrating our body with the rest of our being and enjoying the many sensations of pleasure it can yield, if it means loving ourselves so that we can love others, then Christianity has a great deal to offer. But the dourness, coldness and silence of the Church on the subject has been its tragedy. Young people find little panacea for their alienation, isolation and self-doubt within our walls and turn elsewhere for what looks like a better offer. I didn't want that for my daughter.

'I can't do anything with my body'

Abby has grown up in a fairly traditional family unit, though not as nuclear as some, for there is a sense in which a vicarage child also belongs to the church and has the benefit – and the pressure – of being part of a fairly close-knit community with a great deal of peer support and a host of positive adult role models. But was that enough to help her make wise choices? What about my responsibility? From the moment she was born, I was determined she would grow up free from the negativity about her body that seems to pursue most human beings. Instinct told me that the better her body image, the less the impetus to share her body around. Only a girl who needed to prove her attractions would give it away without deep heart-searching.

I used every tool known to a mother to keep the demons of self-loathing at bay. Throughout her childhood I told her repeatedly that she was beautiful, and I didn't have to lie. She was. It wasn't simply a matter of looks. She was instinctively thoughtful, loving and giving, naturally joyful and vivacious. She didn't need to improve on nature, knock her body into shape, or conform to any expectations.

I didn't realize that dissatisfaction with a newly emerging body was a highly contagious teenage disease, for which there is as yet no effective vaccination – not until I heard her read this poem she wrote at a creative writing event at school.

Pleasure or Pain?

Waxing, bleaching, crying, screeching.
Pleasure or pain?
Needles and pins to cover our skins,
Rods and rings through different things.
Pleasure or pain?
Sugaring and shaving, dieting, craving,
Nature waning, money draining.
Pleasure or pain?
Gimmicks and creams to fill us with dreams,
Struggling for beauty beyond calls of duty.
Puffing and panting, raving and ranting,
Desperate to meet the standard, but find that you're
  stranded

Between pleasure and pain.
Highlights or lowlights? Lemon? Or egg whites?
Curly or straight: heated debate
Or rollers.
Spot cream and nail file, perfume and hair style,
Pleasure or pain?
Skin cream and make-up as soon as we wake up.
Lipstick for pride, at least on the outside.
Teeth straight and white, reflecting the light,
A dazzling smile for an insecure child
Hiding.
From dressing up old, where youth is sold,
To trying to look young when spring has sprung.
Pleasure? Or pain.

ABBY GUINNESS, AGED SEVENTEEN

For teenagers every extraneous pimple, hair or fold is a major disaster. The media, advertising, peer pressure – and unwitting mothers – create the perfect culture for those pernicious germs of discontent. They devote hours to holding back the forces of ugliness arrayed against them. This is how Abby described her inspiration for 'Pleasure or Pain'.

I was struck by inspiration one night as I sat with bleach on my face, grease on my hair and streaky tan on my legs. The ooze of my situation made me wonder if it really deserved the title of 'pampering'. It seemed more a kind of masochism that all females must ritually indulge in.

I was fully qualified in titivation by the time I was seventeen, and realized it must have been inspired by my mother. Who else? She was the queen of make-up and her publicity photograph for BBC radio was fondly known as 'The Jewellery Advert'. A real Jewish mama, and I wouldn't have her any other way. Glamorous works for me, it just seems an awful lot of effort.

Hair removal, filing my nails, make-up, I learned them all from her. But copying her wasn't always straightforward. When I was nine she marched me to the bathroom and before I was allowed to leave the house, made me scrub off the make-up I had

*put on. I was only allowed to pierce my ears when I was twelve.
I pierced my belly button when I was sixteen – without her
permission.*

*It was Mum who first plucked my eyebrows while I lay on
her bed straining to keep my eyes open and feeling hot tears roll
into my ears. She demanded that we follow 'the natural line of the
brow'. When I gathered the courage to do it myself I found it hurt
less and was satisfying until I was baring uneven and ridiculous
eyebrows. They grew back and the next time I followed 'the
natural line of the brow'.*

*The poem born on that night felt like frustration with
men, who demand such perfection of us. On further reflection
I don't believe they do. Some have categorically told me they
don't and were surprised I should think so. It seems that women
competitively encourage it in each other. Maybe it is my own
frustration at striving endlessly to be the perfect image of a
capable and naturally beautiful woman, like my mother.*

Ouch. Did I really do that to her? It all goes to show that we
can never take anyone further than we have been ourselves –
especially our children, for, unlike other acquaintances, they
have access to our hidden side and an unfortunate tendency to
model their behaviour on what we do and what we are, rather
than on what we say. I still remember my mother telling me to
put a bit of lipstick on before we went out. In the Jewish community a girl always has to look her best. We had to hook and
haul in the best catch, and who knew when we might not fall
over him?

Abby knew I found it strange when the turning heads and
wolf whistles were suddenly aimed in her direction, not mine.
'Move over, Mother, it's my turn,' she said. The cheek of it! She
was only fifteen. But while gravity has been taking its toll on
my flesh, the cuddly little bundle with soft, round belly, elastic-
band creases and a dozen dimples has metamorphosed into a
sylph, with masses of dark curls tumbling down her back,
where a pert little bottom perches on top of a long, slender pair

of legs. And not a broken vein, age spot or extraneous bulge in sight.

I don't want my mum or anyone else to think I am scarred by negative body image. Despite the pressures of society with its constant debate about the effect of waif-like models in fashion and advertising, I feel positive about my body. I admit, a great deal of it is luck. I do have a good figure, thanks to my genes and a healthy lifestyle. I worry much more about an unpredictable complexion and Neanderthal hairiness than I do about fighting flab.

During my teenage years the worries about my appearance were very real and very time consuming.

I had a friend at school who was crushed and almost seriously damaged by a boyfriend who told her that she should lose weight. She started to take diet pills and have highly erratic eating habits. There was nothing that I or my other friends could say or do to redeem the situation. His opinion was worth ten of ours.

Another friend in the same group was crippled by low self-esteem and constantly miserable, until eventually a few blokes showed an interest. Most of them treated her abysmally, but the seeds were sown, she knew she wasn't repulsive and a transformation occurred.

I spoke recently to a young teenager mortified by her appearance because the boys she liked weren't interested in her. But however much I spouted my past experience and told her to wait because the time would come, it didn't help. All she needed was a man to tell her she was attractive. And that isn't always going to happen at fourteen.

It has to be true that having faith in a God who loves you unconditionally is the basis of self-worth. I hated reading <u>Bridget Jones's Diary</u>, because the ultimate conclusion seems to be that getting a man is the only way to find personal fulfilment. But just as Mum admits that when you have a husband you rely less on God, knowing that God loves you will not give you the same rush *of pride that you get from a wolf whistle or someone calling you beautiful. So much as I hate to admit it, and as adamant as I am that relationships should only be attempted when both parties are able to stand alone, men and women are co-dependent because they find their self-confidence in each other.*

So much for our long discussions about the way looks are only skin deep. The old *teshuqah*, that need to appeal to a man, simply will not leave a girl alone. Abby recognized from an early age that there is no accounting for taste or chemistry, that men don't necessarily marry pretty women and pretty women don't necessarily marry handsome men, and that the most gorgeous people may not be in a relationship. But in today's celebrity-conscious world, in the competition between the inner and outer life, the skin wins – at first, anyway.

Body and soul

Advice to Daughters

Beware the men who seek
the soft and changing tone
and overlook the bleak
white armature of bone.

He is a fool who loves
only the dimpled face.
It is the bone that moves
ungainly, or with grace
to fill a singing space.

And time will come and hone
his sharp and eager beak
upon the flesh alone,
and then the bone will speak.

EVANGELINE PATERSON[3]

The only person in the Bible to win anything because of their physical attractions is Esther – and her reward was a booby prize if ever there was one. But Leah with the squint and poor complexion becomes a great matriarch. The prophet Isaiah says of the Messiah that 'he had no beauty or majesty to attract us to him', and that there was 'nothing in his appearance that we should desire him' (Isaiah 53:2). No matter how he has been portrayed since, he had no Hollywood appeal to make us fancy or follow him.

The Bible goes out of its way to make the point that looks count for nothing, so they obviously exerted an influence even then. When Samuel goes to the house of Jesse to pick a king for Israel, he is automatically drawn to the tall, fashionably dark, macho older boys, not the little red-headed runt of the pack who is out minding the sheep. Don't let physical appearance be your guide, God says to Samuel. 'The LORD does not look at the things people look at. Human beings look at the outward appearance, but the LORD looks at the heart' (1 Samuel 16:7 NIVI). God always did love David's heart, for it remained strong and loyal and true to the very end. Whatever his looks, he comes across as a very attractive human being.

I once made a television programme about a woman minister who'd had a cancerous tumour removed from her face. As I went to meet her for the first time, I remember wondering how I would feel. Typical to focus on my response, rather than her ordeal of facing the camera. A tall and lovely young woman walked towards me with her hand held out in welcome, and to my embarrassment I found myself asking if it was her. Of course it was. She had a patch across the upper half of one side of her face, but the inner life radiating out of the other half was so attractive that I didn't register anything else.

On the other hand, I shall be eternally grateful to my friend Sue, who saved me from the greatest folly of all time shortly before my relationship with Peter began, when I was becoming ever more embroiled with the most devastatingly handsome of men. He was built like a tank, and had the longest eyelashes I had ever seen.

'Beautiful, isn't he?' Sue reflected one evening as we had a girlie drink together.

'Mmmm,' I responded.

'Like a Greek god.'

'He is,' I sighed.

There was a momentary pause to give us both time to appreciate the attractions of such a gorgeous specimen of mankind.

'Pity he's so boring.'

I was dragged unceremoniously from fantasy into the real world, exactly as she knew I would be.

'You won't be distracted. You will wait for Mr Right,' she said.

The real person outlives the body, which, however gorgeous, finally falls apart. At seventy-five, Hugh Hefner, founder of the *Playboy* magazine empire, keeps a harem of seven almost identical, live, plastic blonde Barbie dolls. What is sad is not so much that thanks to Viagra they all sleep with him, for Ruby Wax never managed to establish that fact during her recent television interview, but that to remain in the harem they must stay exactly as they are and never, never grow old.

'What will you do then?' she asks.

'It won't happen for ages,' they mew.

'But it will,' she pushes.

'Not with plastic surgery,' they insist.

The apostle Paul's recipe for eternal beauty is much less surgical, though it can be radical and costly. It involves remaining God-focused throughout our lifetime. If we keep our eyes on him, we become more, not less, attractive as the years go by, for we are transformed on the inside from one degree of glory to another until, eventually, we become the very image of him (2 Corinthians 3:18). It is a wonderful and very graphic promise. 'She's the image of her father,' they used to say of me when I was a little girl. I liked it because I loved my dad.

This doesn't mean that the Bible has a Greek dualistic view of human beings, that the body doesn't matter while the inner life does. The New Testament adopts the Hebraic view, that body, mind and spirit are one and have equal importance. We will never become disembodied spirits floating through the eternal ether. We will have new, identifiable bodies. Coming to terms with our bodily identity now is therefore fairly important.

Adam and Eve didn't have a body image problem. God was pleased with his design, and they were merrily naked. After the fall, however, when women came to be valued for their reproductive capacity, physical attraction inevitably began to matter. Enter the fear of rejection. It is almost as if a gene is passed through the generations of women which urges us to mistrust, not enjoy, what God has made. Instead of filling us with a sense of delight and wonder, our bodies have become a source of embarrassment and shame.

Whenever I look at myself in the mirror I still get angry with the gynaecologist who left me with the horizontal scar across my belly ten years ago. What really makes me mad is that it never once occurred to him that I would mind. Like a plumber, he dealt purely and simply with my decrepit system and thought I ought to be grateful.

It will take centuries for surgeons to realize that they deal not just with bodies but with the emotions as well, and that the two are inextricable. Body image is about feeling, not fact. That's why it's so irrational. That's why parental reassurances do little to comfort a teenager whose face has erupted into a tiny spot just before an important date. That's why there are couples who dearly love each other and have been together for years, but who make love with the lights off, missing out on vital visual stimulus. Women can tell themselves until they are blue in the face that despite the fashion for hard, gaunt, boyish bodies, many men prefer lush softness and curves and somewhere they can lose themselves, but they don't believe it.

It isn't only women who struggle with those feelings, either. Peter asks me from time to time if I still find him attractive now that he's bald. 'No darling,' I say, 'I only married you for your full head of hair.'

At a Sheffield clergy conference, lecturer in theology and television producer Angela Tilby said, 'There is a wariness and unease in the body language of some Christian men. A tendency to sloping shoulders, wringing hands and a bowed head. Not the straight upward gait of imam and rabbi. Compare the Christian minister's wife with her Jewish or Muslim counterpart. She is clearly a jolly nice woman, well scrubbed rather than sexy, whereas Mrs Cohen and Mrs Patel frequently manage to be both.'

'But I just have nothing to wear'

> I also want women to dress modestly, with decency and propriety, not with braided hair or gold or pearls or expensive clothes, but with good deeds, appropriate for women who profess to worship God.
>
> 1 TIMOTHY 2:9–10

> Your beauty should not come from outward adornment, such as braided hair and the wearing of gold jewellery and fine clothes. Instead, it should be that of your inner self, the unfading beauty of a gentle and quiet spirit, which is of great worth in God's sight. For this is the way the holy women of the past . . . used to make themselves beautiful.
>
> 1 PETER 3:3–5

Our most obvious expression of sexuality is in what we wear. Clothes are never simply functional. They always say something. The French Lieutenant's Woman would probably never have become disastrously embroiled with the French Lieutenant had she gone out that fateful night in a sensible brown anorak rather than shrouded in a mysterious black cape.

I have always struggled with the idea of 'a gentle and quiet spirit', feeling somehow that 'a mouth on legs' was more my style. That and 'appropriate deeds' seem a very dull alternative to the Jewish obsession with gold and diamonds. It's true that Jews love razzmatazz.

Hymie Goldberg is walking along the street (it must have been the Sabbath, for Jews never walk anywhere at any other time, they take the Porsche) when a flying saucer lands in front of him. Out of it climbs a Martian in a wonderful gold lurex suit. 'Oh,' he says, as the strange being shimmers towards him, 'I just love the suit. Does everyone on Mars wear clothes like that?'

'No,' says the Martian, 'only we Jews.'

It was a shock when I first became a Christian to find that, in the rather repressive evangelicalism of the 1960s, I was considered 'fast' because I wore fairly provocative clothes, very short skirts and a great deal of make-up. I had a unique bright red sleeveless dress, bought for me by my mother for a Bar Mitzvah. It was cut away at the shoulders and had two rings of white stitching on the front in a very interesting place. I had no idea it was causing problems in the University Christian Union, until I was told so in no uncertain terms by a female friend. But then, she had been brought up in the Brethren, and to my total incredulity insisted on wearing an old-fashioned brown felt hat to church because that was what her mother would have wanted.

So, should Christian women give gold and pearls, highlights and lowlights, Calvin Klein, FCUK, indeed all 'adornment', a wide birth and reflect their beliefs, as Tertullian suggested, 'in mourning and in rags', covering up their latent sexuality with dull colours and drab, unlovely clothes? In the 1950s and '60s it was a sign of piety to be terribly 'mish' – to dress like a missionary on furlough, out of touch with the latest styles, in dated hairstyle, tweedy skirts and sensible brogues. Extreme feminists joined the evangelicals in urging women to make themselves as unattractive to men as possible so that they wouldn't be weighed up in a sexual way and valued accordingly.

In a world where men are bombarded with explicit sexual imagery, it isn't fair to give them the deliberate come-on. We often underestimate the impact of our clothing. It would be useful to be a man for the day, for how else can a woman appreciate the struggle they face when that testosterone is tickled several times a day by billboards, hoardings, the TV and magazine shelves – not to mention the flash of flesh on the pavement? Perhaps I should have a little more sympathy for the early Church Fathers. For a man, 'I need you to admire me but not touch me' is a mixed message.

On the other hand, we cannot be terrified or tyrannized into denying what makes us uniquely feminine. A friend of mine who was a missionary in Morocco told me that, although the women wore the full *burqa* when they went to the mosque, the men there would line up outside and ogle their feet as they came out. Male desire cannot be curbed simply by imposing restrictions on women. From neckline to hemline, shoes to earrings, there are as many possibilities of turn-on for a man as there are varieties of the species.

Fashion for what is considered attractive has constantly changed. The Romans admired thinness, but in medieval times plump was erotic and in vogue. Necklines were cut so low that a woman could fully bare her breasts, but revealing an ankle was too daring by far. In the nineteenth century a lady had a corseted waist and was delicate, frail and pure, while a good-time girl was heavy, blousy and robust. Only half a century ago the idea of women wearing trousers was greeted with shock and dismay, as Dorothy Sayers makes clear when she talks, tongue in cheek, about the issue being 'so distressing to Bishops'.

> We are asked: 'Why do you want to go about in trousers? They are extremely unbecoming to most of you. You only do it to copy the men.' To this we may properly reply: 'It is true that they are unbecoming. Even on men they are remarkably unattractive. But, as you men have discovered for yourselves, they are comfortable, they do not get in the way of one's activities like skirts and they protect the wearer from draughts. If the trousers do not attract you, so much the worse; for the moment I do not want to attract you. I want to enjoy myself as a human being, and why not? As for

copying you, certainly you thought of trousers first and to that extent we must copy you. But we are not such abandoned copy-cats as to attach these useful garments to our bodies with braces. There we draw the line. These machines of leather and elastic are unnecessary and unsuited to the female form. They are, moreover, hideous beyond description. And as for decency – of which you sometimes accuse the trousers – we at least can take our coats off without becoming the half-undressed, bedroom spectacle that a man presents in his shirt and braces.[4]

Ankle-length dresses or miniskirts, platform or stiletto heels, long nails and starvation diets – it is amazing how many fashions and beauty rituals, so often designed with men in mind, inhibit a woman's freedom and reduce her competence. And Western foibles are tame compared with the neck stretching, foot binding or genital mutilation found in other cultures, all performed in the name of female attractiveness.

When the apostle Peter calls on women to be 'gentle and quiet', he is addressing wives with unconverted husbands, urging them not to rise to their partners' taunts and arguments. Instead, they should wait and let the transformation in their lives speak for itself. They won't want to spend his money on the things they spent it on before – the designer labels, expensive hairdos and other status symbols that were regarded as rather risqué in Roman society. That should really make their men sit up and think.

Nothing captures for me the intention of the apostle Peter's words like the story Naomi Gryn tells of her grandmother, Bella, in her introduction to the autobiography written by her father, Rabbi Hugo Gryn, describing his childhood in Berehovo and time in Auschwitz. When the Nazis invaded the little Hungarian town, Bella buried her Sabbath candles, kiddush cup, eight-branched chanukiah used at the Feast of Lights and Hugo's excellent school report of that year in the garden. They were still there, just as she had left them, when she returned from Auschwitz and she eventually managed to smuggle them out to Hugo, who had settled in England. 'For my father,' writes Naomi, 'that these family treasures had survived the war was a powerful parable about the values that his mother cherished most: not her furs and jewellery, but the symbols of a Jewish home.'[5]

Even Jesus tackled the subject of clothes. Perhaps he'd heard one of his female followers complaining that she just had nothing to wear. 'See how the lilies of the field grow. They do not labour or spin. Yet I tell you that not even Solomon in all his splendour was dressed like one of these . . . will he not much more clothe you. . . ?' (Matthew 6:28–9). The lilies of the field are not grey or beige. They are a riot of colour. Nor did King Solomon appear in public in a hair shirt or a polo shirt and washed-out tracksuit bottoms. He dressed to impress – even if he didn't resort to Oxfam shops or second-hand dress agencies for recycled bargains, as I often do. It's fine to look a schmuck – a nice Yiddish word meaning a slob – from time to time, but if dressing up at all, even for an occasion, makes us feel uncomfortable, it may be an interesting reflection on our feelings about our sexuality.

First impressions are important. In my work in public relations, I dress to represent the company. In my work for the kingdom, I represent the King. There are times when it is important, not so much to power-dress, but to look and feel efficient and in control. It worries me when Abby says, 'You're not going out like that!' because she is my best barometer of fashion. Does she mean I would be embarrassed if I went out 'like that', or she would be embarrassed if I went out 'like that'? Either way, when she speaks, I listen. I would advise every woman to find a younger shopping accomplice, for while it is important to be ourselves, no one can be short-sighted enough to dispense with a little honest advice. I shall leave the last word on the subject to her. The following was inspired by my arrival home one day from Marks and Spencer with a pair of gold moccasins with tassels on them.

Loyally standing up for my generation, I would say the average teenage girl has far more fashion sense than her mother. Middle-aged designer labels get about exciting as Principles, a name designed to appeal to those desperately trying to uphold some. Newer fashion labels like Hussy and Porn Star may revolt mothers, but they are appealing to fashion-freak teenagers, whether they live up to the name on their clothes or not.

Somehow, mothers magically forget their own days in the spotlight of fashion and follow the unwritten dowdiness rule for over-forties. If parents could bear to look at photographs of themselves as teenagers, they would doubtless notice how remarkably similar they look to their children (apart from the disastrous haircuts of the '70s). My dad had Buddy Holly glasses. As for Mum's flared trousers and platform shoes ... enough said.

Haven't parents noticed that most teenagers quickly grow out of the gothic era, the ripped jeans trend or the 'Is it a skirt or is it a belt?' phase? Why do they spend so much time fretting over it when it is a normal and predictable part of growing up? Why can't we give teenage girls a break? If they're not embarrassed, why should we all be embarrassed for them? It's probably the only time they'll ever want to experiment wildly with their image; extreme self-consciousness soon overcomes them, and after the necessary student years a daughter will settle into a highly acceptable wardrobe.

A mother, however, is far more difficult to tackle. They have a habit of festering in a Littlewoods-dominated world, and daughters can forget any hopes of them 'growing out of it'. Who started the notion that once you have children nobody cares what you look like? Remember, once your children are old enough to notice, they will be more embarrassed by you than you ever are by them.

Mothers and daughters have a mutual duty to dress each other well. This works in both their interests when they need a wardrobe to raid. The first key to a successful shopping relationship is tactful honesty. A deferential comment about too *much cleavage and people getting the wrong idea is usually better received than, 'You're not my daughter if you go out looking like a tart!' The stronger the maternal reaction, the stronger the filial defiance, the larger the cleavage. The second vital rule is never try and dress the other in what you would wear yourself. (Another helpful factor is for mothers to flex their plastic!)*

What else does a girl need to know?

Apart from enjoying her femininity to the full, what else helps a girl develop the self-assuredness she is going to need to change the world? First and foremost, she needs basic information. One of the main aims of the teenage pregnancy campaign is to encourage parents to talk to their children about sex. A friend told me recently she was amazed to hear that her student daughter had been horrified when she was admitted to hospital with a suspected ovarian cyst, because she thought she only had one ovary and was in danger of losing her ability to have children. Abby is totally mystified by a male student friend who has to go out of the room whenever the girls mention periods. His mother never told him about the female reproductive system and now it is such a mystery that it scares him rigid. Who thought old-fashioned attitudes to sexuality disappeared with gaslights and gramophones?

My grandmother, like many young women in the free and flapper 1920s, knew nothing of the facts of life on her wedding night, and was so horrified at her rude enlightenment that she ran home to her mother. She was sent promptly back and told to get on with it. (Not to put up with it – Jewish women are much more earthy than that.)

My mother never bothered to mention it to me. She said she assumed I knew – at what age, I'm not sure. Since I was about sixteen when she first broached the subject, it would have been strange if I hadn't known something, so I learned about it in the usual sniggering, giggling manner girls do, which wasn't perhaps the best.

Abby thinks I was the one to explain the facts of life to her – so I may have got something right – courtesy of Nick Butterworth and Mick Inkpen, who produced a wonderful little book called *Who Made Me?* with graphic illustrations of mischievous little sperms chasing after a serene-looking ovum, and Mum and Dad wriggling around having a great deal of fun in the process.

I can never understand the fuss some people make – especially men – about women who breastfeed in public, a sure giveaway of a deep discomfort with their own bodyliness. Peter and I felt it was important to have a relaxed approach to nudity with the children. It is natural and neutral outside the sexual context – but I did draw the line when the children were in their late teens and my heading for the bathroom seemed to be an unspoken sign that Mother was a sitting duck, available for deep, heart-to-heart chats. Sorry ducklings, don't follow me. I'm not being prudish, but I do like some dignity. And the bath is my private space, to which I retreat at the end of the day to think my own thoughts.

Many children grow up feeling uncomfortable about their own bodies because the genitals are never mentioned, and they assume that whatever is shrouded in silence must be bad. Girls – and many boys – are rarely told about the clitoris, despite the fact that it plays an essential part in female sexual response. This is most certainly not the case in Judaism, where a man is expected to give his wife pleasure on the Sabbath and festivals. (Nowhere, incidentally, does the Law suggest that a man is entitled to the same.) A sensitive rabbi, preparing a young man for marriage, would ensure he knew how. Judging by the number of women who have come to us over the years in near despair over the lack of sexual pleasure in their lives, I often wonder whether it shouldn't be a compulsory part of church marriage preparation too. We take far too much for granted.

Women also need a sense of celebration, not that Victorian shame which still seems to dog so many sexual relationships. In some communities the consummation of a marriage was cheered on from outside the door or window. It can't have done much for the couple, but at least it made the point that such a major commitment was public, communal and worthy of a party.

In Judaism, where body, mind and spirit are one, sexual embarrassment is far less. The religion which gave birth to the Song of Songs, one of the most erotic love poems ever written, is light years away from the early Fathers' style of Christianity, dogged as it was by the idea that sex was the most unfortunate mistake God ever made. The poem is full of belly buttons, boobs and other bumps which are a delight to children, if anyone would bother to read it to them.

We are just too intense about it. Sex was an incredibly funny thing for God to create. One of the Jewish holy books says that after creation was finished, God watched Adam and Eve enjoying sexual intercourse. That is what prompted him to say that he'd done a good job – in other words, 'That idea of mine has certainly gone down well.' True or not, there is no doubt that God gave human beings a special form of play, with a twinkle in his eye, probably to prevent us becoming too pompous.

When we were on holiday in the Ibiza house, Peter and I regularly went for an afternoon 'siesta'. Then, one year, we realized from that 'we know what you mean' look from the children that our code had been cracked. 'Okay,' we said, 'if you're so clever, you answer the phone and the doorbell, and give us a break.' Teenagers have their uses.

I am not advocating that girls need to know all the intimate details, simply that we need a more honest, open, joyful approach to a vital part of our lives, so that they will know there is a treasure worth waiting for, worth keeping for the right person.

'My smear test didn't give a clear result. I have to have another one,' I moaned at the girls in the office one day. 'If it doesn't work this time, I'm not having any more,' I said, clattering away at my computer keyboard, without thinking, as you do. 'After all, I'm hardly high risk. I've only had one partner.'

There was a sudden silence at the desk opposite.

'One!' Angie said. 'Only ever one?'

Unwittingly, it seemed I had lobbed a grenade across the room.

'Why, how many have you had?'

Angie used her fingers to count. She had to go through the process several times.

'S-seven, I think . . . at the moment.'

Her most recent relationship had just come to a painful end after seven years.

'Doesn't it get boring? The sex, I mean.'

'No,' I said. 'Gourmet sex, like good wine, takes time to perfect.'

'I envy you,' she said wistfully. 'Here I am, a bit of a shipwreck really, nearly fifty and no man, no sex, and no chance of any kids now.'

In fact, her most recent betrayal and desertion has shown Angie how much she has depended on her partners for her confidence, and she has called a halt. Instead, she is going for the university degree she always wanted.

I didn't want Abby to learn the hard way. She needed to know what the boundaries were – unlike the student member of our church, raised in a Christian family, who told me that since she had unintentionally thrown away her virginity at a party one night, what did it matter who she slept with now? I understood her pain, but not her defensive comment, 'Where does it say in the Bible that we shouldn't?' That one encounter hadn't robbed her of forgiveness or the chance to start again, but her successive relationships were robbing her of any chance of retrieving her self-respect.

The joys of waiting

It is God's will that you should be sanctified: that you should avoid sexual immorality; that each of you should learn to control your own body in a way that is holy and honourable, not in passionate lust like the heathen, who do not know God; and that in this matter no one should wrong or take advantage of a brother or sister.

1 THESSALONIANS 4:3–4 NIVI

It is interesting that in this earliest piece of the New Testament, Paul is so unequivocal on the subject. Self-control is a major theme in many of his letters – a despised and neglected concept in today's hedonistic society, but the key to empowerment for those who find and keep it. One young woman told her minister how hard it was to resist the pressure at school to give up her virginity. He said to her, 'Just say to your friends, I can become like you in a minute, but you can never again become like me.'

I hope Abby is given the grace to live out these ideals she wrote when she was eighteen. I don't claim responsibility for them. Having older role models as her peers, including a school nurse, to whom she could talk openly and freely, has certainly helped.

When two people in my year at school had sex, everyone knew about it. We were in Year 10, the 14–15 age group, and there were probably a few experienced yet silent people dotted around the place, yet for some reason, it suddenly became the most talked about subject for a whole week. Eventually, people came to the conclusion that it was boring and went back to playing football or cricket, or wandering around the school grounds aimlessly passing the lunch break.

The publicity undoubtedly put pressure on the least confident people, who began to wonder if something was wrong with them. Those with more self-esteem and maturity (I love saying that, because I was one of them) thought they were foolish and vowed to wait.

By the time we reached the sixth form, one by one my friends succumbed and whispered secretly about their dreadful experiences with the morning-after pill. I have to say, I am sure there were more virgins than ever owned up – probably around 70 per cent – though most of those would be the boys, because the girls were seeing older people out of school.

University is apparently the place to lose your virginity and join your peers in more knowledgeable conversation on the subject. In my first term, a game of truth or dare revealed that seven of the ten of us there were virgins. I've been told that by the end of our three years there will only be me left, but I don't believe that's true. I know a lot of people waiting 'for the right person'. My reasons for not having sex are probably only half God-focused and half plain common sense. The risk of pregnancy, sexually transmitted diseases and cervical cancer, to name just three, make it pretty clear that sex is not to be undertaken lightly.

Dad once explained to me that whether you think sex is a gift from God or not, it creates a spiritual bond between a couple, and though the couple might split up, that bond can never be broken. I realized how right he was when I witnessed a friend of mine so tangled with her sexual partners that she couldn't extricate herself. There had been three, but when the next one came along she would end up cheating on the old one. She kept trying to decide on just one, but the other two would always be around tempting her back into the intimacy they had shared.

Another of my friends was cheated on by her boyfriend of two years, which caused her immense pain, and a third kept getting mixed up with boys from the Navy. In a frank discussion in our common room, each said they wished they had waited and they were jealous of my reserve. I was lucky enough to be looking forward to sex, while they were all hurt by it and sick of its consequences. To be fair, though, I don't think I really had all that much reserve. I just hadn't met anyone I wanted to sleep with. When you think about it, sex is really quite a strange and undignified thing to do, and I would need to trust my partner and feel at ease before I was able to undertake any sort of intimacy.

I didn't want anyone to see the dimple on my bum or the stretch marks on my thighs unless I knew they would take me for ever, warts and all, those I have and those I'm going to get.

In the car on our way for a day's shopping, Mum and I discussed why sex has been so misrepresented to my generation. She observed that people now see sex as an entitlement and so Christianity is seen as depriving people of that right. When God created sex, he gave it as a gift to married couples in order that they might have a close bond, enjoyment and the ability to reproduce. It is not a commodity, it is a bonus to make that one relationship special. Humans are the only creatures designed to have intercourse face to face, and among the few who gain pleasure from it. Why, then, does it cause more heartache than pleasure? Why have we got it wrong? There is nothing exciting about a wedding day if the couple are already sexually active together. Who cares about a bit of legal paperwork? But when two people commit themselves to each other, knowing the reward they're going to get at the end of the day, that's really worth celebrating.

People can be so selfish when it comes to sex. They think, 'It's my decision,' or, 'It only affects me.' But if a man leaves his wife because he and his new partner 'deserve to be together', what about his children, his wife and the devastation he leaves behind? What about the example it sets to the next generation that personal happiness is all that matters? What about the friendship groups of the couple? I have seen whole groups of friends shattered by broken relationships. Sex can make people lie, it makes them secretive, guilty and deceitful.

I admit that getting older and meeting more people you find attractive means the urges are stronger. People say they have sex by accident. Can it be an accident? It's not really like crashing a car or dropping a vase. Personally, I can't see how it could just be a whoops-a-daisy and look what we did. Sex is extremely appealing, there isn't any way around it. It can be hard to keep control. Being accountable – to friends, mentors or parents – and having someone know about your situation can help. I hold on to the fact that when it is right, it will be a million times better than

getting it wrong, and the only sure way of knowing you will be
together for ever is to agree to get married and work at your
relationship. Sex as God intended is, I hope, I'm sure, worth every
second of waiting.'

Abby's innocent hopes and aspirations contrast painfully with the bright young graduates, so like her, working in the White House, who are seduced by power and become entangled with much older, married men. Writing in the *Guardian* about the disappearance of White House intern Chandra Levy, who was having an affair with congressman Gary Condit, journalist Sharon Krum asked why so many intelligent young women working in DC, like Monica Lewinsky, fell into this particular trap. She spoke to the ex-intern and *Washington Post* columnist Sally Quinn. 'We presume that because young women today – beneficiaries of equal opportunity and affirmative action – are able to claim power for themselves, they are immune to a powerful man ... But Quinn says that feminism only goes so far in DC, and then basic human behaviour trumps ideology.'[6]

The problem is that human behaviour has a tendency to conquer the Christian values as much as any other ideology, and every woman of every age needs to be alert to that danger, to recognize the lure and abuse of power, to know how to handle temptation, pressure and seduction.

The joy of making love

When I presented a local radio debate on teenage pregnancy from a sixth form college, one of the female students said, 'At school they gave us the biological facts, but never told me what it would feel like to fall in love.' Emotion, not disembodied desire, is more likely to rob a girl of her senses. 'Women need a reason to have sex,' says Billy Crystal in the film *City Slickers,* 'men just need a place.'

A man may spend his entire life in search of the key to female sexual arousal, and it is as simple as this: romance begins to turn the lock. To open the door, and keep it open, requires a great deal of gentleness, patience and imagination. It is an art that can take many years to learn. That is why it needs long-term commitment and dedication, and it begins, not in the bedroom, but in the kitchen. Women are often so exhausted by running the home, the garden, the children and the dog, sometimes on top of a job, that they have little energy left over for grand passion at nightfall.

American sex therapist Dr Archibald Hart says that when the poor sexual technique of some men is added to the equation, it is hardly surprising that women are not always very interested. 'Men who want a better sex life not only need to learn how to be better lovers, but also how to carry the emotional and physical burden of housework and child-rearing. To put it bluntly: many men only have themselves to blame for their low sexual satisfaction.'[7] If only older men could mentor younger men in this area, talk to their sons and pass on their best tips, as they do in football or computing – but it just isn't as acceptable a subject of conversation.

Women do have a sex drive, but it is easily driven underground by a cumulation of minor knocks. We are complex creatures sexually, martyrs to our hormonal cycles, worn with juggling dozens of different plates, heavily dependent on mood, atmosphere and harmony. We barely get round to acknowledging the first rumblings of desire before we're engulfed by such a torrent of testosterone that we're left feeling winded.

Unfortunately, to the bewilderment of most men, the male physique does little for us, which is why the current obsession with looks can leave us a little cold. The first time I saw the film of D.H. Lawrence's *Women in Love,* there were two elderly ladies in the row behind me. At the moment when the two leading men wrestle stark naked in front of the fire, their rippling biceps glowing seductively in the firelight, one whispered loudly to the other, 'Lovely carpet.' Personally, my mood is heavily dependent on seeing a tidy bedroom, but that's probably very Jewish.

I don't understand why God made such discrepancies between men and women, but that's how it is and that's what we explain to couples we're preparing for marriage. In very simplified terms, for women intimacy is the way to sex, and for men sex is the way to intimacy – and outside a deeply committed, loving relationship, that's a potentially lethal cocktail.

The dictionary defines 'intimacy' as 'close or warm friendship', but the word has become synonymous with sexual relations. Without the former, however, the latter are not intimate at all. As we have seen in the creation story, the male sins in the area of relationship and, unless the benefits of redemption touch his life, he will always have struggles in this area. Some men find it difficult to express their feelings. Many find it impossible to admit weakness. But for real sexual intimacy, vulnerability – that original Adam-like nakedness – is essential, otherwise, even within marriage, the sex act is simply a way of satisfying the appetite, as members of the animal kingdom do. There is no such thing as 'making love' to anyone as closed down and shut off as a snail.

Yet no human being, sexually active or not, can survive without intimacy. Single and celibate, Jesus nonetheless had a number of 'intimates' – John, who lay at the Last Supper with his head on Jesus' breast; Peter and the other disciples, with whom he could be transparently honest and completely himself; Mary and Martha, whose company he sought when he wanted to unwind. If we cannot find intimacy as a single person, we will never find it in marriage, and certainly not in sex.

When sex becomes a trial, as it evidently does for many couples, it may mean that there are unresolved differences and resentments in the relationship. Even within a deeply caring relationship, the sex act can be blighted by past experience or an abusive childhood. In his work among those with special needs who lack confidence and feel passed over by the world, Jean Vanier has seen how the Christian community can be a safe place where all people, male and female, married or single, find healing, restoration and joy.

One of my greatest hopes for my children has been that they would grow up knowing that it is possible to be hopelessly and completely in love with the same person throughout an entire lifetime, and that I am as filled with passion for their father now, as much as, if not more than, I was on the day we married, enjoying more and more the great gift of our union.

I suddenly realized the other day, with a sense of shock, how few years I have left to enjoy it. I suppose that as we get older it may become a little less frequent, a little more difficult – though by no means impossible. Peter's grandfather was seventy-two when Peter's father was born. Admittedly, his wife was twenty-seven! I have always thought that when one partner has a terminal illness the saddest moment in the relationship must be the last farewell to love-making, that very tangible expression of all that we have been for each other for so many years. Jesus makes it clear that there is no sex in heaven. There are probably very good reasons – there must be something far better. All the same, I had better make the most of it now.

Notes

1. Dorothy L. Sayers, *Are Women Human?* (Eerdmans, 1971), pp. 117–18.
2. Jean Vanier, *Man and Woman He Made Them* (DLT, 1985), p. 159.
3. Evangeline Paterson, 'Advice to Daughters' from *Brining the Water Hyacinth to Africa* (Taxus, 1983).
4. Sayers, *Are Women Human?* pp. 22–3.
5. Hugo Gryn, with Naomi Gryn, *Chasing Shadows* (Penguin, 2000), p. xxx.
6. *Guardian*, 16 July 2001. Chandra Levy's body was found about a year later.
7. Archibald D. Hart, *The Sexual Man* (Word, 1994), p. 130.

CHAPTER 8

The Mothering Woman

You can't frighten me. I have children.

FRIDGE MAGNET

The ability to bring a child into the world is a gift given uniquely to women. Nothing can generate quite such joy or pain. For the single woman, it may be her greatest regret, a dull, nagging ache, so much a part of her that she is only troubled by it when she is caught off-guard; for the woman with fertility problems it can seem the greatest mockery, a denial of all her hopes and expectations by a capricious, ungenerous God; for the woman who decides not to have children, it makes her a pariah among other women, especially in the Church; for the woman who cannot bond with her child, it means endless self-recrimination and guilt; and for the woman who loses a child, there is no grief, no bewilderment, so great.

Even for those blessed with the ability to raise their children in a secure, loving environment, being a mother is the most demanding role they will ever face. In none of the many relationships entrusted to woman is it more essential to speak words of life, and in none can that be more difficult. Thus far, I have been spared most of the heartbreak, yet even so, I would have to say that mothering is a great deal more than and nothing like it is made out to be.

Having a child changes most women overnight. Suddenly, from some untapped, hitherto undiscovered source deep within, there wells up emotion more powerful than any other. It is a fierce, frightening, protective, all-consuming kind of devotion. Now you know you will kill or be killed in defence of the cub. But then, as the months go by, you discover that this little tyrant also has the ability, in tandem and in equal measure, to provoke bouts of temper, impatience and intolerance you always thought you were far too nice to have.

One thing is certain: mothering has very little to do with the bland, pious and idealized images of the glowing, phlegmatic Madonna that have pursued women from Renaissance times to Cow and Gate adverts. There she sits in serene soft focus with a gurgling, contented cherub at her breast. She obviously doesn't suffer from cracked nipples.

As a child I swallowed the saccharine image whole and thought it an unkind freak of nature that I had been given a mother with the gentleness and serenity of King Kong. The softness inside wasn't immediately obvious. I told myself that one day I would live the dream. I would have a gingerbread cottage with honeysuckle growing up the wall, and newly washed, sweet-smelling nappies wafting gently in the breeze as they hung out in the summer sun. In reality, stuck without a car in the middle of Greater Manchester, these were my wilderness years. If just one person had told me I might make a better mother of teenagers than babies, it would have released me from the guilt induced by the stifling and restless boredom I felt. But, blessed with the ministry of encouragement, friends simply said, 'Just wait, it gets worse.'

Like most women, I wanted to be a good mother, and had a very definite ideal of what a good mother should be – endlessly patient, caring, selfless and giving. Yet once the children came I constantly failed to live up to my self-imposed standards, and was consumed with the fear of getting it wrong and damaging them for life. What if my two cherubs suddenly metamorphosed into drug-taking, glue-sniffing, promiscuous little pagans? It would all be my fault.

Children come without a manual or personalized growth plan. Our major role models are usually our own parents, and that can be the very example we most want to avoid. Then one day we hear them speaking to our children – only in our voice. I marvel that my children are as well adjusted as they seem to be. Yet as I look back now, I don't think child-rearing has to be completely directionless and arbitrary. There are certain basic, ageless principles, laid down in a manual for living that survives the test of time.

The Bible contains an encouraging mixture of mothers who get it right and mothers who get it wrong. One thing is sure: there is no area of our lives where women, and even men, are more vulnerable, more susceptible, to fatal fond indulgence like King David, or to desperate scheming like Rebecca.

In Matthew's gospel the mother of James and John asks Jesus if her two sons can have a special place on either side of him in the kingdom (Matthew 20:20–21). There is no attempt to disguise the naked maternal ambition. She has invested all in her two fine boys, and is prepared to voice her aspirations. What else should a Jewish mother want for her boys than the best? Jesus doesn't criticize her maternal pride. It's her concept of success he tackles. It's too human, too hierarchical – that's what she needs to know.

Among the many positive models of mothering in the Bible are Hannah, the mother of Samuel, and Eunice and Lois, mother and grandmother of Timothy, who prepare and release their children for a lifetime of service. In the nineteenth century, letting a child go to Africa, Asia or India as a missionary was heartbreaking. Once he or she went to the other side of the world, a mother would probably never see her child again. We can guess the immense pain behind the sacrifice expressed in these words written by Amy Carmichael's widowed mother in response to Amy's calling.

Yes, dearest Amy, He has lent you to me all these years. He only knows what a strength, comfort and joy you have been to me. In sorrow He made you my staff and solace, in loneliness my more than child companion, and in gladness my bright and merry-hearted sympathiser. So, darling, when He asks you now to go away from within my reach, can I say nay? No, no Amy, He is yours – you are His – to take you where He pleases and use you as He pleases. I can trust you to Him and I do . . . All day He has helped me, and my heart unfailingly says, 'Go ye. . .'[1]

When it comes to letting go of a child, we have the prime example in the most famous mother who ever lived, although women have been robbed of any chance of identifying with her by the pious, desexualized, inaccessible icon that history has made of her. In his *Genesee Diary,* the great spiritual sage Henri Nouwen says that meditating on Mary's gentleness and softness enabled him to keep in touch with his feminine side, dispossessed in an aggressive, competitive male world. But was Mary really soft and gentle, or is that wishful male stereotyping? My feeling is that she is a flesh-and-blood Jewish mama waiting to be rediscovered, a real woman with the joys and struggles of any mother, and as tough as a Scouser bringing up her family in a deprived part of Liverpool.

Mary, an amazing mother

The account of Mary's pregnancy is recorded by Luke. 'I have carefully investigated everything,' he says, just like a doctor with meticulous attention to medical details. He has obviously interviewed Mary at length about her obstetric history and established that this was a perfectly normal pregnancy and childbirth – it's only the conception that is somewhat out of the ordinary. Luke is so impressed with the story, and with the woman who recounts it, that he tells it through her eyes – one of the few scriptural narratives told from a woman's perspective.

The village of Nazareth was so small that even the Galileans would only have passed through it on their way to somewhere else, yet this is the birthplace of one of the world's most exceptional women. Her name is actually Miriam, which means 'strong', for she is not unlike her namesake in the Old Testament, the first female worship leader, who was a tough old boot. That's why God has singled her out. Her calling will require unusual reserves of inner strength and resilience.

Meanwhile, back at the heavenly ranch, the angel Gabriel receives the commission he has been awaiting for hundreds of years, since he appeared to Daniel to tell him it would take seventy times seven years for the Messiah 'to finish transgression, to put an end to sin, to atone for wickedness, to bring in everlasting righteousness' (Daniel 9:24). The time has come at last to announce to the world that the prophecy is fulfilled. He is beside himself with excitement. God probably warns him, 'Don't get carried away, Gabriel. Remember, you're an angel and she's a mere girl. Don't frighten her.'

But Gabriel forgets, and, carried away by the moment, cries out to Mary, 'Greetings, highly favoured one. The Lord is with you.'

And she is terrified out of her skin.

Take two. Gabriel remembers what he has been told and starts again. 'Don't be afraid, Mary, you're going to have a son – he will reign over the house of Jacob for ever and his kingdom will never end.'

Typical of any woman faced with the impossible, Mary asks the practical question, 'How? I haven't slept with anyone.'

It is a question born of faith, not doubt. Since the day of her birth, the Scriptures have been the very foundation of her life. She knows with absolute certainty that the Messiah will come – but how? And what has it to do with her? It's the logistics that bother her.

The power of God will 'overshadow' her, explains Gabriel with great delicacy. And if that was still as clear as mud, she can always go and visit her elderly, infertile cousin Elizabeth, now six months pregnant – a visual sign, if ever there was one, that with God nothing is impossible.

Mary is satisfied – and that is extraordinary in itself. She has just been handed the humiliation of an illicit pregnancy, disgrace for her family and the possible loss of the man she hopes to marry. But there doesn't appear to be any prolonged heart-searching. It takes no more than a moment to yield her autonomy, her ambitions and her future to God. 'May it be to me as you have said.' This is simply the culmination of a life-time of surrender.

Every human being who has ever chosen to follow God comes inexorably to this moment of decision, like Mary, or Ruth, or Esther, when he asks us to choose between our dreams and his plans. Many of my career ambitions had to be abandoned when I moved with Peter away from a city to the north-west coast. It felt, and often still feels, as if some part of me died, but that was nothing compared to the challenge Mary faced. Could she have said 'no'? I think she could, but God knew her well enough to know that she wouldn't. After all, the most important cosmic event in history hinges on that 'yes'. Her acquiescence is vital in terms of what she will be for the child she will carry, for she will raise a son who will take after her in his unflinching obedience to God.

'Blessed is she who has believed that what the Lord has said to her will be accomplished!' says the elderly Elizabeth (Luke 1:45). I'm not sure I would have wanted Mary's blessings. God's plans do not carry an automatic exemption from suffering, illness or pain. At this stage she is aware of the enormity, but not the implications, of her calling. For Mary, the stigma was merely the start. She would face an uncomfortable birth in surroundings she would never have chosen, banishment from her village and the life of a refugee, the bewilderment of her son's ministry, the terror of watching him face trumped-up charges and the devastation of his terrible death. At Jesus' *brith*, or circumcision, the prophet Simeon warns her that a sword will be plunged into her heart – hardly the most encouraging picture to give a mother at such a joyful celebration. But Mary knows now what to do with disturbing information. She simply tucks it away inside herself, like a handkerchief in a pocket, trusting that it will be there when it's needed. Moment by moment, we are only given as much as we can cope with.

Like Esther and Ruth, however, Mary is no passive victim of circumstances. She grabs God's will by the throat, with joy, not self-pity, and in the great prophetic tradition of Jewish women like Miriam and Hannah, she proclaims the greatness of God and the coming of his kingdom. Her Magnificat is full of Old Testament echoes, the words and themes she has loved from childhood, but now they have personal significance, for a little nobody from nowhere has been given a place with her heroines in the history of her people, as they wait for God's promises to be fulfilled. God is the master of topsy-turvydom – for one day, when this extraordinary child of hers comes into his own, all the poor will be empowered, all the powerful brought down to size.

For the first twelve years, Jesus' childhood is much like any other. After that 'silent night, holy night' of Bethlehem, where 'all is calm, all is bright', there must have been many other nights shattered by noise when Jesus screamed the house down, as babies do. Along came the other babies, Joseph's children, and, packed into a basic, tiny home, didn't Mary sometimes lose her temper when Jesus got under her feet, or messed with the sawdust she had just swept up from under Joseph's workbench?

The turning point comes when Jesus is twelve, shortly after his Bar Mitzvah. His parents manage to lose him in a crowded Jerusalem during the Passover, one of the three pilgrim festivals they would attend annually as a family. In fact, Joseph and Mary are a third of the way home, a full day's journey on foot, before they notice Jesus isn't with them. Mary must have been beside herself with guilt and distress, and her relief when she finds he hasn't been trampled to death or kidnapped by white slavers is tangible. Instead, he is safely in the temple discussing theology with the rabbis. Only when the initial relief wears off does the anomaly of it strike her. He's only twelve, a child, for goodness' sake. Though he goes home willingly and never treats her with anything other than respect, from that moment, in some subtle way, his priorities have changed. His first loyalty is no longer to her, and, given her strength of character, she isn't going to find that easy. She begins to see that there is more to this child than she imagined. It is a salutary moment when the roles are reversed and we learn from our children.

Mary must have been close to her eldest boy, especially after Joseph died. The firstborn son took on the family business and became the breadwinner. Then, while her other children married, as they usually did, Jesus stayed at home and presumably became her companion and confidant. Later, when he met the widow of Nain, he knew exactly how she felt.

Yet from the moment of his conception, Mary has always known that this special child cannot be hers to hold for ever. She must have lived in dread of the inevitable separation. If letting go of our children is the greatest gift we can give them, it is also the most painful. On the day that Joel left home and our church, where he had been music director for nine months, to work in London, I went up to his empty room and found a single plectrum lying in the middle of the floor. I sat in a heap, feeling desolate, and grieved for the church's loss as well as my own.

When Jesus' ministry finally begins, it is not at all what Mary expects. Her quiet, respectful son mixes with the rabble, makes the worst sort of friends and has a fascination for the wrong sort of women. 'Isn't this Mary's son?' the local people sneer. Her reputation is ruined once again, because of him.

On one occasion, she is so worried about him that she sets off with his brothers to find him – presumably to give him a piece of her mind – but can't get near enough because of the crowds. Worse still, a message is relayed back to her: 'Whoever does the will of my Father in heaven is my brother and sister and mother' (Matthew 12:50).

Was she stung by this apparent snub? She might well have been, but it is necessary. Jesus is not disrespectful, but he has to resist the attempt to keep him tied to her apron strings. He does not belong to her alone, he has the work of the kingdom to do. The umbilical cord is finally cut.

Mary now becomes one of a group of women from Galilee who leave Nazareth and follow the other disciples, providing for their needs, on a path that ultimately leads to betrayal and death. She can no longer intervene and make things right for him, pick him up and put him on her knee as she did when he was her little boy, save him from all hurt and harm, as we all instinctively want to do for our children. A sword is indeed plunged into her heart and the pain is almost unbearable.

As he hangs on the cross, Jesus sees it. His last human act is to hand her to his brother John for safe-keeping. 'Take care of her for me, John. Be to her what I would have been if I could. But I can't.'

She doesn't need to stay in that terrible place and watch his last agony, but she does, and presumably brings him some minimal comfort simply by being there. Finally, once it is all over, he is taken down from the cross and laid in her arms, where she cradles him one last time before laying him gently in the grave. This feels like the death of all the promises of God.

Yet disappointment and disillusionment do not cripple someone who has learned to wait and trust as she has. She too had her moments of resurrection. In the book of Acts she was with the other disciples, waiting patiently for Pentecost and the coming of the Holy Spirit, and she was empowered with them. She became a mother to the infant Church, a force to be reckoned with. Legend has it that when the persecution of Christians in Jerusalem broke out she went with John to Ephesus to help lead a difficult, touchy congregation. For the greater part of her life she was single and alone, a widow whose child was cruelly and publicly put to death, but she didn't wallow in her misfortune, or opt for an early, easy retirement, sitting with her feet up in front of the fire.

No wonder God loved her. But when a member of the crowd shouts to Jesus, 'Blessed is the womb that bore you, and the breasts that you sucked!' he responds, 'Blessed rather are those who hear the word of God and keep it!' (Luke 11:27–8 RSV) – firmly resisting any notion that Mary is greater than any other mother. Much as he loves her, he has lived with her and knows, like any other child, that his mother is not the perfect woman. At times she was difficult, at times demanding. Occasionally she got it completely wrong. But when it came to faith and obedience there have been few to equal her.

Mary is no bland or faded Madonna. Like many women in difficult circumstances, she is strong and determined, practical and resourceful – a survivor. She is every woman who has ever given up or lost a child, every woman whose 'yes' to God has cost them their all, every woman who has walked alone in later years, yet remained faithful to the very end.

Pregnancy and babyhood – the desert years

Life's tough enough without having
someone kick you from the inside.

RITA RUDNER

I had a Jewish delivery: they knock you out
with the first pain; they wake you up
when the hairdresser shows.

JOAN RIVERS

Pregnancy was not what I expected and I felt dreadfully let down. For nine months I waited in vain for a serene, contented glow to suffuse my entire being and illumine all who came into contact with me. I think the very idea must have been created by men, who, feeling they ought still find a pregnant woman attractive, confused the inability to move with contentment.

The first time I experienced morning sickness – now there's a euphemism if ever there was one for that dreadful, all-day nausea – I was gutting chickens and thought I must be getting squeamish. It was three in the afternoon, not the morning, and I was barely six weeks pregnant. Before we married I told Peter I had a stomach of iron and was never sick, but for a full eight months, I never stopped. I was sick behind every tree, wall and lamppost in our street, while tutting passers-by muttered that there was only one thing worse than a drunken man, and that was a drunken woman. Having conceived a much-wanted baby, how was it possible almost to long for a miscarriage – anything to let me feel that the sea had stopped heaving and I was on land again? I felt I was going to die of it, and was greatly reassured when I read that Charlotte Brontë had.

But once a little seed has miraculously overcome all the obstacles and successfully tunnelled its way through the female underground system, there is no turning back. As the pig said to the hen over a cooked breakfast, 'You may be involved, but I'm committed.' And only God knows what that commitment will involve.

Nausea was just the first in a series of never-ending joys. Gradually, as the flesh expands, the skin creaks, groans and stretches like hardened leather, then cracks into fissures from naval to buttocks. Folds and pouches appear in the most extraordinary places. Purple veins make their way to the surface, then fork, split and thread into dozens of spaghetti junctions. The teeth disintegrate, fillings fall out, gums ulcerate, abscesses form in every area of decay – but at least the dentistry is free.

I told myself that Joel would be an only child. But it is one of life's mysteries how quickly the memory of pregnancy and childbirth passes into oblivion. Bruised and battered, stitched up like a Christmas turkey as you are, nonetheless any recollection of nausea, indigestion, stretch marks, swollen ankles, high blood pressure, discomfort, embarrassment and pain as you have never known it, melts at the first sight of the bundle of hospital linen on your lap.

On top of all the discomforts associated with my first pregnancy, Abby sat on top of the cord and the placenta in the uterus, which may well have been comfortable for her, but meant I had a skull pushing my intestines into my diaphragm. I lived on antacids. The only comfort was that, since Joel had hurtled down the birth canal from amniotic gloom into daylight like a deep-sea diver coming up for air, having a second baby would be easier still. I was wrong.

Abby's near nonexistence has always left me with the feeling that she was a special gift. In the summer before she left home for university, grieving for her going, I wrote down all I wanted to tell her about what she meant to me, in the form of a letter.

Dear Abby

In some ways I wonder whether it wasn't a mistake to come to Ibiza this summer of all summers – the last before you leave for university and the nest finally empties – for this house has been our only constant home down through the years and it holds so many memories. If your childhood is anywhere, it's here, and that's why I seem a little overwrought!

I keep getting glimpses of you as you were, with a little melon-shaped belly, elastic-band wrists, wispy tendrils escaping from an excuse for a pony tail, and smooth olive skin, so beautiful I could hardly believe you were mine. I wanted to stop the clock and keep you just like that. But then, each stage was wonderful and had its compensations.

And here you are preparing for university, excited about the future, and here am I living in the past. Yes, I imagine it can be exasperating. I don't want to regret what has gone or use it to hold you back, but these memories belong to you. They tell the story of who you are today and that's why I want you to have them, for the more you understand your past, the more you can embrace your future. And there is nothing more I want than for you to see your dreams come true. I also want you to know how greatly loved you have always been, but I'll write it down, rather than go all mushy on you.

You were always a surprise from the very beginning. We never expected to have a daughter. All our friends seemed to have two, or even three, of the same – all boys or all girls. Mixtures weren't in fashion. We automatically assumed therefore that we would have another boy. So when the consultant came out of the operating theatre, and presented Dad with a baby girl, he was speechless with shock.

The indomitable Miss Baker, who was ready to sacrifice a night at the theatre for the sake of your safe arrival, thought it was due to the trauma of your dramatic delivery and reassured him you were all right. But actually, I think we had both been very much at peace throughout the entire ordeal, very sure that you were safe in your heavenly Father's hands. But your earthly father could hardly say, 'Actually, it's her gender that has reduced me to this state.'

And there you were, in his arms, long before I was able to touch or see you, staring up at him from a bundle of blankets, as if you knew already who he was. And if he held you then as I saw him hold you later, it will have been with immense pride and tenderness.

I know he gave you back to God, just as we did together with Joel, seconds after his birth. We always thought of both our children as a gift, not a right, a temporary bequest entrusted to us for those all-important years. I never realized how temporary that was, how fragile my hold, how much it would hurt to let you go, until now, watching you stand on the threshold of independent womanhood. What happened to the precious moments and days which slipped through my fingers before I could catch or keep them?

I had badly wanted to give you a tranquil, gentle introduction to the world. Joel's birth had been disappointing. Wired up like a battery hen, a state-of-the-art techno-patient, I was a victim of medical science. Two midwives moaned about their nightlife and their men over the top of my bump, pausing just long enough to deliver the baby, cut the cord and dump him in my arms.

But in the end your birth was wrenched from my hands with a violence which left us all a little breathless. Dad said that the young nurse who took you up to the ward was shaking so much that she could hardly manage to press the lift button.

'Ten minutes before brain damage. But we did it. Emergency procedures worked. Seven minutes. Isn't she lovely?'

They wheeled you to my bedside.

'We have a daughter. Look at her.'

I was aware of Dad's voice somewhere in the distance. I desperately tried to make some kind of enthusiastic-sound, but all that emerged was a groan. I felt as if I had been run over by a steam-roller.

'Make her look at the baby,' I heard a strange voice say. 'Otherwise she'll worry. She may think the baby hasn't lived.'

I remember thinking, 'Go away you silly old bag. Of course I know she's alive. Just get me the morphine.'

Throughout the entire traumatic series of events, from the moment I felt the cord come slithering down like a giant snake, as they rushed me on the trolley to the theatre through endless hospital corridors, on my knees, head down, so that the cord would continue to function and not starve you of vital oxygen, I knew with a certainty beyond reason, with a calm which defied circumstances, that you were meant to be. But I couldn't look at you then.

Later it worried me. I was terrified you might grow up with some deep-seated sense of rejection, because you were alone that first night, not touched, cradled or fed. But neither the pregnancy nor the birth followed the textbook, nor any plans I might have made. We were studying Clinical Theology at St John's and many of the students claimed to have been damaged by their pre-birth or birth experiences. I had visions of you in years to come confiding in a counsellor, 'I think my problems all stem back to the dreadful night of my birth when my mother didn't want to see me.' Yet I could not believe that a loving God would penalize you for what was neither my fault nor my choosing.

I awoke at about four in the morning longing to see you, but of course you weren't there. They had taken you to the nursery so that I could sleep, and being a perfect patient I didn't want to be difficult by asking them to bring you to me. So I waited in the darkness, counting the minutes until day, praying that none of the trauma of the past nine months would do any lasting damage.

I needn't have worried. You are naturally the most joyous, free spirit I have ever met. I love that unladylike laugh which echoes across the hillside here and alerts every crowded room to your presence. Never lose it. I fought so hard to preserve it. I love the way you have always danced, instinctively like an African child, in the dullest churches to the direst hymns. There were times when I was tempted to stop you, to say 'shush, sit down, keep quiet', but that would have reflected my hang-ups, made you self-, not God-conscious.

When they eventually brought you to me the nurse asked if I wanted to feed you, bearing in mind it wasn't always easy after a Caesarean. Joel had screamed every time I had held him anywhere near my breast and opted instead for fast food from a bottle. It had left me feeling a bit of a failure and a freak. The staff nurse placed a pillow over my stomach to cushion the wound, and laid you on it. You opened those heavily lashed, dark, almond-shaped eyes of yours and looked me full in the face, and I felt as if I had been hit, full on, by a tidal wave. I was shocked by the fierceness of the protectiveness I felt. It sounds silly but it mattered that you were a girl, one like me, a potential woman. I decided there and then to make the world a better place for women, the world you would inherit. I wanted you to have access to the moon, and the sun and the stars too, not to be earth-bound by artificial human ties. I could no longer understand how any man or woman could look at their baby daughter and tell her that in God's scheme of things she was an afterthought, second best, that it was a pity she wasn't a boy, for her horizons must now be limited.

Amazingly you fed and went on feeding, hungrily and happily. No screams, no rejection, just pure, untroubled tranquillity. 'I have calmed and quieted my soul, like a child quieted at its mother's breast; like a child that is quieted is my soul.'[2] The relationship between God, our mother and his, or should I say her child in this case, is as intimate as it can be.

He, no more than I, would willingly inflict pain on a beloved child. So, as I did throughout your traumatic birth, I entrusted you to his eternal care.

The only person with the power to disturb your tranquillity and sour your spirit was me. As I held you for the first time in my arms that suddenly seemed an awesome responsibility. There were plenty of times, when, like any baby, you screamed for no reason I could fathom and after several hours, I wasn't as patient as I might have been. It was later, as you let me know that you understood everything I said, that I realized that every cynical, harsh and unloving word would drive out spontaneity and joy, diminish confidence and tarnish the world that would claim you soon enough.

Your Great Great Aunt Lucy Guinness, a pioneer missionary and writer, who had her children in her late thirties and died when they were very young, wrote, 'What in me impels my child to rise or fall?' I have always found that worrying, but have tried to live up to its challenge, even if I haven't always succeeded.

Today you lie stretched out on the terrace in a patch of sunlight, flexing one smooth and graceful limb after another, like a cat. The future looms unspoken between us. You are poised on the threshold of a new adventure that may eventually take you far away from me. I am so glad that because of your faith you go with an openness and freshness, not with the jaded, haunted look of thousands of young women who throng the paseo *every night in search of some new, temporary pleasure.*

I am so proud of the lovely young woman you have become. Brains are a help in this world, but Dad and I always believed character came before academic achievement. We place you firmly in the hands of one who loves you even more than we do, as we always have ever since that day when you so nearly didn't make it at all. You go with all our prayers and blessings, as well as the crockery, furniture, bedding . . .

Mum

Babies and I never really went well together. As my friend Serena puts it so appositely, 'Some are born mothers, some become mothers and some have motherhood thrust upon them.' When the press announced a new phenomenon known as 'the mum-at-home breakdown syndrome', I could quite understand it. I didn't have much patience with another individual crowding my space, interfering with my routine and disturbing my nights. It all stems from my big Myers Briggs 'J', the personality check that tells me I value order and planning. Having the carpet, walls and every other available surface smeared with jam, chocolate and banana was enough to drive any woman, let alone a 'J', to depression. I was cut off, deprofessionalized, deskilled, depersonalized by life alone with a mini-tyrant inside four brick walls. And when I did go out, I seemed to become invisible, the lot of any woman with a hyperactive toddler imprisoned in a buggy.

I'm the sort of person who prefers intercourse with independent beings, capable of serious, mature conversation, who entertain themselves and then put their own toys away. That came, faster than I could have imagined. But meanwhile, I had never been so tired in my whole life. The comedian Milton Berle said, 'If evolution really works, how come mothers have only two hands?' There is no such thing as a nonworking mother. And I'm not an expert. I only had two.

The growing years

It's easier to become a parent than to be one. It's also easier to get rid of a husband than a child. A child is for ever, so the first principle of having one is to nurture one you like. But how? What blueprint is there?

> Like an eagle that stirs up its nest,
> that flutters over its young,
> spreading out its wings, catching them,
> bearing them on its pinions,
> the LORD alone did lead him.
> DEUTERONOMY 32:11–12 RSV

On holiday in France one year I watched, not an eagle, but a beautiful snowy white barn owl teaching her babies to fly. She lined her two up on a high window ledge, carefully explained to them what they had to do, then gave an impromptu demonstration – in other words, 'Do as I do, not just as I say.' Mesmerized, they watched her sweeping and diving, but when she flew back onto the ledge, they were reluctant to follow. They put out one claw, then the other, weighing up the risks, manifestly terrified of dropping fifty feet to the earth below. Patiently, she coaxed and encouraged them. She probably explained what wings were for. Then eventually, hesitantly, they flew a few yards, before diving back to the ledge for safety. By the end of the evening, they had developed a taste for freedom and there was no holding them back. We watched the three of them swooping and swirling joyously in the night sky.

During those early years of high dependency, children observe their parents and model their behaviour, uncannily, on what they see. Yet all the time the crack between them and us is steadily growing into a crevice. They were nurtured inside us, but become their own people. It is vital to relate to and respect that otherness. The first time Joel was cheeky to us, when we had barely taught him to speak, I was completely taken aback. 'Hang on a minute, boy, we decided to have you. Who do you think you are? You wouldn't be here if it wasn't for us.' But I didn't will Joel into existence. God did. 'And if we are made in God's image,' a friend said to me, 'then so are they. We need to know that with more than just our reason.'

In my heart, no matter how much I wanted to keep them at my side, I knew my children would have to fly, so I let them try out their wings almost as soon as they were born. Since Abby was only five when I went out to work full time, there was little choice. I warned her that if she wanted sandwiches rather than school dinner, she could make them herself. I can still see her, barely able to wield a knife, sitting at the kitchen table, honey from ear to ear, in her hair, up her nose, down her uniform, anywhere but on the bread. 'It's not that I like being sticky,' she announced one day, 'it's just that I've got used to it.' What a heel I felt, until she said with smug satisfaction, 'The other children complain about what their mums put in their sandwiches. They're silly. They should make them themselves.' So early independence wasn't such a bad thing after all.

When Joel was born I set off on a one-woman mission to raise the first real new man. If anyone could do it, I could. Imagine my shock when the Sunday school teacher informed me that my three-year-old son, when asked to tidy away the toys, had announced, 'Let the girls do it.' Where had he seen that? How did I fail so soon? I had to admit to myself reluctantly that this was a person, not a clone. Nonetheless, if I had anything to do with it, this male person was going to be thoroughly house-trained.

When he was a little older he was happy enough to conjure up the evening meal if I gave him a pound of mince, but heaven help me if I suggested what he might do with it. Creativity is an integral part of true freedom and independence. So we occasionally ended up with polka-dot casserole – black specks floating in a milky substance. Today, unlike his dad, he's a brilliant cook.

Just as he took control of his birth, Joel continued to do everything with gusto and determination. Our children may inherit our genes, our allergies and occasionally our neuroses, but they have their own character. All it needs to mature and grow and fulfil its potential is a conducive environment – protection, information, discipline, the stability of the parents' relationship if that's possible, but most importantly unconditional love. Above all else, deep in his or her spirit, a really secure child will know that love does not have to be deserved or earned. It is never temporarily withheld, never knowingly unkind. It covers a multitude of parental sins and failings. I think we have apologized to our children as often as they have had to apologize to us.

Affection and touch are the building blocks for discovering meaningful relationships and real intimacy in later life – for boys as well as girls. When I'm abroad I love to watch Italian men with babies and children. They adore them. It doesn't matter whose children they are, they cannot resist picking them up, throwing them in the air, kissing and cuddling them, while making the sort of goo-goo, gaa-gaa noises that would make a traditional macho man cringe.

For many centuries people have been hidebound by supposed male and female roles in child-rearing. But who defines what they should be and who should do what? The Bible gives no guidelines or advice in this particular matter. Making children and rearing them needs to be the parents' mutual activity and interest – which is why it can be fraught if they are apart. Peter and I discovered that when it came to comprehending our children and their very different needs, our complementary styles were very helpful.

When she was around eight or nine, for a number of years Abby had mega-tantrums. Peter tended to confront her and demand that she 'stop that behaviour immediately', which only made the kicking and screaming ten times worse. In the end he left me to deal with her. It took me a while to realize that she just couldn't bear to be seen to be in the wrong, whether she was or not. Any allegation of misconduct would throw her into a rage. When she was little, and even when she was older, if I took her on my knee and explained the nature of the problem with a cuddle, calm and good behaviour was usually restored. Again this is a tender, wonderful picture of the motherhood of God. 'As one whom his mother comforts, so I will comfort you' (Isaiah 66:13 RSV). He knows the most effective way of dealing with a wayward child. He never withholds his love.

Adolescence

Lullaby

Go to sleep, Mum,
I won't stop breathing
suddenly, in the night.

Go to sleep, I won't
climb out of my cot and
tumble downstairs.

Mum, I won't swallow
the pills the doctor gave you or
put hairpins in the electric
sockets, just go to sleep.

I won't cry
when you take me to school and leave me:
I'll be happy with other children
my own age.

Sleep, Mum, sleep.
I won't
fall in the pond, play with matches,
run under a lorry, or even consider
sweets from strangers.

No, I won't
give you a lot of lip,
not like some.

I won't sniff glue
fail my exams
get myself pregnant.
I'll work really hard and get a steady
really worthwhile job.
I promise, go to sleep.

I'll never forget
to drop in/phone/write
and if
I need any milk, I'll yell.[3]

At sixteen Abby was half-child, half-woman. She still laughed uproariously at loud body noises, English tourists with no dress sense, spoonerisms and parental faux pas. She blew enormous gum bubbles which exploded in her face and sent us running for the white spirit, flew kites, lay on the floor without her shoes on, oblivious to its effect on the scent in the room, and told me off if I teased her father – though she did it to her heart's content. All the most important things in life were piled up somewhere in her bedroom, if she could but find them among the mounds of files and papers, empty glass bottles and other clutter gathering dust on her shelves, under her bed or tucked in corners. She was exuberant, warm, curious, open, fun-loving, irresponsible, wide-eyed and full of wonder, head-strong yet totally dependent at the same time.

The secret of relating to teenagers is to like them. They don't actually enjoy being criticized. They get heartily sick of hostility, yet they meet it everywhere, usually from unpleasant elderly people, jealous of their youth and exuberance, whose rudeness sets them the worst possible example. 'I'm older than you, so I can be as unpleasant as I please.' Age is no excuse for bad manners.

I was spared any of the sullen sulking I was promised. The early years of companionship paid off, except that it still took time to persuade Abby that mutual trust and respect involved keeping her word about what time she promised to come in at night, and asking before she borrowed clothes, make-up, tights and underwear. My sister-in-law embarrassed my niece to death by calling her mobile in the middle of a crowded students' union to find out where all her knickers had gone.

Abby's chubbiness took a long time to melt – but it did, almost overnight, in one great hormonal explosion. No wonder teenagers can be difficult. They have such a lot to contend with. My friend Rosemary thinks men's heads are dislocated from the cervical cord at birth. She takes as evidence for her argument her lovely, pubescent son Mark – sensitive, thought-ful, raised and predisposed to be an entirely new man, yet whose emotions, she claims, still wander around like dismembered ghosts trying to find a body to inhabit.

I know exactly what she means. Every now and then, Joel and I had to have a lengthy discussion about what it meant to be part of a family. He was forever pursuing projects with such single-mindedness that nothing and no one else mattered. He has the steamroller mentality which earned his Guinness ancestors their millions and is shared by his father, uncle and grandfather, but if he isn't going to flatten out some poor little woman one day, it needs the modification that only the efficient, consistent workings of its emotional parts can ensure.

A daughter has different learning curves. I knew that food was often a bargaining point between parents and children, a way of gaining control and establishing independence, especially from a Jewish mother, for whom food is the panacea for all ills, but I couldn't stop myself getting more than just a little neurotic when, for a time, she almost stopped eating. On reflection I exaggerated the problem, but I was terrified she was becoming anorexic. I wish someone had explained to me that very few women become serious anorexics. Abby's faddy food phase, when she was around nine, turned out to be a sign of major distress at her primary school in Coventry. One day, on the way there with her dad, she had a major panic attack. Peter had the wisdom to take her back home, talk with her and pray with her until the matter was resolved. 'Oh,' she said, as he laid his hand gently on her head and asked for the Holy Spirit to fill her, 'I feel as if thousands of petals are falling down inside me.' The panic attacks never came back.

My mother always said, 'The best years are when the children are little. At least they don't argue back.' I didn't believe her. I was too tired, too consumed with struggling to survive. Could child-rearing get worse? Well, it simply gets different. When they were little and tucked up in bed at night, at least I knew where they were. But once they're behind the wheel of a car, if they're out a moment past midnight, a thousand terrifying images assault the imagination and keep a mother from her sleep.

It's so perverse. When they're at home there's no access to your computer, TV, video or shower. They invariably beat you to the toilet, are in your favourite armchair, in front of you at the mirror, and even between you in your bed. You wish they were out, so that you could settle down, just the two of you, to those newly rediscovered, more mature pleasures in life. Yet you must hold on to every wonderful moment of their presence, for you know with a sinking heart that the day will come all too soon when you long for them to disrupt your routine and rob you of your privacy.

> Oh, time! be slow!
> it was a dawn ago
> I was a child
> dreaming of being grown;
> a noon ago
> I was
> with children of my own;
> and now
> it's afternoon
> – and late,
> and they are grown
> and gone.
> Time, wait![4]

The nest empties

A Wish for My Children

On this doorstep I stand
year after year
to watch you going

and think: May you not
skin your knees. May you
not catch your fingers
in car doors. May
your hearts not break.

May tide and weather
wait for your coming

and may you grow strong
to break
all webs of my weaving.[5]

Empty nest syndrome? Not I. I'm a professional woman. I have my career. I always laughed at those who were upset when their children left home. 'I can't wait,' I used to say jovially. 'Life is far too full.'

Then suddenly the years melted away, the months became weeks, the weeks days, and then she was gone. It never occurred to me that I would lose a friend. Perhaps if she had been more difficult, thrown a tantrum or two, argued, spoken down to me. There were moments – but that's all they were – moments. And now I wonder who will advise me on my spur-of-the-moment purchases or tell me what to wear. Who will say, 'Stop worrying, Mum, it'll be all right,' when I have a house full of guests, set the table with fancy serviette arrangements, or throw together a perfect pavlova?

The room that used to be full of knick-knacks and bric-a-brac, piles of papers, clothes and lists is so painfully bare that it echoes. Oh, bring back the mess! I'll never complain again. Her scent still lingers – a touch of the Calvin Kleins mixed with a hint of foot odour. I don't like to think of her now, enclosed in such a small space. Her en-suite room at college is so small she says that if she were a boy she wouldn't have to bother getting out of bed to go to the loo.

I passed her bedroom door three times last night when I couldn't sleep and each time the sight of all that emptiness left me with a gnawing sensation in the pit of my stomach. I stood there in the early morning chill, remembering the comforting sight of the sliver of light beneath the door when I came home late from a social engagement. I would knock softly. 'Yes.' I would perch on the edge of the bed. She'd be sitting reading, then would pause to look at me, waiting for an explanation, as if I'm the errant child about to justify my lateness. Then she would relent, move over and make room for me to get in next to her. We would chat about the evening's events and giggle at the foibles of friends. Eventually I would prize myself away. It's hard to say 'goodnight'.

I blink – but there's no stream of light under the door. Will I ever get used to this emptiness? The books say you must bond with your baby – but no one helps you unbond. And this is for ever – the beginning of a new life for her. Dear God, please let it be the beginning of a new life for me, before I drown myself in self-pity. The past has slipped through my fingers like water – yet the future waits. My most productive years are yet to come, aren't they?

I am so glad now, as Peter and I look at each other across the meal table and come to terms with the empty spaces on either side, that I didn't invest all in my children. They always understood there was a pecking order, that our first commitment was to one another. We always knew that one day there would be just the two of us, just as we also know that one day one of us will be alone. It does fine-tune one's priorities.

I was fascinated to see this process from Abby's perspective. It was evidently as hard for her as it was for us.

I'm sure that the body has a subconscious preparation routine for leaving home. I have a great relationship with my family. I wasn't unhappy at home, but at eighteen, my body was itching for a new adventure. I was desperate to get out. My mind had prepared itself to dispatch and the escape route was university, a whole world of independence, an abundance of opportunity and a plethora of mistakes to be made and faced.

I was struck by sadness in the weeks before I made the momentous leap to freedom. Although I would be back for each student vacation, I would never truly live and belong at home again. An inbuilt grieving system was at work, thinking of my parents alone at home. I'm so glad I've left. I realize I haven't stopped knowing them. I've begun to know them in a new way, and it's better for both of us.

My parents have been faced with living alone together again after twenty-one years and they seem to have taken to it rather well. I feel I ought to apologize for coming home and interrupting their shorthand conversation to ask what the heck they're talking about. Aside from that, we relate to each other now as adults. They ask me for advice and tell me things they used to talk about only in code. I ask them for advice and still talk in code – there are some things parents shouldn't know.

There are things I have realized through leaving home. The way things are done in my house isn't the way they are done everywhere else. What has always been normal suddenly doesn't seem so logical, like why keep the wet and dry rubbish separate when the stuff to be recycled has its own box anyway? Little things they do, like never answering the question they have been asked, have become infuriating. My parents have foibles. They are faulted, heaven forbid. What's worse, they're ageing. How dare they? They're not old, but they are definitely ageing, and it seems inappropriate and thoughtless of them to do so while I am not around to supervise.

The woman is greater than the wife or mother

> The woman is greater than the wife or mother and in consenting to take upon herself these relations she should never subscribe one iota of her individuality to any senseless conventionalisms or false codes.[6]

Mothering may well be one of the most important jobs a woman can do, but it takes a very short part of a life. It must always take its place in the context of the rest of our lives, and never become all-consuming, otherwise what is left when the children are grown up and gone? It can be fatal to try to find fulfilment through our children. They are, as Kahlil Gibran said in *The Prophet,* like arrows from our bow. We have no control over their destiny. If they do provide us with fulfilment, it is a bonus, not an entitlement.

God forbid that I should end up with that typical Lancashire epitaph, 'She was a wonderful wife and mother'. I have told Peter he can put anything he likes on my gravestone – that I was a scintillating hostess, a source of endless fascination and frustration, an undervalued writer, fun in bed – but please, not that I was a wonderful wife and mother! We women are indeed so much more than the roles and stereotypes imposed upon us.

The Bible does not define men or women by whether they have children or not. Mothering is not for everyone, and the best mothers are not always the biological variety. My favourite Aunt Ida was unable to have children. It was a source of immense pain to her, but she became a surrogate mother to me. The unconditional love she lavished on me built my confidence and made an enormous difference to my life. I felt angry on her behalf when complete strangers would ask her why she never had children, as if every woman has the choice, as if it were any of their business anyway. I wanted to shout at them, 'She has!'

Jewish mothers can be masters at pulling the emotional strings. How many of them does it take to change a light bulb? None. 'Don't worry about me. I'll just sit here in the dark.' When I was baptized at the age of twenty-one, one of the world's most reluctant rather than joyous disciples, I thought I might never see my mother again. It was certainly the end of all her dreams of seeing her daughter marry a nice Jewish boy under the traditional canopy in the synagogue. But what I thought might mean the end of our relationship turned out to be its making. In time, and with great sorrow and reluctance, she accepted my decision. Now we were two individuals with our own minds and no illusions about the future.

The writer Susan Hill wrote, 'The moment you have children yourself you forgive your own parents everything.' I see now that life wasn't easy for my mother. She never had the opportunities she so freely gave to me. Her world was constrained by the numerous expectations imposed on the women of her background and generation. None of her intelligence, shrewdness and character was ever really put to its best use. There are women who cannot understand this or forgive the failures they see in their mothers, and it blights their lives.

Whoever we are, whatever our roles, women as much as men are all called to take up our cross and follow our master. Yet many women use the excuse, 'I'm only a wife and mother. God can't possibly ask anything of me at the moment while I have such an important calling. He can't expect me not to put my children's needs first.' Then somehow the 'children's needs' dominate the rest of their lives, and they miss their chance of speaking life to their wider world.

Yet who am I to speak about such sacrifice? I can't imagine what it must be like for my sisters in some developing countries whose children are taken into slavery or die of starvation. Mine haven't even gone to live abroad yet. Nor have I sent a son to war. On holiday on the Greek island of Leros one year, I deliberately went into the tiny British cemetery where seventy-nine British soldiers lie buried, having heroically lost their lives defending the island in the Second World War. I laid a stone on the grave of the youngest – he had been a mere seventeen years old – the traditional Jewish way of remembrance. Each of these boys was some mother's son, and had one of them been mine, I would have wanted a British visitor to give up a few minutes of their holiday to go there and say, 'We haven't forgotten your sacrifice.'

In the days of the great Roman persecution of the early Church, Christian mothers were forced to watch the massacre of their children. Their faith and courage are beyond comprehension. I cannot say what I would have done in their shoes. We can only take up the cross minute by minute and, like Mary, who said 'yes' and paid the price for it, trust that we will be given the grace to know our priorities when they are put to the test.

Notes

1. 16 January 1892, quoted in Elizabeth Elliott, *A Chance to Die, The Life and Legacy of Amy Carmichael* (Revell, 1987), p. 55.
2. Psalm 131:2 RSV.
3. Rosemary Norman, *In the Gold of the Flesh*, ed. Rosemary Palmeira (The Women's Press Ltd, 1990).
4. Ruth Bell Graham, *Sitting By My Laughing Fire* (Word Books, 1977).
5. Evangeline Paterson, *Lucifer at the Fair* (Taxus, 1991).
6. Elizabeth Cady Stanton, quoted in Margaret Forster, *Singular Sisters* (Penguin, 1984), p. 224.

CHAPTER 9

The Working Woman

It doesn't quite fit with an image of competency and confidence to break down at work and have a good cry in a meeting, not in front of a dozen or so hard-boiled managers, so I swallowed the golf ball in my gullet before the telltale signs of distress welled up and out and drenched the brilliant draft communications strategy my colleagues were shredding with such relish. After all, why let frustration, disappointment, humiliation, or whatever other emotion was driving me to display such weakness and vulnerability, spoil their fun?

I had wrestled with the document for hours. I'm a journalist, not a strategist. I love stories not theories, creative thinking not abstract planning, meaningful words not management-speak. But there is one thing I have had to learn about the world of work: no one these days ever says 'I can't', or even 'I won't'. Expediency requires chewing a 'Teach Yourself' book, swallowing it whole and becoming an expert in five minutes – with the jargon to prove it. On a positive note, this means that some of us are being stretched in ways we never imagined possible. On the other hand, the fear of snapping can make many normally pleasant people pretentious and defensive. As I discovered that afternoon.

I have no degree in communications theory. I let myself be guided by instinct and experience, as well as the manuals, and I thought my strategy was quite good. On reflection, I suspect the people round that table thought it was too, hence the barrage of negativity – from four females. That was what really hurt. Naively, I've always believed in sisterhood, a world where women have an unspoken understanding to support each other in the workplace because we're not as combative or competitive as the men. We women, I thought with a sense of our superiority, are relational, caring, collaborative, sensitive, supportive team-builders.

Not round the table that day. Four venomous harpies with bared fangs and flexed claws inflicted more than superficial wounds to my pride. I managed to stay calm and, at the end of the meeting, made myself smile and thank them all for their time and contribution. It felt like proper team leadership, not to mention Christian duty, but it left me with an ache in the heart – and in the cheek muscles.

My first major confrontation with female posturing had wreaked havoc on my unwitting, but nonetheless misguided sense of female superiority, and had left me determined to gain a comprehensive understanding of the underground currents that can make women unkind to one another. All of us had worked hard, sometimes against the odds and a great deal of male competition, to achieve the senior management positions we were in. Why had we so little compassion or encouragement for one another, and what did that say about the impact of women on society, now that few of the doors remained shut in our faces?

As I left my office at NHS headquarters that fateful day, feeling minced, boiled and bottled like a marmalade orange, all I could think of was that, after fifty years of fighting our way from the fringes, had women really come to this, to taking our hard-earned, unique contribution to the workplace for granted?

Middle-class women of my mother's generation never had such opportunities. Although working-class women had always been farm workers, domestics and factory hands, doing what was seen as 'women's work' – the jobs the men didn't want to do, as late as the 1950s a single woman who was a teacher, office or health worker would be expected to resign her post when she married. Some married women kept their status a secret for thirty years for fear of losing their jobs. Then came the 1960s, the contraceptive pill and a crack in the door into some of the professions and businesses.

This wasn't entirely as twentieth-century as it seems. There was, and still is among the most orthodox of Jews, the tradition that a man's highest calling is to study the Torah, so he is blessed if he can find a wife with the strategic ability to run the home and the family business. The husband with the ideal wife in Proverbs 31:23 'is respected at the city gate, where he takes his seat among the elders of the land'. What did these wise men do all day? They debated and interpreted the law, handed out advice and judgement – and left their women to be the breadwinners.

A vigorous woman is hard to find

A good woman is hard to find,
   and worth more than diamonds.
She shops around for the best yarns and cottons,
   and enjoys knitting and sewing.
She is like a trading ship that sails to faraway places
   and brings back exotic surprises.
She's up before dawn preparing breakfast
   for her family and organizing her day.
She looks over a field and buys it,
   then, with money she's put aside, plants a garden.
First thing in the morning, she dresses for work,
   rolls up her sleeves, eager to get started.

> She senses the worth of her work,
>> is in no hurry to call it quits for the day.
> She's skilled in the crafts of home and hearth,
>> diligent in homemaking.
> She's quick to assist anyone in need
>> and reaches out to the poor.
> She doesn't worry about her family when it snows;
>> their winter clothes are all mended and ready to wear ...
> She designs gowns and sells them,
>> brings the sweaters she knits to the dress shops ...[1]

If ever woman was capable of multi-tasking, this woman is. Among her lines of business are real estate, farming, market gardening, fabric design and fashion retail, to name but a few, and her prowess in sales and marketing comes on top of her outstanding ability as a housewife. Far from admonishing her for neglecting her family, the writer praises her for working from dawn to dusk to support them, and holds her up as an example to follow.

The Hebrew adjective *chayil*, traditionally translated 'virtuous' or 'of noble character' (or far too weakly as 'good' in *The Message*), actually means 'forceful' or 'vigorous'. A merchant ship in full sail was big and bold, almost brash. It ploughed its way through the ocean with such grace and power that smaller ships gave it right of way. I'm not sure that this particular picture of woman would really be a favourite in most churches. It hardly fits the age-old stereotype of gentle, acquiescent domesticity. In fact, in terms of image, it's more New York Jewish, upfront and direct, than mild and deferential.

The Proverbial Woman is no meek little creature dependent on the protection and provision of a man. She has her own land and her own bank account. 'Her arms are strong,' says the NIV translation (v. 17). She's a tough cookie, both physically and mentally, a shrewd negotiator and businesswoman, so woe betide anyone who mistakes her for a soft touch. Yet the hard-nosed career image and highly pressured life don't make her a harridan in the home. Her husband and children adore her.

They rely on her, for she is organized, dependable, even tempered and wise. She doesn't make them pay for the stresses she encounters in the workplace. Their lives run like clockwork, there is always food in the fridge and clean underwear in the drawer. This paragon of virtue does not owe her organizational ability, integrity and strength of character to management or lifestyle textbooks, but to her godly principles. Work, home and faith are fully integrated in her life.

Manifestly, this is not a universal prototype. Not all women have such financial resources, but I wonder why this model of godly womanhood has been so stalwartly ignored for so long. Admittedly, it's a hard act to follow, but shouldn't a role model expand our boundaries? In his commentary on Proverbs, Derek Kidner describes her achievement as 'the full flowering of domesticity'. It seems to me that there is a great deal more than domestic prowess in the text, but he was writing in 1964, before it was really acceptable for middle-class women to earn a living. Even so, he is forced to admit that this woman's world is 'no petty and restricted sphere', but rather, 'Here is scope for formidable powers and great achievement.'[2] I would add, both in and out of the home.

Doomed to be domesticated

Throughout most of the post-war years, the Church supported the secular, middle-class notion that a woman's place was limited to the home, whether she loved or loathed it, was contented or frustrated. In its reactionary fervour it often still rides roughshod over women's feelings and calling, limiting them to the 'restricted sphere' of playing second fiddle.

Peter maintains that the innate equality of woman with man, both at home and in the workplace, came almost as a revelation shortly after he had left teaching to go to St John's, Nottingham, to train for the ministry. He feels that due to the fall he was 'the victim of a deeply ingrained chauvinism of which I was simply unaware, and which wasn't highlighted for me until I attended a sociology lecture at Nottingham University. I suddenly realized that despite a good working relationship with senior female colleagues I still thought of them as earning pin money. Even then, a man can be very egalitarian in his working relationships with his colleagues, yet still expect a woman in the home to back him and support him, subsuming her wishes to his. It is a shock when she develops her own career and the whole structure of the relationship has to be reordered.'

It was as well that he had that revelation when he did. Within a year I had started writing, mainly as a way of getting my head and hands out of the nappy bucket. I had a friend who produced a Monday evening religious programme for commercial radio with a wide secular audience. 'What you need to keep your listeners with you is a serial,' I said to him off the top of my head one day. 'Write it,' he said. Never one to resist a challenge, I did. I told the story of my Jewish upbringing, my search for meaning and slow, dawning realization that Christ was the Messiah – and it ran and ran. Whenever the children were at playschool or asleep, at lunchtime, in the evening, in the early hours of the morning, I slaved over a hot word processor.

The serial came to the attention of a Radio 2 producer, and I found myself with a 'Pause for Thought' slot on Derek Jameson's breakfast show and the chance to write and present religious television programmes. One day in the bath, I said to God, in that state of semi-reverie praying can be, 'When the children are older, you know what I'd really like to do? Become a television researcher.' I had never really considered the financial benefits of work. Having been on Family Income Support, they turned out to be extremely useful, but were not a priority. I simply loved having such creative opportunities.

Abby had been at school a month when the phone rang, and the Head of Religion at Central Television offered me a full-time post as a researcher. 'What will we do with the children after school? How will we manage?' I said to Peter. 'We will,' he reassured me. 'I can be at home doing administration, and if I can't, someone will help out.'

The job involved a lot of travelling and occasional overnight stays. Peter and I had to learn to juggle our respective roles. Neither of our ministries was more important than the other. Each took precedence in turns.

On reflection, I think there were times when the children would have loved to be greeted on their return from school by the smell of fresh baking and a stereotypical mother, round and rosy cheeked, in cosy sweater and pom-pom slippers, with a dusting of flour down her pinny and in her hair.

'Why aren't you there when we get in from school like other mums?' Abby asked.

'Because Dad is. How many other children have Dad waiting for them?'

She thought about it for a while and ran off, satisfied. When it came to playing, Dad was always more fun anyway.

Peter felt he ought to try his hand at cooking, manifestly a doddle for a trained engineer, and thought that for his first little trick he might try croissants. A yeast and puff pastry mix for such a raw beginner? I described in detail the difficulties he might encounter, and he and a fellow clergyman decided to plug the gap in their education with a cookery course. They seemed to spend most of their time fending off questions from curious old ladies trying to work out what job would give two men a day off in the middle of the week. After twelve weeks he graduated successfully with a great deal of theory, but little practice. The problem was, he didn't enjoy cooking enough to resist disappearing into his study to do just a little bit of sermon preparation or to make a few vital phone calls, while the casserole was burning to a cinder on the ring. His lasagne was excellent, but it took all day to make and involved around a week's worth of pans, to the disgust of our two reluctant dishwashers. In the end we excused him from duty, except in times of dire emergency and desperation. At least he tries.

At the end of the day, as in so many other domestic partnerships, we discovered that ultimately there can only be one chief executive in the home – whichever one ensures that the children have clean school knickers on a Monday morning. Since that privilege usually falls to the woman, it is small wonder that 80 per cent would work only part time given the chance. A successful career has cost women more than we ever imagined. A survey in *Good Housekeeping* in 2002 revealed that 90 per cent of women believed that better opportunities had made life more pressurized, less manageable and less enjoyable.

'Women don't want to go back to the bad old days,' said journalist Polly Toynbee, 'but we're living through a tough transition period, a half-made female revolution where old and new cultural expectations clash to create unbearable pressures.' A woman's stressed brain, she said, was like a washing machine, churning with thoughts of shopping, dinner money, birthday cards, cleaning, ironing and a thousand other worries as they strive to prove they're as good at their job as any man. A friend of mine whose husband's pay was such that she had no choice but to work from virtually the moment her baby was born said to me wistfully, 'Most women's lives are a compromise, juggling to do the most they can with what they've got.'

John Drane of Aberdeen University says the reason women feel so torn by the workplace is that, 'Whereas men have generally inclined to put career consolidation ahead of idealism and intimacy, women more usually consider the effects that their lifestyle choices will have on others, especially those with whom they are in close relationships.'[3] The alternative for some career women is to forgo a spouse and children altogether.

Perhaps, however, the Church could make the most of the opportunity by providing breakfast clubs, after-school clubs and holiday play schemes, and by demanding more flexible working policies – to improve quality of life for men and women. A recent survey in the USA of 2,000 children of working mothers discovered that children did not necessarily want more time with their parents. What they really wanted was quality time – parents who were not stressed out of their minds, irritable and distracted when they got home.

Nonetheless, while Western men are beginning to come to terms with the independence of women, it is unthinkable elsewhere in the world. In Africa 80 per cent of the food is produced by women, yet they do not own land or have any rights. Certain forms of fanatical Islam deny women the right to drive, ride a bicycle or venture out with their face uncovered. Even in societies where women do manage to break out of the restraints that deny them their freedom and earn a little money, male fear and resentment can bubble over into dire and desperate aggression – such as in the Mexican border town of Ciudad Juarez, where, since 1993, around 250 young women, mainly workers in the American factories just south of the border, have been raped and murdered.

Meanwhile, in the West, despite many new opportunities, women are finding it difficult to get to the top and still do not have equal pay, though the situation is changing slowly. The latest Institute of Management survey shows a major increase in the percentage of women executives – from 8 per cent in 1990 to 22 per cent by 2000. Women now occupy at least 10 per cent of the top jobs in all industries except engineering.

Why can't a man be more like a woman? Gender differences in the workplace

We were on holiday in rural France, on a makeshift 'beach' in a bend of a river, cordoned off for swimming. On a platform ten yards out, with no verbal communication other than whoops and shrieks, a dozen twelve- to fourteen-year-old boys endlessly wrestled and manhandled each other overboard in the effort to be the only one left standing. Despite the occasional half-hearted warning whistle from a lifeguard, they went on throwing each other in, dragging themselves back onto the platform and getting themselves thrown in again for several exhausting hours, oblivious of any risk to life or limb.

As I watched this masculine, adolescent rough-and-tumble, I wondered whether boys ever grew out of it and whether, in fact, most of the manufacturing industries and management structures throughout the world are simply a more refined version of this particular game. Each boy was determined to be the last one left on the platform, master of his universe, and when he achieved it, albeit for a moment, he jumped and cheered and thumped himself on the chest.

It took a long while before they realized that superiority could be accomplished by cunning as well as by brute force – that creeping up from behind could be more effective than confrontation in launching another boy into the water. Whoever was pushed overboard was far less likely to pull their attacker down with them.

We went through a phase in the 1980s of believing that man and woman were basically the same, that 'anything he could do, I could do – and probably better'. It was, of course, a nonsense. His physical strength meant he was always going to win a race or a game of squash. By the 1990s we were beginning to accept the idea of gender differences and writers like Deborah Tannen, Professor of Linguistics at Georgetown University, were confirming that men and women behave very differently, and this is reflected primarily in our conversational styles. In fact, she says, women are often prevented from rising to key positions by the way in which we communicate. It is a very strange irony that one of our unique and essential design features, our ability to 'speak life', should become the means to deny us the opportunity to do so.

Some of the differences are biological and innate. Research based on observing children at play shows that boys tend to be more 'project' orientated, while girls are more 'people' orientated. After an hour, two boys will have concentrated so hard on the task that they will know little more about each other than they did at the start. Two girls, however, will have discovered each other's age, family status, likes and dislikes. The task will have been secondary to the relationship. Men compete, women connect – it was all in the Genesis story long before the socio-linguists became aware of it.

Those differences, however, are modified and developed by cultural and social expectations as children grow up, which is why we have to be very careful about making sweeping generalizations about men and women. Boys in a group become competative and play at one-upmanship. When they are out at night in a gang, they walk in pyramid formation. They boast, brag, swagger, banter, hand out their orders and hold forth with confidence, deploy any number of little strategies to ensure that, whatever they feel like inside, they are the leader and not the runt at the bottom of the pile. Men like my introverted, gentle husband always feel slightly insecure in all-male groups, unsure whether admitting fear and self-doubt won't be seen as weakness.

Groups of girls, on the other hand, are more likely to link arms and walk side by side. They make suggestions to each other, they don't give instructions. They don't want to be called bossy. They can't obviously boast, because all girls are equal and being superior isn't nice. They don't like to sound too confident or certain, lest they draw attention to themselves. So when they grow up, however bold or retiring their personality, they will have learned to adapt their conversational style to what is regarded as an acceptable feminine way of speaking.

That day at the river beach, when Abby and her friend Helena swam out to the platform to join the boys, they played a very different game. They sat quietly on one corner, enjoying the sun and chatting, ostensibly ignoring the performance around them, but watching, always watching. And as soon as the boys were out of the way, they stood up together and dived gracefully into the water. Deborah Tannen describes the way in which these dynamics affect our different styles of communication in later life:

Conversational rituals common among men often involve using opposition such as banter, joking, teasing and playful put-downs, and expending effort to avoid the one-down position in the interaction. Conversational rituals common among women are often ways of maintaining an appearance of equality, taking into account the effect of the exchange on the other person, and expending effort to downplay the speaker's authority so they can get the job done without flexing their muscles in an obvious way.[4]

The different styles have a major impact on the workplace. Men tend not to ask questions, as it may reveal their ignorance and put them in a 'one-down' position. Women do, and may be considered incompetent for it.

Since they are more used to vying for centre stage, men tend to appear more confident – although, if they are like my husband, there's a strong chance that the more certain they sound, the less sure of themselves they actually are. They ensure that the boss is kept informed of their achievements, prepare the pathway to promotion and then negotiate bigger pay packets than their female colleagues.

Women, on the other hand, tend to temper what they say, lest they be accused of self-aggrandisement or of sounding aggressive. We are more tentative, more aware of the impact of our words on the recipient and the feelings they might provoke. In the context of the NHS, a female doctor or nurse will usually be far less direct and forthright in breaking bad news. Women downplay their certainties, while men downplay their doubts. Since women prefer consensus, a female manager or headteacher may seek out the opinions of others, but that can be counterproductive, for it may suggest that she doesn't know her own mind. Not only that, but unless she explains quite clearly that she reserves the right to make the final decision, those whose views do not affect the outcome of any consultation may feel annoyed at her apparent high-handedness.

Since men are more used to aiming for the superior position in a hierarchical world, they will feel more comfortable about handing out their orders. Few women can deliver a list of instructions, no matter how reasonably and sensitively, without someone accusing them of being 'Mummy' or 'schoolmarmy'. The press said Margaret Thatcher was bossy. Actually, she *was* the boss. Journalists haven't yet criticized Tony Blair for being the nation's 'nanny', though many of his policies are equally, if not more, prescriptive.

The differences between men and women in the workplace are evident on the journey in. When we lived in Coventry, I was part of an ever-expanding group of women who commuted into Birmingham. We had an enormous amount of fun, sharing our holiday snaps, family anecdotes, favourite TV programmes, shopping haunts and restaurants. As the group grew, so did the noise. No subject was taboo and giggles soon began to turn into raucous laughter. Every day the same men got on the train, but they never acknowledged or addressed each other or formed themselves into a group. They stayed in their own individual little worlds, hidden behind their newspapers, and, as the weeks went by, their hostility became palpable. They moved further and further down the train away from 'those women', occasionally raising their eyes above their paper and half-moon spectacles to stare at us in disapproval.

This is the era when women's particular gifts and qualities, our people skills, our preference for teamwork and collaboration, are supposed to bring a new and welcome dimension to the workplace. This is supposed to be our chance to excel, but we still rarely make it to the top because men like those on the train dismiss our chatter as 'small talk'. It may well oil the wheels of the average office, but they do not lay any store by the relationships it creates. To those men we were a group of silly, senseless females, not serious workers, although we all went to responsible jobs.

So what are women up against?

A whistlestop tour through the images of the working woman as she has been portrayed in the media, that wonderful creator of caricature and former of false opinions, will give us an idea of the stereotypes with which women have to contend.

After the end of the Second World War women who didn't go back into the home, and even some of those who did, were seen as formidable and unfeminine. In the 1950s and '60s, big, busty battleaxes like the *Carry On* matron or the Peggy Mount house harridan were the butt of a great deal of fun. They emasculated weedy, wimpy little men. What had Ena Sharples of Coronatron Street done with hers? The man who put them in their place was regarded as a hero.

In the 1970s the idea of female independence was still incredibly threatening. Women only went to work out of necessity, and when they did they worked in shops like Mrs Slocombe in *Are You Being Served?* and were divorced, sad and couldn't get or keep a man. No career woman had any chance of a happy, fulfilled domestic or emotional life.

In the 1980s, enter the vamp. The powerful *Dynasty* woman with false eyelashes and shoulder pads to mask her insecurities clawed her way onto the stage. This was the Thatcher era, when powerful women knew how to squeeze a man where it hurt. They were desirable, but disastrous in the long term. The film *Fatal Attraction* personalized and polarized the struggle between the evil career woman and the good little housewife and mother.

In the 1990s, in *Prime Suspect,* Detective Inspector Jane Tennyson forced her way to the top by being as tough as a man. The roles had been reversed. The long-suffering men in her life had to compete for her attention, and her relationship with them was often subsumed by her passion for her job. Career success and domestic happiness were still not compatible.

The dawn of the new century has heralded a new type of working woman, who supposedly gives voice to the anxieties and neuroses of countless of her kind. Like Bridget Jones, Ally McBeal is the single girl with a big man-shaped hole in her life. 'Society is made up of more women than men and if women really wanted to change it they could,' she claims. 'I plan to change it. I just want to get married first.' On the outside McBeal is a legal bigshot, on the inside she is an insecure, vulnerable, hurting little girl with no self-esteem because she has no man. Life on the other side of the glass ceiling turns out to be one huge disappointment. Domestication is what a woman really wants, but the show ends and McBeal never gets it.

It has taken over half a century for the media to come full circle from a Bette Davis comment in one of her early movies. 'One career all females have in common is being a woman. Sooner or later we've got to work at it – no matter how many other careers we've had or wanted. In the last analysis nothing's any good unless you can look up just before dinner or turn around in bed and there he is. Without that you're not a woman, you're something with a French provincial office or a book full of clippings, but you're not a woman.' That old *teshuqah,* the yearning for male affirmation and approval, still pursues us and prevents us having the impact we could and should have.

If research is now telling us that the new, house-trained man is a figment of our imagination, could the media also be right in indicating that few female workers defeat the stereotypes and successfully bring a wholesome femininity into the workplace? To return to that awful day when my brilliant communications strategy was shredded by my female colleagues and I was left a crumpled heap, it certainly would appear that it isn't happening in mine. Much of Deborah Tannen's theory appears to disintegrate in the face of female posturing. In many ways it seems worse when it comes from a woman than from a man. It feels like a betrayal, for if our calling is to speak life to the world, we turn it on its head and speak death when we resort to the put-down. Someone's self-esteem, enthusiasm or confidence invariably takes a knocking.

A few days after that apocalyptic meeting I asked a colleague how she felt it had gone, fully expecting her to commiserate with me. She didn't. She told me how pleasantly surprised the female managers from her hospital had been. Fortunately, I was using the phone, so she couldn't see how far my jaw had dropped. What I had overlooked was that the communications strategy had grown out of the joining of two NHS trusts, each deeply hostile to the other. Her managers had come, fearing that because I had written the strategy rather than someone from their own trust, it would put my trust in a superior position. In other words, I had set myself up to be knocked down. Female egalitarianism demanded that I be put in my place for pushing myself forward. The men, quite happy with my apparent one-up position, simply read what I had written and took it at face value with an occasional 'Mmmm, very good' or 'Yes, that seems fine', while the women resorted to comments like, 'We don't use language like that in a public strategy,' or, 'Our managers won't accept that.'

In the end, my refusal to challenge their rudeness, my aim to be collaborative and all-encompassing, my silent prayers that I would not rise to their barbs or spill my insecurities all over the table, won the day. I had been suitably chastised. They were pleased with their achievement. The strategy was still intact – almost – albeit in jargon. On that occasion I saw quite clearly that women's communicational style is not necessarily superior to men's. In fact, it can be counterproductive.

Professor of social sciences Judy Wajcman believes women have no choice but to become more like a man if they want to be successful. Her comparative study of senior men and women managers showed that, although female executives were being encouraged in business school to forgo the more aggressive style, they managed in much the same way as senior men. 'Like their male counterparts, women find it hard to be soft.'[5]

All the managers who were interviewed believed there were differences of style – the male in terms of command and control, the female as more co-operative and consultative. A staggering 80 per cent of the men claimed they wanted to manage in a more consultative, collaborative manner – in other words, more like a woman. The problem they identified was that the culture of British business, driven by downsizing, left them with no choice of style. A tough market economy has produced a more hierarchical structure, more control from head office or government. One male manager gave a frightening description of what the workplace has become, but it explains a great deal. 'We have returned to the sixties' military style of management by brutality, shout louder, hit them harder and threaten them to death until they are frightened and they do what they are told.'

Wajcman concludes that in this kind of hostile environment women have no option but to conform to a macho ethos. 'My research shows that to be successful women have to learn to tailor and adapt how they manage to the dominant masculine culture.'

Christian psychiatrist and theologian Paul Tournier, who argued in the 1950s that once women became the bosses the 'feminine' qualities of emotion, feeling and relationship would be restored to every aspect of Western life, would be profoundly disappointed.[6] Deborah Tannen too, with her argument that men and women must learn to understand their conversational differences to become more accepting of each other's behaviour, would feel let down.

Yet, if Wajcman's assessment of our work culture is accurate, there is no doubt that if we are going to be taken seriously and embrace our God-given calling to bring Tournier's spiritual balance to the workplace and the Church, women will need to sound more confident. This does not mean we need to become men. Far from it. It means that, without resorting to black power suits, we dress and speak in a way that says we want to be taken seriously, and we reject the cultural conditioning that makes us apologize for our very existence. It means we stop believing or pretending that we are not confident, capable and gifted. It means we admit that in our hearts we really are the Proverbial Woman, vigorous, dignified and strong, and start to sound like it. It means we run the risk of being called bold, bossy and unfeminine, both by men and by other women.

There is never any excuse for not being gracious, courteous and affirming of others. A failure to acknowledge their status as God's beloved creatures is simply spiritual pride. But there are times when, like Jesus, we may find ourselves having to be a little more confrontational than we might like, particularly if we have to deal with an 'alpha' male or 'king chimp', and there are still a few of them in key positions at work and in the Church. In their need to prove their supremacy to other males, an 'alpha', macho male will enjoy having women who fawn on him. He is threatened by intelligent, confident, capable women.

I have been in national church situations where I knew my upfront, Jewish, nonservile approach was proving too much for one or two of the more high-profile men. My friend Chris, once a respected senior manager in Marks and Spencer, maintains there are two ways of dealing with men like that. We can be manipulative, flutter our eyelashes, collude and pretend to swoon in their shadow to get what we want. Or, when the lion roars or stamps his feet, we can remain unfazed and, using all our best gifts of communication, seek to bring him from a childish into a reasonable or adult state, hoping that in the end we will earn his grudging respect. The latter approach, though harder, seems to me to be more in keeping with the *knegedu*, or 'eyeball to eyeball' treatment described in Genesis.

'Women, if they but realized it, have such wisdom and negotiating skills at their fingertips,' says Chris. 'No man at the top will ever have to make the decisions the average woman will make in a lifetime. We don't need to become tough or manly, but simply put the best part of us – our adult relational skills – to good use. It's in a man's nature to want to dominate, but women have always had the power to help them develop a gentler, more egalitarian approach. The trouble is, we allow emotion to govern our reason. We think our power lies in their wanting us. But we deceive ourselves. Men want anybody who says, "I'm here for you, I'll be your mother." If we want to change things we need to understand that.'

Chris makes no pretence of any religious interest whatsoever, but this secular explanation of how men and women should relate is the closest equivalent of the creation story I have ever heard. Woman resists *teshuqah,* her need for male approval, uses her communication skills instead to help man yield his need for domination, and bingo, equality and complementariness. Thank you, Marks and Spencer.

Of course, the problem with making sweeping generalizations is that there are always exceptions to the rule. The 'alpha' male is only one small category of men – even if they have to be top dog, but then, both cream and scum rise to the top. There are all the other rows of men in the pyramid – the 'mothering' or 'nurturing' man, who often ends up in human resources (or 'human remains' as one of my colleagues calls it), the enthusiast, the introvert, the intellectual, the team player, the gentle and sensitive type, and so many more. Ultimately, we wouldn't want men to be anything other than male – certainly not an extension of us. Where would be the fun in that? But for a man, if he is honest, the higher he rises, the lonelier work becomes. He doesn't make friends as women do. He watches his back, his side and his front, and there is nothing more welcome than a straightforward, supportive female colleague he can trust.

Chris believes that, because they are more hardened to competition and posturing, men are more mentally equipped to cope with the cut and thrust of the Western business world. If she is right, then maintaining our uniquely feminine style – asking questions, consulting the team, treating our colleagues as equals – is more, not less, vital in the workplace, particularly in its present hostile state. The secret is to become more direct, more honest, more challenging, without losing our sensitivity to the way others around us are feeling.

The rights and wrongs of the workplace

After several years at Central Television I was wooed by a brand-new BBC local radio station in Coventry to present a three-hour daily programme. It was a flattering offer and certainly seemed the right move at the time, but within a year the station manager was promoted and replaced by another, determined to move his own cronies in. My days were numbered. It was a terrible blow to my pride, and a financial worry. As my initial anger began to subside, I realized I had a choice – to give control of my life to the new station manager and rail publicly against the injustice of his behaviour, or to place myself firmly in the hands of God, knowing that no human machinations could disrupt or deflect his ultimate plans. As I made a conscious decision to yield control to no one but God alone, the more at peace and the less bitter and resentful I felt. With all the dignity I could muster, I told my new boss firmly and gently that I would not allow him to break my contract. I also made up my mind that while I worked out my last months, I would not criticize him to my colleagues.

The hatchet continued to fall. One by one the other presenters found themselves without a job.

'You're better out of it,' my ex-PA said on the phone one night, shortly after I had left. 'The atmosphere is awful – weeping, wailing and screaming in the corridors. You didn't behave like that. Was it because of your faith?'

Meanwhile, Peter had seen an advert for a job that seemed to fit our identikit ideal parish. We had wanted to move back to the north, and now we were free to do so. As far as the children's education was concerned, it turned out to be the answer to our prayers. And a new career in communications in the NHS opened up for me, work I have now been doing fairly happily, on and off, for almost ten years.

Six months after our move, the new station manager of BBC Radio Coventry and Warwickshire, a man in his forties, dropped dead in the car park. No one will ever know what contribution stress made to his coronary, but I was relieved that I had tried, at least, not to add to it. The station was virtually closed down. Almost all my former colleagues were out of work. And I had learned an invaluable lesson – that in plenty and poverty, promotion and redundancy, God knows exactly what he is doing.

Nonetheless, while we wait with open palms for our daily bread, we are not called to smile sweetly in silence if it is deliberately withheld, comes with conditions, or is rammed down our throats by the human institutions that often make the mistake of thinking they own us. Too many women unwittingly play the pushover, but speaking life may mean standing up to the system and speaking up for justice and for the values that really matter.

There is no excuse, for example, for not being paid, and on time. 'Workers deserve their wages,' said Jesus, even for preaching (Luke 10:7 NIVI). The Levitical law says it is wrong to withhold pay – even if it resolves cash flow problems.[7] And claims for genuine injury should be paid in full (Exodus 21:19). Furthermore, Paul tells young Timothy not to 'muzzle the ox while it is treading out the grain' (1 Timothy 5:18), a Hebrew idiom, the equivalent of 'Don't kill the goose that lays the golden egg.'

It is ironic that the Church, which tends to exalt full-time Christian work over secular work, pays a pittance for it. Few institutions are more prone to abusing and exploiting their workers in the name of Christian service, killing off their gold-laying geese in the process. Why is a fee so rarely offered for speaking at women's meetings? I was once invited to speak in Bournemouth. We lived in Manchester at the time, a car journey of around six hours each way. 'We would be very happy to offer you a cup of tea.' There was no offer of expenses, a meal, or overnight accommodation. But there was a PS: 'Your husband could always drive you. We'd gladly give him a cup of tea too.' Presumably, being a helpless woman, I wasn't capable of driving that far by myself. I wrote back, said I would go for the price of a return train fare, and never heard from them again.

Admittedly, that was twenty years ago. Yet there still seems to be a common assumption in the Church that a woman must have a man somewhere paying the bills – even the ones incurred by the invitation itself – and that she is free and financially secure enough to do endless amounts of voluntary work.

Even a babysitter is entitled to a reasonable wage and proper conditions of service. Voluntary work is a great deal more satisfying if terms and boundaries are carefully agreed, and expenses paid in full. Of course life consists of a great deal more than its value in pound signs, and it is imperative for our peace of mind that our motivation and self-esteem is not woven into a pay cheque or pay rise. Nonetheless, there are correct ways of acknowledging a person's worth.

No matter how crucial the job, every worker is entitled to time off. My previous boss in the NHS was a man who knew how to thank and apologize – rare but important courtesies in the workplace. If he saw a light in my office when he left the building at night, he would knock, put his head round the door and say, 'Go home to your family. Whatever it is you feel you have to do, it will wait.' And he was right. It amazes me how often subsequent bosses, often female, have put me under pressure to work late, or an extra day, because 'it's absolutely vital'. Yet it is more likely to be the result of disorganization and mismanagement, and I am beginning to be a little less tolerant of picking up other people's problems.

Leisure is not an optional extra. It is a spiritual requirement. Observing a Sabbath is one of the most ignored commandments in our shop-till-you-drop society – at our peril! Rest and recreation were given not just for our enjoyment, but because they are necessary to us. If God set us an example, who are we to argue?

More often than not, it's we who drive ourselves – out of fear, guilt, perfectionism or a desire to please. It's hard having the guts to say 'no', to be the first to clear the desk and go home, to admit to ourselves we cannot live up to our ideals. With its compulsory observance for a full twenty-four hours, from sundown to sundown, Sabbath is a useful tool against workaholism. 'I have to go home now – it's my religion!' may well be worth a try. So is gentle but firm assertiveness. When she was chairman of a health trust, whether she was in the middle of a board meeting or not, at the official end of the working day and at lunchtime on Fridays, Rabbi Julia Neuberger used to say, 'I'm off. It's time for the family.' It was her way of challenging a work-obsessed culture, of saying that home was a place of equal importance, and of giving permission to her colleagues, especially the men, to leave. They found it life-enhancing.

There is a disproportionate number of successful Jewish career women. They appear much less neurotic about reconciling woman as mother and worker. It could well be that Sabbath has helped them to maintain the vital balance of work and play. According to the Chief Rabbi Jonathan Sachs, the Hebrew writer Achad ha-Am once said, 'More than the Jewish people kept the Sabbath, the Sabbath kept the Jewish people.'

Some seem to think Jesus put an end to any need for a Sabbath. Far from it. He put an end to Sabbatarianism – the legalistic observation of it – but he loved the Sabbath, that weekly opportunity to climb off the merry-go-round and catch a glimpse of what eternal rest will be like. To maintain our *shalom*, a healthy integration of body, mind and spirit, we need space for reflection and recreation, time to mop the floor and wash our smalls, and a chance to be fully involved in a local faith community. All are essential if we are to maintain our God-focus.

When I speak about the workplace, the most common question women ask me is, 'How do I handle bullying?' No one should have to put up with bullying at work. Recognizing it and naming it is the first weapon in our armoury. Other defence techniques are implicit in the life and words of Jesus. He was shamelessly bullied throughout his ministry – first by the Pharisees, then by the authorities. He was beaten, mocked, scorned, demeaned and belittled, but was never anyone's doormat. He was made a public spectacle, yet he bore it with a dignity and courage that left his integrity intact and ultimately earned him the grudging respect of most of his persecutors.

His secret is revealed in the Sermon on the Mount (Matthew 5:38–41). 'Turn the other cheek' does not mean, 'Let yourself be a pushover'. A slave would have been slapped across the face with the flat of the hand. If he offered the other cheek, his master would have had to slap him with the back of his hand, hard to do with any real panache. In fact, the master might well have looked a bit of a fool. Turning the other cheek was tantamount to saying, 'I'm not a slave – why don't you try slapping this cheek too?' As with the instruction, 'If he asks for your coat, give him your cloak too', it was a form of passive resistance. A man without coat or cloak would have had to explain why he was inappropriately dressed, and it wouldn't have reflected well on any citizen who had divested him of his entire winter wardrobe.

Jesus was the master of this particular art. Confronted by abuse, he maintained an assertive stance, never conceded an inch, and usually managed a short but pithy retort. I wish I could think of clever answers when I'm in that position, but they never make it from my mind to my mouth in time. Occasionally, simply calling the person concerned a bully might work, especially in the presence of a sympathetic public. Humour can be more disarming, however.

It would appear that women are less accustomed to conflict and attack, and are therefore less able to deal with it. The real secret is to remain completely unfazed, or, if that isn't possible, to look it. It is imperative, in the face of bullying, to breathe deeply, hold the head up high, look the abuser straight in the eye and never, never let him or her know how intimidated you feel. 'It is fairly exhilarating,' one woman manager said to Deborah Tannen, 'to be able to stare hostility straight in the face and manage to remain unmoved.' It took her thirty-five years to learn this particular trick.[8]

Bullying should always be reported. New working directives on whistle-blowing make it a little easier and ensure a measure of confidentiality, but it is always a courageous step to take. It feels like an admission of defeat. It means becoming the centre of even more unwanted attention. It risks provoking the wrath of workmates, for bullies will always have their cronies. In the end, however, going public could be doing countless colleagues a favour, for some may have been suffering in silence for years. It may well be a laying down of one's life for one's friends, a risk one has to take, and 'If I perish for it, I perish.'

This is especially true of one particularly nasty form of bullying – sexual harassment. Unfortunately, every institution, including the Church, has its share of sexual predators who feed their need for power by playing cat and mouse with every woman in their sphere, cleverly covering their tracks by pretending to be a domesticated pussy rather than the rapacious tom. It may even be the boss or the minister.

In my naivety, when I first began working in the religious department of Central Television I was shocked when one particular director, who made a public show of his Christian piety, called me into his office for some very unwanted prayer and attention. 'Don't worry about it,' one of my colleagues confided in me, when I sheepishly shared my concerns with her. 'He's done it to a lot of the women. We think it's probably his diabetes getting out of control. Just make sure you're never alone with him.'

That was easier said than done when we ended up on a film shoot together at the Swanwick Conference Centre in Derbyshire, and I had a bedroom with no lock on the door. I heaved a huge chest of drawers across before I went to bed, but spent a sleepless night, full of terrors, convinced I heard him outside.

One Friday evening some months later, after we had all left for home, he tried his technique on a woman in another department. By Monday morning he had been suspended amid a blaze of publicity in the tabloid newspapers.

The incident raised many questions for me about why we in the religious department had felt such a misguided sense of loyalty and sympathy that we had colluded in his behaviour. Of course his diabetes had nothing to do with it. Common sense should have told us that. Some were genuinely fond of him and didn't want him to lose his job. Others knew his wife and didn't want to upset her. Our producer, who knew what was going on, had offered his team no protection or support.

Unless women are prepared to say when they find touch and sexual innuendo embarrassing and uncomfortable, however difficult that may be, it will continue unchecked. Perpetrators will never stop at one or two victims, and even if the initial accusation isn't acted upon at once, the effect is cumulative and vindication will finally come.

It can take time to investigate allegations of bullying or sexual harassment. Meanwhile, if life becomes intolerable, or if management is not prepared to listen or offer support, then it may be necessary to find work elsewhere. In those circumstances, when dignity, integrity and self-confidence are severely threatened, there is no shame in walking away. That is the company's loss. One of our congregation, a male nurse called Alan, left the NHS because of a bullying superior, took a drastic pay cut and found a job with physically disabled young people instead. He is a different man. He has never felt so happy or fulfilled in the workplace in his life.

Give work your best shot

I would earnestly ask my sisters to keep clear of both jargons now currently everywhere (for they *are* equally jargons); of the jargon, namely, of the 'rights' of women, which urges women to do all that men do, including the medical and other professions, merely because men do it and without regard to whether this is the best women can do; and of the jargon that urges women to do nothing that men do, merely because they are women, and 'should be recalled to their sense of duty as a woman' and because 'this is woman's work' and 'this is men's' and 'these are things women should not do' which is an assertion and nothing more. Surely woman should bring the best she has *whatever* it is to the work of God's world without attending to either of these cries. . .[9]

Work deserves our best. The creation of the tabernacle in the wilderness required an extraordinary variety of workers: designers, engineers, managers, jewellers, carpenters, teachers, perfumers, weavers and embroiderers. Every skill is a gift, and each has its own contribution to the whole, however mundane or lowly the work might seem.

The apostle Paul tells the slaves who have become Christians at Colossea to 'work at it with all your heart, as working for the Lord, not for men, since you know that you will receive an inheritance from the Lord as a reward' (Colossians 3:23–4). In other words, don't just work because you're being watched and want to create an impression.

Every day, in workplaces all over the world, magazines are shoved into drawers, private correspondence and phone calls come to a dramatic halt, and lacklustre performers spring into action as the boss's familiar footsteps are heard in the corridor. Thousands of pounds of public or company money is wasted every time those footsteps retreat. According to Paul, Christians have a boss whose back is never turned, and therefore a different perspective altogether. It means they cope more easily with the frustrations of the workplace, the boring routine, the lack of supervision and appreciation, the demanding or unreasonable boss.

We may not agree with our chief executive, manager or headteacher, but having argued our case as strongly and politely as we know how, we have no option but to be over-ruled. At the end of the day, even if they are wrong, even if they are arrogant (1 Peter 2:18), they are paid to be the boss and are accountable, whether they know it or not, to the Boss of Bosses. Grumbling behind their back will change nothing on this earth. They're human, for goodness' sake. The truth has a way of coming out in the end. Resourceful as we are, women should be able to find a circuitous route round virtually any problem. Constant criticism, argument and the refusal to accept authority is wearing rather than constructive. There's a wonderful old Eskimo saying, 'Never criticize anyone until you have walked in their moccasins.' We can always do a better job than the next person, until we try it.

Giving our all unreservedly does matter (Ephesians 6:6–7). Christians are called to forgo the usual destructive cynicism of the workplace and live a radical lifestyle. We are being watched. God's reputation is at stake. And if we do have the privilege of becoming managers, there is an onus on us to treat our staff with courtesy and respect, not with rudeness or threats, making work as pleasant, challenging and creative as it can be (Ephesians 6:9).

Years ago, when she was chief executive of the Bro Taf Health Authority in Cardiff, I met Dr Gill Todd when I spoke at a meeting for female heads of NHS trusts. A deeply committed Christian, she had brought another young woman with her, whom she was mentoring and preparing for a future senior management role. The young woman explained that Gill would give her up-and-coming young managers a small geographical area of their own, so that they could get to know the local population and commission the health care it needed. It was a visionary, creative approach to training, and they respected the trust she placed in them.

Too many women who have had to fight their way to the top 'pull the ladder up' on younger female colleagues, instead of offering them opportunity and encouragement, because they don't see why the next generation should have it any easier than they did. Flexible working hours and allowances for childcare appear unnecessary luxuries that mock their dedication and sacrifice. Or perhaps they simply feel threatened by younger talent. This is not women giving their best. This is women behaving badly, jealously guarding their territory without sisterly understanding or compassion. It isn't new. Some early women missionaries thought their pioneering work so difficult that when they went home on furlough they recruited only men. More recently, a well-known female church-founder deliberately handed her 'baby' over to a group of male leaders before she moved elsewhere. Only men, she told me, were up to the task. Manifestly she thought herself unique amongst women.

Ultimately, Paul says to Titus, we are to 'adorn' the Gospel – to make Christianity attractive with our hard work, diligence, efficiency, honesty, loyalty, humility and all those other qualities that haven't been high in the popularity stakes for a very long time (Titus 2:10 RSV). Conscientiousness and integrity are no guarantee of popularity. The need to be liked is a terrible tyrant. So is ambition. They can keep us from challenging the status quo in the interest of our students, patients or customers. Who says the punters have to be sacrificed in the name of productivity, or even to fulfil unreasonable government requirements? We have a moral obligation to tell the truth, and 'truth is always subversive'.[10] Yet only the truth makes people free.

Sometimes, in the name of justice, we may have to look demotion or even redundancy squarely in the face. I once had a job I loved, but had to pack up my belongings and walk away from my office when my appointment was used to attack the integrity of a senior colleague, who was also a close friend.

Work can never be our entire world. Yet in a mysterious way, when it is sanctified, made holy because we treasure it as a gift of God, it becomes so much more than a job. It is a calling. A first-rate teacher inspires her pupils, a good manager instils self-confidence and self-worth, a caring health professional speeds up the recovery of her patients, a professional housewife makes her home a place of recreation.

We have been given the privilege of toiling in God's garden. One day it will be fully restored to its paradise glory. Meanwhile, we turn the soil and cultivate the flora and fauna as carefully and lovingly as we can, dealing with the briars and thorns along the way, knowing that the little bit we achieve is only a tiny part of an overall weeding process until that great and final day.

Notes

1. Proverbs 31, from Eugene Peterson, *The Message, The Old Testament Wisdom Books in Contemporary Language* (NAVPress, 1996).
2. Derek Kidner, *Proverbs*, Tyndale Old Testament Commentaries (IVP, 1964), p. 184.
3. John Drane, *McDonaldization of the Church* (DLT, 2000), p. 175.
4. Deborah Tannen, *Talking from 9 to 5, Women and Men at Work: Language, Sex and Power* (Virago, 1994), p. 23.
5. 'We Can't Take "Man" out of Management', *Guardian*, 7 November 1998. Professor Judy Wajcman is at the Research School of Social Sciences at the Australian National University. Her research, 'Managing Like a Man', was carried out while she was a research fellow at the Warwick Business School and published by Polity Press.
6. See Paul Tournier, *The Gift of Feeling* (SCM,1981).
7. 'Do not hold back the wages of a hired worker overnight' (Leviticus 19:13 NIVI).
8. Tannen, *Talking from 9 to 5*, p. 190.
9. Florence Nightingale, in appendix to *Notes on Nursing, What It Is and What It Is Not* (1860), quoted in Forster, *Significant Sisters*, p. 95.
10. Anne Lamott, *Bird by Bird, Some Instructions on Writing and Life* (Anchor Books, 1994), p. 226.

CHAPTER 10

A Woman of Experience and Maturity

Beautiful Women

Age 3   She looks at herself and sees a queen.

Age 8   She looks at herself and sees Cinderella.

Age 15   She looks at herself and sees an Ugly Sister (I can't go to school looking like this).

Age 20   She looks at herself and sees 'too fat', but decides life's too enticing to stay at home.

Age 30   She looks at herself and sees 'too fat', but decides to worry about it tomorrow and goes out anyway.

Age 40   She looks at herself and sees 'too fat', but decides at least she's clean, so she goes out anyway.

Age 50   She looks at herself and sees 'too fat', but decides it's too late to do anything about it and goes wherever she wants to go.

Age 60   She looks at herself and reminds herself that at least she can still see her reflection in the mirror, and goes out without her glasses.

Age 70   She looks at herself and sees wisdom, experience, laughter and ability and goes out to conquer the world.

Age 80   She doesn't bother looking, just slaps on an old felt hat and goes out to have fun.

Perhaps we should all reach for the felt hat sooner. I don't know who charted this female journey to self-acceptance; it was sent to me in the post, downloaded, I imagine, from the Web. I would like to think it was true, but I fear that, in our ageist society with its cult of youth, it may contain an element of wishful thinking.

As this world's pleasures slowly loosen their grip and eternal joys become more real and more imminent, we should, in theory, be released from the earthbound necessity to conform, satisfy and please. But I meet few truly liberated eighty-year-olds, largely, I think, because they fear the consequences.

A few years ago I found myself on the speaking circuit of a group of women's literary lunches, where the average age of the membership was around seventy-five. Those who managed to stay awake to the climax of my post-luncheon address were treated to a rendering of Jenny Joseph's wonderful poem, 'When I Grow Old I Shall Wear Purple', long before it became an almost cult phenomenon. There were loud, affirming cackles throughout – whether because they thought they were purple-wearers or still planned to become purple-wearers I couldn't quite work out. The truth was that a group of less likely geriatric delinquents would be hard to find. Their perms, frocks and brooches were utterly conventional. They referred to me as 'Mrs Guinness' however many times I told them my first name, and spoke to each other in the same formal, deferential language.

But if you can't blow a raspberry at the establishment at seventy-five, when can you do it?

'They're angels,' said an elderly lady from the hospital bed opposite a friend of mine who had just had a bunion removed. The friend could hardly believe what she was hearing. The young nurse subject to such admiration and deference had denied the older patient the commode several times and had been repeatedly rude and unpleasant.

'No, she isn't,' my friend retorted. 'She's anything but an angel.'

But the older woman had no intention of letting truth penetrate her reason and either destroy her illusions or galvanize her into assertive action. It was manifestly safer to live with physical discomfort and keep the peace, rather than threaten the nurse with reporting her to her manager, as she should have done.

Meanwhile, nothing disabused the nurse of her views – that all old ladies are weak and ineffectual, willing butts for her frustrations and passive victims of her anger. It is staggering that there needs to be a government directive to NHS staff to remind them to show elderly people courtesy and dignity. Even the best of nurses tend to shout at them as if they're automatically deaf, or, worse, speak to them as if they're children. 'Come along now, Gladys, let's just pop you into bed, shall we?' And they take an arm that quivers to order and 'just pop' her with barely disguised intolerance into whatever out-of-the-way piece of space is ascribed to her.

If I were Gladys, I'd tell that nurse where to pop herself in the most robust English available to a Christian, or swing a fast right hook. But Gladys wouldn't dare do either. A lifetime of ladylike subservience, of never acknowledging or expressing her own needs, of putting everyone else first, has left her defenceless. She submits to the indignity of being called by her first name, which she hates, and plays the nurse's game by pretending to be the frail, hard-of-hearing, helpless old biddy with the cracked, worried little voice everyone associates with old age.

Woe betide anyone who treats my seventy-three-year-old Jewish mama as a pathetic old dear, despite her shock of silver hair. Her voice has never lost its inimitable ability to shatter glass at a hundred yards. And she can still reduce the most hardened workman to pulp with her Thatcheresque gift for wielding words like a machete.

'I'm sorry,' grovelled the male manager of her local Tesco's when she complained loudly and in full about the quality of the service one day. 'The problem is the girl on the till.'

Now, if there is one thing my mother cannot abide, it is a pompous male manager who blames his defenceless, unsuspecting junior workers – especially if they're female. She drew herself up to her full five foot, looked him straight in the eye and remonstrated, 'On the contrary, a store is only as good as its manager.'

At eighty-four, my mother-in-law, a strong-willed, determined woman, used to snap, 'I'm not an old lady yet!' when we tried to take her arm to help her across the road. When her body finally began to give up, a junior doctor arrived at her hospital bed and said, 'We're going to operate, Mrs Guinness.'

'Oh, are you?' she replied. 'Well, it's my body and I think I'll be the judge of that.'

'Of course,' he demurred, a grudging new respect in his eyes.

There was an eighty-four-year-old woman in the New Testament who was equally outspoken, a wonderful role model for any woman who fears that the ageing process may creep up on her unawares and divest her of her usefulness before her time.

Anna, defier of convention

There was also a prophetess, Anna, the daughter of Phanuel, of the tribe of Asher. She was very old; she had lived with her husband seven years after her marriage, and then was a widow until she was eighty-four. She never left the temple but worshipped night and day, fasting and praying. Coming up to them [Mary, Joseph and the infant Jesus] at that very moment, she gave thanks to God and spoke about the child to all who were looking forward to the redemption of Jerusalem.

LUKE 2:36–8

The spirit of prophecy had been silent in Israel for over 300 years. The traditional view was that God would only speak directly to his people again in the dawning of the new messianic age. According to the Pharisees, one thing was sure – no prophet would ever come from Galilee.

On every account Anna defied the conventions of her day. She was a prophet, she was a woman, and she was descended from Asher, a tribe which had settled in Galilee. She even preceded the fulfilment of the prophecy of Joel at Pentecost that women would prophesy.

This widow was not a frail little nobody, a burden to her family and society. Anna had only had seven years of marriage when her husband died – much like my husband's grandmother, Grace. Grace was only twenty-seven when she married the ageing preacher and writer Henry Grattan Guinness. He was forty years her senior and their relationship caused a great stir in evangelical circles. But they were blissfully happy and had two sons, born when Grattan Guinness was seventy and seventy-two. Many years later, in old age, she would speak wistfully, with girlish pleasure, of the seven years they'd had together and say that those years had provided her with more than enough passion to last a lifetime. She never married again, but challenged the conventions of Edwardian society by going out to work so that she could bring up her two boys alone.

I imagine that Anna, like Grace, must have been a feisty individual. They must have been fairly tough to survive alone as women in their respective societies. Who knows why Anna chose never to marry again, at a time when it would certainly have been the norm? Perhaps she too had been married to an irreplaceable man, and felt that since there could never be a human substitute, God might now have other plans for her life. Perhaps, since there is no mention of children, she felt she had been given an unexpected freedom to serve God in a special way, and was loath to give up that possibility. Either way, God had certainly become the centre and focus of her being. She was one of a group of people like the contemplative monks and nuns of today who lived in Jerusalem and were known as 'the quiet of the land'. They had such a burden for the world that they withdrew from society and devoted themselves to praying for the coming of the Messiah. Most of Anna's life had been spent in worship, prayer and fasting, never knowing whether she would live to see the fulfilment of her hopes and dreams.

After all those years in the temple precincts, one day must have dawned much like another. Out of the corner of her eye she notices a young couple slowly climbing the steps with their precious bundle in their arms. She smiles to herself as she observes that special radiance of all new parents – despite the exhaustion and broken nights. She turns away, but something different about this particular family makes her look twice. Her spiritual antennae start to work overtime. Her throat tightens and her breathing speeds involuntarily. She cannot take her eyes off them as they continue their hesitant approach towards the high altar, bringing the traditional gifts of thanksgiving. Suddenly they are intercepted by old Simeon, who, despite the teasing and mocking laughter of the other sages, has always insisted that he will see the Messiah with his own eyes before he dies.

So Simeon has sensed something too. There can be no mistake. She can contain herself no longer and rushes over to them just in time to hear Simeon declare he is now ready to die in peace. Her stomach turns cartwheels of joy. She can hardly believe the privilege she has been given. Gently, she takes the precious baby into her own arms, then hurtles round the temple like a virago, calling out loudly to all the scholars and teachers and holy men and women who have been waiting and praying only for this moment. Mary and Joseph wonder what kind of an eccentric has taken hold of their baby, but they are too bewildered to interfere, and besides, he doesn't make a murmur. As for Anna, what does she care how others will see her? This is her moment, and as every cool and shady corner of the temple yields its curious, leaving their studies and come, one by one, blinking into the light, she holds the baby high above her head and publicly proclaims him the Messiah of Israel.

I imagine Mary and Joseph were glad to have Jesus safely back in their arms. Quite possibly they were not aware, as others were, since Dr Luke recorded it for posterity, of the significance of the restoration of the prophetic voice. It means that a new messianic age has dawned. Anna, daughter of Phanuel or Peniel, which means 'face of God', for it was at Peniel that Jacob wrestled with God, knows she has come face to face with the living God. In her maturity she becomes the first woman to proclaim to the world the good news of the incarnation.

Mature achievers and the tale of Beatrix Potter

Theoretically, once a woman passes the fifty-year landmark, she should be freer and more confident than she has ever been. Her children may have grown up, her expertise and wisdom is at its best, while her energy, if not at its height, shows no sign of running out. Even industry, unkind to a fifty-something man, is beginning to recognize the worth of a confident, mature woman. Even some daytime television presenters are now over forty. And occasionally, even in the Church, older women take centre stage, or at least pioneer new ventures.

Age need be no obstacle for an energetic, determined woman, motivated by faith and vision. It may even be an advantage. She is no longer held back by the sexual ratings game or by the need to please. The respect she gains is entirely for her character alone. Some of the most heroic women of faith have been well past their prime when God's call came, yet the timing seems planned to precision.

At forty-seven Corrie ten Boom was a sedate, middle-aged single lady who had lived a very ordinary kind of life in her small but much loved native town of Haarlem. All that changed in 1939 when war broke out and the occupation of Holland meant the persecution of Dutch Jews. She prayed a prayer not unlike Esther's, a dangerous thing to do: 'Lord Jesus, I offer myself for your people. In any way. Any place. Any time.'

During the early years of the war Corrie and her sister Betsie hid Jews in a secret room above their home over their father's watch repair shop, but were eventually betrayed to the Gestapo and ended up in Ravensbruck concentration camp. The physical indignity suffered by two sheltered, middle-aged women was immense, but their inner spiritual life remained intact as they prayed for those who subjected them to such humiliation. In 1944, shortly before Corrie was released, Betsie died, but Corrie fulfilled her last wishes by travelling the world to preach the power of forgiveness. Her ministry was only ended when she was in her eighties after a stroke left her paralysed.

Mother Teresa, surely the most famous Christian woman of our time, was born in Albania to a peasant family in 1910. She was forty when she set up a new order, known as The Missionaries of Charity, to work among the poor in Calcutta, in her sixties before her work gained any international recognition, and in her eighties when her public witness had its greatest impact. She urged every human being to smile five times a day at someone they didn't like, and, like Corrie ten Boom, attributed her life's achievement to placing herself entirely at God's disposal. 'Put yourself completely under the influence of Jesus, so that he may think his thoughts in your mind and do his work through your hands, for you will be all-powerful with him who strengthens you.'[1]

Helen Taylor Thompson was in her late sixties when she led the fight in the late 1980s to save a dilapidated Christian charity hospital from the bulldozer, not knowing what she was supposed to do with it. She was in her seventies when the Mildmay Hospital in London became one of the foremost centres in the country for the palliative care of people with AIDS, largely due to her ongoing struggle for resources and funding. Mildmay had one of the first mother-and-child units, where extended families of children, parents and grandparents could stay together throughout those crucial last days of terminal care.

New Zealander Colleen Redit founded her Haven of Hope ministry in her garage in Madras when she was in her twenties. Her aim was to try to provide poor young women – who had no opportunity of further education and no future except an arranged marriage and endless years of childbearing – with the means of gaining some financial remuneration. They were taught to sew and knit to a very high standard, and she arranged the sale of their wares overseas.

Colleen couldn't bear to turn anyone away, and over the years increasing demand for help and shelter from so many destitute little girls and young women gave her the endless headache of acquiring bigger rented premises. But it wasn't until February 1994, when Colleen was fifty-four, that she faced the greatest challenge of her ministry.

By now hundreds of girls were coming to her for help and the Christian Missions Charitable Trust, as it was called, was providing organizations like TraidCraft with some of its most beautiful items and its workers with a basic wage. Because of her reputation and dedication, Colleen was offered a piece of land at cut price. She asked for a month's grace to think about it, and on the very last day received a promise for the 10 per cent downpayment she needed to begin work on the large glass-fronted building on Lammech Avenue. This centre of creativity and hope for so many hundreds of Indian women, still supervised by Colleen, who was now well past retirement age, was paid for in full without begging, pledging or borrowing in August 1995.

My favourite older woman who decided to forgo a comfortable retirement made no statement about her Christian faith, but her achievement was so special, and her personal bequest to many so great, that I think her story deserves to be told. In 1923, when she was fifty-eight, children's story writer and illustrator Beatrix Potter embarked on a new career that would bring pleasures more lasting than any of her books, delightful as they are. She had no idea when she bought Troutbeck Farm in the Lake District that on her death eighteen years later she would bequeath the entire Monk Coniston estate – 4,000 acres of land, fifteen farmhouses and dozens of cottages – to the National Trust.

Throughout the 1920s, while agriculture was in the doldrums, the well-to-do came to the Lake District in droves, looking for holiday homes or building plots along the lake shores at their most picturesque vantage points. Capitalists bought up land for businesses, hotels and forests – unaware how corporately destructive to the landscape their individual pursuits might be. But Beatrix Potter could see it only too well, and feared that some of the most pleasurable pursuits would be lost to the public for ever. Despite substantial earnings from bestselling children's books like *The Tale of Peter Rabbit, Squirrel Nutkin* and *The Tailor of Gloucester,* she did not have enough money to buy the Monk Coniston estate outright, but knew, if she was to save for others the part of the Lake District she loved the most, that she had to find it.

Born in London in 1866, Beatrix Potter had fallen in love with the Lake District from her very first family holiday there, when they had rented Wray Castle for three months in the summer of 1882. Only in the countryside, where she could give free rein to her profound affinity with nature, did she feel truly, completely alive. She drew and painted everything she saw, with reverent attention to the tiniest detail. Even the common toadstool became an object of fascination, thanks to her pen.

The Potters were strict, strait-laced, rather unloving parents, who believed that once their only daughter reached her late thirties and was still single, she would devote the rest of her life to caring for them. Her success as a writer and illustrator was a shock to them. So was the announcement of her engagement to her publisher, Norman Warne. They were bitterly opposed to her marriage, and not a little relieved when her intended died suddenly of pernicious anaemia. But instead of playing the dutiful daughter, Beatrix decided to establish her independence anyway and in 1905, seven weeks after

Norman's death, bought Hill Top Farm in the village of Near Sawrey, with its breathtaking views over Esthwaite Water to the hills of Coniston beyond. 'My purchase seems to be regarded as a huge joke,' she wrote to Norman's brother, Frederick. 'I have been going over my hill with a tape measure.'

She continued to live in London, but spent as much time in Sawrey as she could, renovating the house and helping her tenant farmer get the farm in good working order. It was the best possible therapy for grief, and the next few years were Beatrix Potter's most fruitful as her 'friends' at Hilltop provided the inspiration for Jemima Puddleduck, Jeremy Fisher, Tom Kitten and Samuel Whiskers. But her stories always had an undertow – a bleaker side. Her sketches were delightful, but nature was not kind. Her characters were forever threatened, or even eaten, by hostile forces, and in many ways appealed more to discerning adults than to children.

In 1909 she bought a second farm in Sawrey – Castle Farm – with professional advice and support from a local firm of solicitors, W.H. Heelis and Son of Ambleside and Hawkshead. William Heelis, the bachelor partner specializing in land contracts, was very taken with the determined woman writer from London and soon proposed to her. Beatrix's parents were furious. She was forty-six and they were getting frail, but in 1913 they finally gave their consent, and she and Willie began their new life together in Castle Cottage in Sawrey. From now on, writing and drawing were superseded by her interest in farming.

In 1923 she acquired Troutbeck Farm and then, when its tenants died in 1926, she decided to run the farm herself with the help of local shepherd Tom Storey, who encouraged her to build up her celebrated flock of Herdwick sheep. But it was in 1929, when she was sixty-four, that she faced her greatest challenge. The Monk Coniston estate, comprising 2,500 acres of land around Lake Coniston, including seven farms and some of the area's most magical vistas and glorious beauty spots like Tarn Hows, was more than she could ever afford. But in 1930 she clinched a cliff-hanging deal, having persuaded the newly formed National Trust that she and they should each buy half of the estate, which would be theirs on her death. She wrote:

> Those of us who have felt the spirit of the fells reckon little of passing praise; but I do value the esteem of others who have understanding. It seems that we have done a big thing; without premeditation; suddenly; inevitably – what else can one do? It will be a happy consummation if the Trust is able to turn this quixotic adventure into a splendid reality.[2]

Managing the entire estate until she was well into her seventies, Beatrix Potter was a familiar figure in her tweed skirts, gaberdine coat, green wellingtons and battered hats, choosing tenants, collecting rents, repairing hundreds of dilapidated buildings, putting up fences, mending walls and supervising the felling and planting of trees. Willie kept the accounts, and her lavish spending on ramshackle buildings was a source of constant marital disharmony. But she was determined to do everything she could to hand over her estate in pristine order.

This was a woman who managed to gain acceptance and respect in an exclusively male world. Children found her rather formidable and unapproachable, but she was shy and had no idea how to relate to them. To the locals she was not a famous children's writer. She was just Mrs Heelis, farmer, Herdwick sheep breeder and supporter of hill farming. 'I am in the chair at the Herdwick Breeders Association meetings,' she wrote to a friend in the 1930s, when she was their president. 'You would laugh to see me amongst the other old farmers – usually in a tavern! after a sheep fair.'

Every summer Peter and I spend a reading and walking week with friends in a house built in the 1920s with lovely views over Esthwaite Water and within walking distance of Tarn Hows. Fellfield belongs to the Anglican Diocese of Liverpool, thanks to the generosity of a previous bishop, who left his lovely home for other clergy to enjoy. There is a restfulness and peace about the place that seems to sink deep into the soul. From the moment I cross the threshold, it always feels like home, and I often refer to it affectionately as my spiritual timeshare. Every year it seems a wonderful privilege to be able to stay there, and every year I'm also glad, perhaps selfishly, that one woman managed to limit the number of properties built in its vicinity. When Beatrix Potter died in 1943, her bequest was the largest ever made to the National Trust. She had effectively saved the Coniston area from the few with means who would have exploited it, for the many without means who dearly love it.

Beatrix Potter simply did what she had to do, and was fortunate enough to have the vision and resources to do it. Helen Taylor Thompson, Mother Teresa, Corrie ten Boom and Colleen Redit had no financial resources when they committed themselves to their life's grand projects, yet they succeeded all the same. When asked by a health authority official how she intended to raise the money to save the Mildmay Hospital, Helen Taylor Thompson said quite simply, 'I get down on my knees and I pray, then I get up and I work.' All these women seem to have worked harder past their retirement age than before it. I think that's why it's probably a good idea, as one gets older, to cut oneself free from ties and be ready for the truly great adventure.

Losses and compensations

There is so much more I would like to achieve and so little time left in which to do it. When I was younger I thought that the mind would adjust automatically to the changes in the body. But it doesn't, and I'm left in an almost permanent state of shock – especially when I catch sight of myself in a passing car or shop window and wonder who the old bag with the saggy skin can be.

One of the nice things about growing older is that the old *teshuqah* begins to lose its power, and there is no need to worry about being attractive to men any more – except one, if we're fortunate to have one, and such odd things are happening to his own body that he doesn't seem too concerned about what's happening to yours. Men swell and droop, moult and sprout every bit as much as, if not more than, a woman, and they find it just as hard to admit that they're not quite the fine specimen they thought they were at thirty-five. My mother-in-law once said to me that you know he's getting old when you say, 'Darling, let's go upstairs and make love,' and he says, 'Sorry, my love, which shall I do? Because I can't manage both any more.'

There is a wonderful justice in the story about the couple who, at fifty, are celebrating their silver wedding. During the celebration a fairy appears (you can tell this isn't a Christian story!) and says that because they've been such a loving couple she will give them each a wish.

'I'd like to travel the world,' says the wife.

One wave of the magic wand, and poof! she has the tickets in her hand.

As his turn comes, the husband pauses for a moment, then says, 'I'd like to travel round the world too – with a woman thirty years younger than me.'

The fairy waves her wand, and poof! he's eighty.

Apart from taking short breaks in Sidmouth and Hove, where the average age of the population seems to be about eighty, I don't know many easy ways of feeling young. Abby and I went shopping for bikinis before our Ibiza holiday this year and tried on the few we could find designed for what appear to be misshapes like us, who don't fit into standard sizes. We both seem to be expanding in the upper regions in a quite unexpected and unwanted manner – she because of university food, I because I'm at that post-menopausal stage when my flesh seems to be realigning itself.

I breathed in, held my breath and almost went purple, but couldn't manage to kid either Abby or myself that I looked anything other than a middle-aged woman who knew she had lost the battle with gravity, but thought, 'Stuff it anyway.' Abby had just heard one of those intimate heart-to-heart talks on Radio 4 by a woman who said she knew the moment the two-piece had to give way to the one-piece. 'She was just your age, Mum,' she said encouragingly. I am suddenly confronted by another experience that mother and daughter can no longer share together. Bye bye, bikini. Another bereavement I can't escape.

Yet there are small bereavements almost from the moment we are born. I remember being surprised when, at eight, Abby told me she missed so many childhood things she was no longer allowed to do because of being grown up. 'You can't suck your thumb in public, or take your comfort rag to school, or be sick on the floor, because everyone thinks you should be old enough to be sick in the toilet.'

I shall simply have to get used to the losses, kiss them sadly goodbye – and dwell on the daily compensations instead. Besides, I still have my moments. Abby and I were shopping in the more sophisticated atmosphere of Ibiza town, where those gorgeous grey-haired continental men with the lean and weatherbeaten good looks know how to value experience and maturity. *'Guapa, guapa,'* we heard behind us, 'Pretty, pretty,' whispered unmistakably into my ear. I turned, fully expecting to see a sophisticated, muscular Spaniard with wonderful eyes and a fine jawline, but found instead two bald-headed, heavily jowelled old boys with paunches, who looked as if they had about 160 years between them, nodding at me appreciatively. Abby had hysterics and they fled.

After all, what is attractiveness? I was fascinated by a recent TV documentary on the face written by John Cleese. He interviewed an American consultant in plastic surgery who was distressed that when he tried to repair congenitally malformed faces, he seemed to make matters worse, not better. So he set off on a quest to discover what constituted beauty, gathered thousands of photographs of so-called beautiful people of every race and nationality, and came up with a prototype of the perfect face. With their large eyes, full mouths, dainty chins and well-proportioned features, many current celebrity faces fitted his model exactly. But, as John Cleese pointed out, and I couldn't have put it more succinctly if I'd tried, today's celebrity status symbols are little more than pond life. Pop and film stars, footballers and TV presenters have done little worthy of fame. Nor have they made any contribution to a beauty that will not survive much past their thirtieth birthday.

He then went on to examine photographs of Nelson Mandela, Mother Teresa, Gandhi and other genuine superstars, people whose faces radiated the strength and beauty of their characters. They were compelling, profound and wonderful faces, proving that attractiveness involves so much more than society's limited, superficial, skin-deep definition. These characters had put a great deal of unwitting effort into creating the crevices, cracks and laughter lines that constituted the faces of their later years. By the time we're seventy, every wrinkle reflects the prevailing emotions in our lives – strength, bitterness, joy, anger, malice, love, purity, achievement and failure. The face is a visible diary or record of all we have felt and done throughout our lives. Ugliness and attractiveness go on growing. Neither dies before their owner.

I am currently wearing a bolshie T-shirt that has 'No, it is NOT my age' stretched across its front. Thence I shall graduate into a delinquent, eccentric geriatric with long hair, big dangly earrings, floaty skirts and outrageous boots, exploring and enjoying all the freedoms denied me by my various roles as respectable worker, mother and minister's wife. I want to be more liberated, not more tied or restricted in later life, but I suspect that's easier said than done. Even as we age we're confronted with a host of expectations – to care for the grandchildren, become tireless at voluntary work, wear appropriate, dull and rather boring clothes, and to submit to the frail, helpless, faded image thrust upon us by our ageist society.

How do we prevent creeping decrepitude? Wearing a bikini may be one last defiance, but it is a bit like King Canute holding back the waves. Abby is convinced there are a number of obvious ways of giving away our age that post-menstrual women often fail to see. She has created this little test. If periods have become a thing of the past, simply tick which of the fashion no-nos listed below apply to you and discover how young and free you really are.

Abby's Fashion No-Nos for Older Women

- ☞ Large floral or paisley patterns
- ☞ Leggings, with a jumper that doesn't cover your front and behind
- ☞ Leggings with court shoes
- ☞ Ski pants
- ☞ Mid-calf-length skirts, especially pleated
- ☞ Tracksuits worn as a set, especially velour
- ☞ Clothes through which underwear shows
- ☞ Waistbands really high on the waist
- ☞ Boobs that hang below your waistline—get a better bra
- ☞ Orthopaedic shoes—no matter how comfortable they are, they're gross
- ☞ Shoes with tassels on them
- ☞ Boots with a fur trim
- ☞ Fluffy slippers
- ☞ Woolly tights without lycra in them—they ruckle at the ankle
- ☞ Pop socks—they were never cool
- ☞ Drawn-on eyebrows
- ☞ Hairy armpits
- ☞ Blue rinses and tight perms
- ☞ Gold handbags
- ☞ Long pearl beads or necklaces—especially when tied in a knot

---

Two ticks or fewer? You're a marvel, a twenty-year-old in mind and body. Three to four ticks? Then, like me, you need to get a grip on your image and your wardrobe to spice up your life and be ready for a new challenge. More than four ticks? Abby thinks you're past it.

It's never too late to create long-term goals

Get even. Live long enough to be a source of aggravation and anxiety to your children.

BUMPER STICKER

What sort of a life do we want? As we get older, priorities and perspectives change. What seemed important once isn't any more. In her lovely book *Bird by Bird*, American writer Anne Lamott says, 'To live as if we are dying can set us free. Dying people teach you to pay attention, to forgive and not to sweat about the small things.'[3] The tragic terrorist attacks in New York and Washington in September 2001 were a salutary reminder of how frail the cords are that attach us to this life.

When the NHS was rejigged yet again, one or two of my female colleagues, a little younger than I am, ended up jostling for power. They rushed round in ever more demented circles, giving every hour to their work, determined to become senior executives. All power to their elbows, I said to myself. I was just glad it wasn't me. Those of us who were a little older sat and watched them with admiration, and not just a little amazement. For us, it just didn't seem worth the effort. We felt there were other calls on our time and commitment, a world of voluntary work and family pleasures, as well as a career.

Then suddenly the door swung open for me, without so much as a tiny push. In fact, it felt as though I had fallen through it, and landed, like Alice in Wonderland, in a senior management job with a bump, a shock and a sense of semi-horror. Even now, my predicament leaves me vaguely schizoid – excited at the challenges of landing, unsought, such a responsible job at my stage of life, and lamenting the freedoms of part-time paid work.

Women have always tended to have very different objectives and goals from men. They will say to someone who admits that their job hasn't been well paid, who were never promoted and have a tiny pension, 'As long as you're happy, that's all that counts.' I have never heard a man respond like that. Men measure achievement in much more obvious ways. For a man, size is always important. Peter finds it difficult that some of his male colleagues seem to judge one another by the numerical size of their respective churches. Churches are big or small for all kinds of reasons, first and foremost because of geographical location. A church in inner-city Liverpool is never going to grow as fast as a church in southern suburbia. Size is no indicator of success; it can be a very erroneous measure.

But if a person has no goals, nor will they achieve them. Men plan, remain focused, and quite often succeed in their aims, even though their drivenness may drive the women in their orbit to despair along the way. 'You can't stop Niagara,' my mother-in-law used to lament, when my father-in-law had launched himself into yet another project. He was still in full flow, finalizing the details and handing out his orders on his death bed.

Women, however, because of our many interests, are not quite so good at having identifiable objectives. We say things like, 'Well, I might try to become the managing director, but, on the other hand, I might have another baby.' We don't always allow for a strong sense of calling, and, if we're not careful, one day can follow another without foresight or focus. I have met very few women who had any idea of what they wanted to do with their retirement. 'Well, I'll just have a holiday, then I'll paint the house, and then I'll just see.' I can guarantee, if there is a man in their lives, 'just seeing' will be an endless round of cleaning, cooking and baking.

Mother Teresa and Corrie ten Boom, like Anna, were single. Colleen Redit has never married. Helen Taylor Thompson has a very supportive husband. But what they all share are dreams, ambitions and a vision for the kingdom of God that extends far beyond the temporary goals of career success and watching children grow up.

As responsibilities fall away, the latter years are a time of unprecedented opportunity, when we can renew, or receive for the first time, a sense of calling. It isn't fair of daughters to see their mother simply as the means to their own freedom, so that they can go out to work. A grandmother may be delighted to childmind, but it is also her right to say 'no'. This is a long-awaited chance to be and do and see. That's why we need to know the right 'yes' for us, otherwise we'll end up saying 'yes' instead to all the endless distractions.

And if Mother says no, she means no. That sounds like an invective against rape – but women always have to be firm in the face of bullying. It is no more acceptable for a daughter to bully her mother than for a mother to bully her child, yet time and time again I have seen grandmothers subjected to emotional blackmail of the worst kind by a daughter who thinks she is totally committed to equality for women. She hints that if Mother will not agree to her demands, the grandchild – that most precious of joys in the whole world – might be removed altogether. Desperate for the grandmother though it is, the daughter's loss is far greater. She's cutting herself off from the only woman in the world who will never tire of hearing her brag endlessly about her child. She is denying her child a life-enhancing relationship.

This is how Abby describes the importance of her grannies in her life.

Grannies are great inventions. Both my grandfathers died when I was young, so my grannies became my main education and entertainment.

My paternal grandmother was a wise and witty woman. I wasn't sad when she died as she was old, ill and ready, confident of her destination. It was about a week later when I cried, remembering how we had made earrings out of string and gems from her button box, how I would eat salad only for her because she would make it into a clock face and test me on my telling the time.

Her recipes for cheese dreams, curried eggs and 'boiled Granny dressing' are part of our family tradition. I always felt a little timid in her five-foot-ten presence, but could never hear enough about her Canadian childhood and wartime motherhood. I used to gaze in wonder at her papery skin, infinitely soft and traced with thousands of sunshine lines. Everyone always said she was a real lady. Her memory makes me hope I will be remembered in that way when I am gone. How wonderful for people to discuss your life with admiration and slight envy.

It was she who impressed on me the importance of etiquette. The word 'ladylike' began to haunt me when I sat, ate, talked or walked. I have to admit I'm grateful for it now, just as I'm grateful for being beaten hands down at Scrabble by one Granny and at Kaluki by the other.

The 'other', my mother's mother, is very different and she is still very much alive, which is useful. One evening, when I was very small, I stood in my favourite Andy Pandy pyjamas and watched eagerly as she prepared for bed. When she finally turned and asked what I wanted, I said, 'I'm waiting for you to take your teeth out.' She thought it was very funny, but then, all my friends' grannies had false teeth and it was a great disappointment to find that I was unlucky enough to have a granny whose teeth were all her own. However, she too is armed with recipes that no one else can imitate: we live for her chopped herring and chopped liver, not to mention the gefüllte fish and chicken soup. The routine evening cuddle is completely reliable, but quickly forgotten when the cards come out with the coppers for betting. There were private celebrations when I grew taller than her, there will be public ones when I finally win a round of Kaluki.

Being a grandparent seems to turn the least sentimental women into fond and doting softies, showing off their photographs at any and every opportunity, as if it is some kind of infectious disease. I hereby vow I will never do it. As the possibility draws ever nearer, I know I will.

Woman as mentor and role model

> Teach the older women to be reverent in the way they live, not to be slanderers or addicted to much wine, but to teach what is good. Then they can train the younger women to love their husbands and children, to be self-controlled and pure, to be busy at home, to be kind, and to be subject to their husbands, so that no one will malign the word of God.
>
> TITUS 2:3–5

Timothy encourages older women to be role models and to train younger women. That means, he says, that they will have to forgo the malice and booze that appear to be the weaknesses of their later years.

The Greek word used for 'to train' is an unusual word. *Sophronizo* means 'to bring to their senses'. According to Gordon Fee, Paul is still smarting here about the problem with those misinformed young women in Ephesus who were using their sexual attractions to lead young men astray. He hopes that the older women will get alongside them, show them how to abandon their pagan ways, and make them 'wise up to their responsibilities'.[4]

There aren't many role models for young women in today's Church and its literature. In a recent book for church leaders called *Leaders on Leadership,* editor George Barna openly admits to believing in women's leadership. In a chapter called *What Leaders Do,* one of his contributors, Kenneth Gangel, calls on male church leaders to learn from the way women lead, so that, 'The newly interractive leadership style can be valued and rewarded as highly as the command-and-control style has been for decades.' So far so good. There's just one problem. There isn't a single female contributor to the book, so that for many women the gulf between what is written there and what it actually says is too wide to span.

When Ruth, our church youth and children's worker, recently helped lead a training day for future leaders, several participators expressed surprise afterwards that Peter had given her such a key speaking role. Ruth was taken aback by their reaction. 'I think in their hearts they were still expecting the inevitable moment when he or another male leader would say "Ruth, go and put the kettle on",' she said. But Peter recognized that Ruth was an important role model for the women who were there, and that giving her the floor would say more about equality in leadership than any words that would pass his lips.

When Peter and I speak together on the subject of male and female equality, I always do the introductions and start the seminar, and though it may seem a small thing, I am amazed at how many people comment on it afterwards. They say, 'You actually model what you say, and it makes such a difference to see you're not just the cherry on the cake.'

With sorrow I have to admit, however, that apart from my husband, few church leaders, male or female, have given me any real support, encouragement, advice or guidance in my own speaking ministry. In fact, I have received a great deal more in my secular, professional life. One or two special men, like Michael Mitton when he was Director of Anglican Renewal Ministries, opened metaphorical doors for me, for which I am truly thankful, but even women tend to pull up the ladder and batten down the hatches. We're not very good at encouraging the young talent right under our noses.

Ruth is currently seeking out a dozen or so female mentors to get alongside a number of young women in their early teens, in order to support them in their faith through their growing years and encourage them into leadership. So far, it's proving rather difficult. It isn't seen as a priority.

Where are the women in their sixties, seventies and eighties, who will mentor four or even five younger women? They will not condemn them – 'Well, I never left my children and went out to work.' Nor will they project their disappointments onto them – 'Take my advice and get a job, otherwise you'll just be a drudge as I was.' They won't expect them necessarily

316 | Woman: The Full Story

to do as they did, but will listen to God's calling together, and will encourage them to fulfil it.

In poverty, persecution, and suffering, Jewish women throughout the ages learned to live with contradiction – vinegar and honey – and passed on their secrets of survival and success from one generation to the next. Life is a gift, but it comes without a guidebook. From our very first day everything has to be learned. What an opportunity for older, wiser women to put their maturity and wealth of experience to positive use, emboldening the next generations to dream even bigger dreams.

Called to change the world

Articles and books on the place of women in the Church often have titles such as *Equal but Different*. It's the 'but' that always worries me. It usually means the writing is a justification for women being 'not quite equal'. I thought I might call this book *Women without Buts* – but it might have had the wrong connotation.

Yet the more I research and write about the subject, the more convinced I am that equality is not just an optional extra for the Church – a matter of cultural and personal preference. The equality of men and women, established in the book of Genesis at creation, affirmed by the ministry of Jesus and the gift of the Holy Spirit at Pentecost, is one of the distinctive features of Christianity, marking it out from orthodox Judaism, Islam and Hinduism. It is a persuasive argument for the contemporary relevance of the faith we believe, and a powerful tool in our hands for changing the world. Such is the influence of women that the World Health Organization has their liberation as one of its prime targets in bringing physical health and wellbeing to the nations. But the nations cry out for spiritual health and wellbeing too.

When Abby was born, I wanted to create a better world for women. I'm not sure that it is. Ideally, I would like to wipe out fanatical regimes that oppress women, hunt out and shoot the perpetrators of female circumcision, castrate men who know they have HIV but impose themselves on women while deliberately refusing to wear condoms, bully the World Health Organization and anyone else with clout into overt political action in every part of the globe where women's rights are ignored and their wellbeing is in jeopardy. There have been occasional opportunities to make a difference, and that is a privilege. I have prayed for years for the freedom of the women of Afghanistan. Prayer empowers us to achieve a great deal more than most women could ask or think. But I have had to learn what I can change, and accept what I can't.

If we can't change the world, we'll just have to make women more confident, more able to live in it. Apparently, when a job is advertised men will see the 75 per cent they can do and apply for it, while women will see the 25 per cent they can't do and don't bother. That's why, from their girlhood, women need more encouragement to be adventurous. Once we take the initial plunge into the unknown, we tend to be more tenacious than the men. 'I get up. I walk. I fall down. Meanwhile, I keep dancing,' said the old sage, Rabbi Hillel. It was more likely his mother who coined the Jewish saying, 'You can't stop the birds of tragedy from flying over your head and dropping their business on you, but you can refuse to let them nest in your hair.'

The emancipated American black slave Sojourner Truth, who set out in 1843 with 25 cents in her pocket to travel the coast campaigning for women's rights, said, 'If the first woman God ever made was strong enough to turn the world upside down, all alone, together women ought to be able to turn it rightside up again.'

Together we have the power to change hearts, lives and whole cultures. We simply don't use that power positively or often enough. The Greek heroine Lysistrata brought a long and pointless war to a very fast end by encouraging her fellow women to deny their men their conjugal rights until they agreed to put down their swords.

On a more contemporary, less dramatic level, the founders of the National Childbirth Trust who campaigned for childbirth to be treated as a perfectly normal, though uniquely special, event, rather than an illness, were initially regarded by a superior, hostile medical profession as a few wacky women. In the end their tenacity was rewarded – even if it was too late for them. Ingrained cultural attitudes were overturned. The mother was given more control. Labour was no longer such a brutalizing experience.

It would have taken much longer for women to achieve their political rights without the determined efforts of the suffragettes. In many African countries and some European countries like Switzerland, women still didn't have the vote as late as the 1960s.

After the liberation of Afghanistan from the Taliban, one Afghan elder said that subduing the influence of women had left his country like a bird with only one wing. Perhaps, like Esther, we women in the West, whose freedom has been won at such a price, have been called 'for such a time as this' to take up our creation calling and speak life and liberty into a sad and needy world. 'The function of freedom,' said the writer Toni Morrison, 'is to free someone else.' Without two working wings, a bird is wounded, grounded, ineffectual. If the Church wants to rise up and fly in these crucial times, it desperately needs the voices of women. Otherwise it will be telling only half the story.

Notes

1. Malcolm Muggeridge, *Something Beautiful for God* (Collins, Fontana, 1971), p. 67.
2. Susan Denyer, *Beatrix Potter and Her Farms* (National Trust, 1992).
3. Lamott, *Bird by Bird*, p. 125.
4. Gordon Fee, *New International Biblical Commentary, 1 and 2 Timothy and Titus* (Hendrickson, 1988), pp. 186–87.

Share Your Thoughts

With the Author: Your comments will be forwarded to the author when you send them to *zauthor@zondervan.com*.

With Zondervan: Submit your review of this book by writing to *zreview@zondervan.com*.

Free Online Resources at
www.zondervan.com/hello

 Zondervan AuthorTracker: Be notified whenever your favorite authors publish new books, go on tour, or post an update about what's happening in their lives.

 Daily Bible Verses and Devotions: Enrich your life with daily Bible verses or devotions that help you start every morning focused on God.

 Free Email Publications: Sign up for newsletters on fiction, Christian living, church ministry, parenting, and more.

 Zondervan Bible Search: Find and compare Bible passages in a variety of translations at www.zondervanbiblesearch.com.

 Other Benefits: Register yourself to receive online benefits like coupons and special offers, or to participate in research.